DIFFERENT
...Not Less

Inspiring Stories of Achievement and
Successful Employment from Adults
with Autism, Asperger's, and ADHD

Temple Grandin, PhD

DIFFERENT...NOT LESS: Inspiring Stories of Achievement and Successful Employment from Adults with Autism, Asperger's, and ADHD

All marketing and publishing rights guaranteed to and reserved by:

FUTURE HORIZONS INC.

721 W. Abram Street
Arlington, TX 76013
(800) 489-0727
(817) 277-0727
(817) 277-2270 (fax)
E-mail: *info@fhautism.com*
www.fhautism.com

ISBN: 9781935274605

To every individual on the spectrum who
believes in finding a sense of fulfillment and
success in life, sometimes against all odds—

May you find valuable information,
inspiration, and hope in the pages of this book.

This book was purchased
through the generosity of the

Didsbury Municipal
Library

**Friends of the
Didsbury Library**

ACKNOWLEDGMENTS

The contributors to this book must be acknowledged, not only for their courage, but also for their candor. I thank them profoundly for their willingness to welcome readers into their lives and tell their stories—the ups and downs, the good times and bad. I absolutely believe their life experiences and wealth of knowledge will help countless others on the spectrum. They are living proof that individuals with autism can achieve great things—even when life seems like an uphill climb.

TABLE OF CONTENTS

First and foremost, this book is the marvelous brainchild of Dr Temple Grandin. It is and has always been very important to Temple that people with autism and Asperger's syndrome find their niche in life. As she famously emphasizes during conferences, "Collecting Social Security is not a job description!"

It is imperative that these outstanding folks use their unique and special skills to help themselves and the rest of the world. Temple came up with the concept for this book last year and has been relentless about her ideas coming to fruition. We applaud her passion.

Many readers will already be familiar with Temple's story from watching the award-winning HBO biopic, "Temple Grandin," starring Claire Danes. Those of us in the autism world were surprised and delighted by the overwhelming number of people who were touched and inspired by Temple's story. Here you will find 14 similar stories, each a singular source of inspiration.

One of Temple's early livestock plans is depicted on the cover of the book. Not only does it illustrate her obvious talent, but we believe it offers a glimpse into what greatness lies in the minds of so many people with autism and Asperger's syndrome. These folks have extra burdens to overcome to be able to share their light with the world, and it is so important that they figure out a way to do so. The stories in this book relate the different paths the contributors have taken to find success—from dealing with the challenges of being "Different" to ultimately discovering that they are "Not Less." Indeed, people on the autism spectrum have more than their share of talent to offer the rest of the world.

It was important to us, and to Temple, that each contributor's point of view be expressed in his or her own voice. As such, you will notice a variety of writing and communication styles throughout the book, which are unique to each individual. Also, as this is a book that delves into the early years of each contributor, there are some instances of mild sexual content. If you are a parent and will be giving this book to a young teen, please peruse it first to be sure the content is appropriate. Please note that some of the names in this book have been changed.

There are words used in this book that may be new to someone who is unfamiliar with the world of autism and Asperger's syndrome. An "Aspie" is used to denote someone with Asperger's syndrome. Aspies use this term proudly, and rightfully so. A "neurotypical" person, sometimes called "NT," is someone who develops and functions in a usual way (ie, neurologically typical). If you have never heard these terms before, it is likely you are a neurotypical person.

A few thanks are in order. First, thank you to the illustrious Teresa Corey, who helped Temple find, gather, and filter all of the original contributions. As there were many interesting submissions from talented individuals, this was no small feat. Also, thanks to Heather Babiar, who edited the submissions and brought them together into a readable and cohesive format. Thank you to Cynthia Williams, who generated the initial interior design, and to John Yacio, who designed the cover and completed the final layout.

A special thank you to Dr Tony Attwood, who wrote such a wonderful foreword, and to the many exceptional contributors.

And, of course, we must thank Dr Temple Grandin, who put her heart and soul into this very important project.

Jennifer Gilpin Yacio

FOREWORD

This is an inspiring book. The stories of achievement will be encouraging for parents of a young child with an autism spectrum disorder and will be especially inspirational for adolescents and young adults who are feeling despondent that autism could deprive them of a successful career or relationship. This book has antidepressant qualities to rival those of medication.

The stories serve to illustrate a cross-section of abilities, experiences, and adversity for mature adults with an autism spectrum disorder. There are clear themes in terms of adversity, such as being bullied at school and having self-esteem challenged by the ignorance and prejudice of peers and coworkers. There are descriptions of the difficulties caused by sensory sensitivity, social naivety, and vulnerability. Some stories explore the time it may take to eventually find a career that constructively uses the qualities and abilities attributable to autism. Where there is a successful outcome, common themes include the discovery of a mentor within the person's family, circle of friends, and colleagues who is able to provide guidance and encouragement, as well as the individual's personal qualities of determination and perseverance.

Other keys to a successful outcome are employment during adolescence in the form of a part-time job and recognition that there is no career that should be avoided by someone with an autism spectrum disorder. The careers described by the contributors include employment in information technology and business, the arts, the caring professions (including becoming a psychologist), and the animal sciences. The contributors provide an international perspective, as well as illustrations of outcomes for both men and women with an autism spectrum disorder who have a range of intellectual ability, from average to superior.

The stories also include "dark" times, including depression, relationship breakdowns, and even a term of imprisonment. However, these have been catalysts for positive change, and the eventual outcomes have been perfect illustrations of being *Different…Not Less.*

Dr Tony Attwood

INTRODUCTION

The individuals who wrote their stories for this book are adults, most of whom are about 50 years old. For many of the contributors, receiving a diagnosis of an autism spectrum disorder helped them to understand their problems with relationships. It was a relief to have an explanation for problems they had in relating to other people. Their journeys have not been easy, but they have all found success by earning a living, and some have even had children. Some of the contributors came from families with modest financial resources, which meant they had to work harder to succeed.

Throughout my life, I have met and worked with many people on the autism spectrum whose condition has gone undiagnosed. Many of them are in technical fields, such as engineering, computer programming, industrial design, and equipment construction. I too am a "techie" and feel that my career is my life. I am what I do. I have observed that "techies" who get into good careers appear to be happier because they are surrounded by "their people." John Robison, in his book *Be Different*, embraces Asperger's syndrome and talks about his good techie life, making special effects for rock bands and learning about electronics from various mentors. At the time of writing this introduction, I was doing lots of public speaking and teaching but not a lot of technical work. In between speaking engagements, I managed to visit a beef plant to fix some equipment problems. It was so much fun being a techie again. I love using my mind to solve problems.

Some of the most important companies in Silicon Valley are led by people on the autism spectrum. Many school systems today would assign a diagnosis of autism to Albert Einstein. He did not speak until the age of 3, and he demonstrated many odd behaviors that are attributed to autism. At an autism meeting, a retired NASA space scientist walked up to me and said that he was sure many of his colleagues were on the autism spectrum. Several books have been written that profile famous scientists and musicians who were likely on the spectrum, as well.

NOT ALL TECHIES

The "techie"-type person is only a portion of the population on the autism spectrum. A huge percentage of autistic individuals do not have primary strengths in technical subjects or art to rely on for employment. They long for satisfying relationships, and this group often has a more difficult time finding work. They do not have easily displayable skills in art, design, music, math, or programming that can be shown in a portfolio. In my livestock design business, I sold clients by showing my portfolio of drawings and photos of completed projects. I sold my work, not myself. Nontechnical people on the autism spectrum often have keen interests in facts about a favorite subject, like history or politics. Though interests can be harder to sell, it can be done. In this book, chapter 1 will begin with the account of a woman whose life became happier and more meaningful when she became a tour guide, allowing her to talk about history.

Autism is a truly continuous spectrum. There is no black-and-white dividing line between the geek, the nerd, the socially awkward person, and the mildly autistic individual. In fact, many people in the general population have autistic traits. A large study conducted in Korea showed that in 7- to 12–year-old children in regular schools, 1.89% had symptoms of autism but had not received an autism diagnosis. I have visited state science fair competitions and have seen many children with autistic symptoms. Some had received a diagnosis, and some had not. Many of the individuals who tell their stories in this book had difficult childhoods, in which they were ostracized by other children and constantly bullied for their apparent symptoms. Yet, they were inspired to succeed by teachers and mentors who encouraged interests in skills and things they were good at.

ASPIE FRIENDS IN COLLEGE

Life was really difficult for me in both college and graduate school. I did not fit in with the other students. The saying, "Birds of a feather flock together," rang very true. During this time, I had several friends whom I believe were on the spectrum but were undiagnosed. My college years were very difficult emotionally. These friends kept me going when I felt depressed. Through the years, I have maintained contact with the friends I made then. Some of them endured many difficulties, but they all managed to support themselves and remain employed. These people were some of the few who sought me out and made an effort to be my friend.

Tim, a short, nerdy kid who loved CB (Citizens' Band) radios, invited me to join his CB club. Nobody else at my college shared Tim's enthusiasm for CB radios or emergency communication. Tim saw me as a kindred spirit who could share his interest in CB radios. We had a great time going to CB Club meetings off campus. Tim went on to become an emergency medical technician, or EMT, and today, he runs an ambulance company.

The physical education teacher, Mrs Estes, also sought me out. She was the weird lady on campus who wore long johns under all her skirts and put together strange mixtures of clothes. When I felt lonely, I often went over to her house just to talk. When I graduated, she gave me a little card and told me that it was a "phone card" I could use to call her anytime if I ever needed advice. Today, if Mrs Estes were a child, I think she would likely receive a diagnosis of Asperger's. Mrs Estes was married to another faculty member and had children, as well.

In graduate school, I became friends with two people who were definitely on the autism spectrum. One of them received a PhD in history, and every year, I receive a card from him. He has been underemployed all his life in specialty retail. He has held three jobs since he graduated in the mid-1970s. One job he lost when the business closed, and his present job, at a large specialty retailer, has been stable for years. Specialty retail is a good job for a "non-techie" type because the employee is appreciated for his or her keen knowledge of the merchandise. Examples of specialty retailing are hardware, men's clothing, sporting goods, electronics, computers, jewelry, books, and furniture. I can also remember the Aspie guy who worked for years at the local hardware store. He knew everything about paint. Everybody laughed at the goofy Superman advertisements he did at the local TV station. It was "Bobby to the rescue for your painting problems."

ASPIES IN MY WORKPLACE

I have worked with all kinds of technical people who are on the autism spectrum but have never received a diagnosis. They have adapted better than some of the people in this book and therefore didn't feel a need for a diagnosis. The reason why the contributors sought out a diagnosis as older adults was because of the serious problems they continued to face. When I first started my career, I often got lonely, and I would go down to the Armour Corporate

Center in Phoenix to talk to Sam. Sam was an engineer, and his work mates would say, "You ask Sam what time it is, and he will tell you how to build a watch." It was so much fun to talk to Sam about building meat plants. He was definitely on the spectrum, and he held a high-level engineering job and frequently visited the meat plants. When I was fully engaged with individuals who loved to talk about engineering, animal behavior, or cattle, I was happy, and I forgot about the emotional difficulties.

Some of the people I work with on my design projects have a certain degree of autism. One, an excellent specialty metal fabricator, has worked on many of my projects. He has a small shop and builds conveyors for many major meat companies. He called me one day all upset because a plant manager had been really mean to him. He told me the entire story, and it became obvious that the manager was using him and had no intention of paying for the equipment he "bought." I understood his frustration and was able to help. I told him that the guy was a jerk and that the best thing to do was to quietly remove the equipment and walk away. I reminded him that he had many good clients and that he needed to concentrate on them. I told him to work with the many other clients who appreciated his excellent, innovative work.

OBSERVATIONS OVER THE YEARS

So many people sent in personal stories for inclusion in this book that it was impossible to use all of them. I tried to pick a wide variety of people who have supported themselves in many different types of employment. I purposely avoided filling the book up with successful, happy people who work in computers or science. During the 30 years that I have been a part of the autism community, I have seen some definite trends. Services for individuals with more severe problems have greatly improved, and sometimes these people have fewer problems integrating into society when compared with a fully verbal individual on the milder end of the spectrum.

In the 1950s, children with severe problems were simply "put away" in institutions, but most Aspies with milder cases managed to remain employed. In the 50s, manners and basic social skills were pounded into all kids. I was expected to be on time, shake hands, and say "please" and "thank you." When you do not instinctively pick up on social cues, learning basic social rules like these is a lifesaver. Recently, somebody wrote on the Internet that I was showing my age, because I emphasized manners and criticized excessive video-game playing. Some job counselors estimate that 65% of teenage boys on the spectrum are addicted to video games. If it could be proven that the video games were helping them learn skills to make them employable, I would not be critical. Video-game companies are short on programmers and software engineers. What I would *like* to see is getting them interested in spending hours *making* the games instead of *playing* them. However, the video-game field is very crowded, and jobs in other types of computing would be easier to get. A September 19, 2011, article in *Bloomberg Businessweek* reported that there are shortages of software engineers, certified welders, machinists, nurses, and people in computer-support roles. There is also a need for electricians, plumbers, and technicians to repair medical equipment. These are all jobs that could be fulfilled by Aspies.

DIFFICULT JOURNEYS

The people in this book have had their difficulties—especially in the area of relationships. For some of these individuals, this arena has been more difficult than employment. One of the reasons why they sought out a diagnosis was their difficulty with relationships. For most individuals on the spectrum, the road to successful employment started with teenage jobs, such as paper routes. Having a paper route taught the basic work skills of being on time and having to do it every day. Today, the paper routes are mostly gone, but a good modern substitute for a young Aspie is dog walking. Like a paper route, it has to be done every day. Other good jobs for teenagers on the spectrum would be fixing computers, making PowerPoint presentations, maintaining and updating Web sites, working in a farmer's market, writing for the church or community newsletter, selling art, or helping an elderly neighbor.

When I was a teenager, I did hand-sewing for a seamstress, cleaned horse stalls, built carpentry projects, and painted signs. The crucial skill that has to be learned is *how to do work that is assigned by other people.* In my design work, I often had to modify my designs to either fit the building site or satisfy some whim of the client. There are some people on the spectrum who can get hired easily by showing a portfolio of artwork or programming code. However, they cannot keep a job because they do not get assigned work done. They are either rigid and inflexible in modifying a project to satisfy the boss, or they refuse to do work that is outside their area of interest. When kids do jobs in middle and high school, it teaches them valuable work skills, such as flexibility and doing assigned tasks. If a teenager is creating a Web page for a real-estate office, he will learn that he cannot decorate it with science-fiction characters. When I made signs as a teenager, I did not paint horses on a sign for a beauty shop. I had to learn how to do work that other people wanted.

Recently, I had a lady walk up to me in the airport and say, "Your book, *Thinking in Pictures,* saved my marriage. Now I understand my engineer husband, and we are able to work things out." Each contributor in this book has a unique story, and my intent is that their stories will provide hope and insight to individuals on the spectrum, as well as parents, teachers, and professionals.

People on the autism spectrum always keep learning. It is never too late to learn new skills, improve relationships, or learn better work skills. To grow, a person on the spectrum has to "stretch." Stretching is a good analogy, because sudden surprises cause fear. Even individuals my age can learn new skills. When I was writing this introduction, I talked to a family member of a woman in her 60s who has autism. Within the past year, she discovered that the way she dressed herself improved her life, and now she enjoys nicer clothes. The mind of the person with autism can always keep learning. It is never too late to change. A person on the spectrum needs an employer, spouse, or friend who will calmly coach him when he makes social mistakes. He has to be instructed on how to behave, like a character in a play. In my own life, I have gained great insight from reading the writings of other individuals on the spectrum.

Dr Temple Grandin

CHAPTER 1

CHARLI DEVNET

Tour Guide and Lover of History

CHARLI DEVNET, BA, MA, JD

Age: 57

Resides in: Croton-on-Hudson, NY

Occupation: Tour guide and legal freelancer

Marital status: Single

FROM TEMPLE:

I chose Charli as the first *Different...Not Less* story because I know her insightful cover letter will offer hope to so many people on the spectrum. After years of struggle and a series of false starts, Charli found positive direction in life through an unusual job that was right for her. Charli's chapter begins with her cover letter, explaining why she would be a good candidate for inclusion in this book.

CHARLI'S INTRODUCTION

Despite my seemingly satisfactory verbal skills, I have been significantly challenged by autism. I know many adults have received a diagnosis of some form of autism, yet—in my eyes—they have such a mild level of impairment that they seem to be able to lead fairly normal lives. Any one of them could provide you with a more conventional career success story. When I first heard about Temple's new book, I was afraid it would only relate the stories of higher-functioning individuals and that those of us who have struggled with near-insurmountable difficulties just to achieve a measure of acceptance in our personal and professional lives would be overlooked. I believe that those of us who are not in the "near-normal" category should also have a voice. Feel free to use my name. I am not ashamed of who I am—not any longer.

For the past 10 years, I have worked at a historical house museum, called "Kykuit," in Sleepy Hollow, New York. Kykuit was formerly the countryseat of the Rockefeller family. I work as a tour guide and, on Saturdays, I sell memberships for the National Trust for Historic Preservation, the present landlord of Kykuit. The name "Kykuit" is a Dutch word, meaning "lookout" or "high place." When the Dutch settled along the banks of the Hudson River back in the 17th century, they assigned the name to a craggy, rocky hilltop 500 feet above sea level. This hilltop was used by the local Indian tribes as a signal post. Now, 500 feet may not seem very high to those who live in Colorado, but here in Westchester Country, it almost touches the sky! A hundred years ago, the richest family in America transformed this barren, rocky hilltop into a little bit of paradise.

This is the best job I have ever had. I love my work for so many reasons. First of all, the site itself is both peaceful and inspiring. Sculpted on the façade of the house are two classical deities, joined together by a laurel branch—Apollo, who represents culture, art, and science, and Demeter, the goddess of agriculture and harvest. Art and nature work in harmony to create a place of wonder—the sweeping views of the Hudson and the Palisades take your breath away, enhanced by the sculpture gardens, fountains, and greenery. The house itself is interesting, but it's the exteriors that are a treasure. John D. Rockefeller, Sr, the oil baron, was a robust, outdoorsy, athletic type of man. Despite his vast wealth, he cared nothing for high society or manmade opulence—he was a Baptist and preferred to spend his money, if he must spend it, on the gardens, golf course, and woodlands.

Sense of Camaraderie with Tour Guides

My colleagues at Kykuit have provided me with a sense of camaraderie that I have not known since junior-high school. The other
guides are all intelligent and highly educated, with diverse backgrounds. Some are retired teachers, and some have a background
in the arts. A few, like me, have worked in the legal field. Now, I
myself am intelligent and educated, and those qualities alone would
never impress me. However, the other guides embody the attributes
that are lacking in me, which I therefore admire in other people—
attributes like poise, sophistication, self-assurance, and possession
of the social graces. They generally consider themselves "artsy,"
and, as such, feel almost obligated to be tolerant of the quirks and
eccentricities of others and have therefore been more accepting of
me than coworkers in the legal or business world might be. However, this was not always the case. At first, in my eagerness to become one of the "troupe," I made comments that seemed witty and
incisive to me but may well have been perceived as offensive, rude,
and gauche. As time went by and we became better acquainted, we
began to get on much better. If I did not find any close friends among
my colleagues, at least we became friendly. On occasion, we get
together outside of work for a field trip to a museum or other attraction. A few years ago, there was a public art "happening" in Central
Park, called "The Gates," and the guides all went down together.
While I might have gone alone, it was much more fun going with
the gang from work.

One of the best aspects of my job is that it allows me to talk and
be the center of attention. For two and a quarter hours, visitors must
follow me around and listen to me speak about matters in which I
am interested and knowledgeable. They cannot change the subject
and have a conversation in which I can take no part—about their

children or their mortgages or where they are going on vacation—nor can they just talk over me as if I were not there.

What I like best about being a tour guide is actually the greatest obstacle to retaining the job. While the wages are low, the job actually requires a high-level skill set. It requires knowledge of both American history and art history (which fall right in my area of special interest). I have always had a keen interest in history and politics, so for any aspects of the material of which I knew nothing—for example, modern art, styles of architecture, and landscaping theory—I quickly picked them up. In fact, I enjoyed having new subjects to delve into. However, a guide also has to be comfortable with public speaking, which presented me with a great challenge. My first season was almost my last. Sure, I could talk on and on—but does anyone want to listen? My presentation was where I ran into trouble. In my first year, I was criticized for speaking in monotone, not looking visitors in the eye, not projecting my voice, having a "flat affect," and being consistently late to the bus at the end of the tour. I came very close to losing my job, as I had lost many others before it.

Developing Confidence

During that first summer, however, my beautiful mother died at the age of 74, from smoking-related lung cancer. Her loss threatened to send me into a serious tailspin. I adored my mother. She may not have been the most nurturing or supportive of parents, as she had difficulty expressing her emotions—but I loved her. Despite the fact that she smoked, she had always taken good care of herself, and I had thought she would die well into her 90s, if at all. Because of my mother's death, I needed the structure and the socialization that my job at Kykuit provided, and I acquired the social skills that were necessary to keep it. I discovered in myself abilities that had lain dormant all my life—abilities that few autistic people ever get a chance to develop: the self-confidence to speak in public, to be articulate and to modulate my voice, to make witty comments that are amusing to everyone (and not just to myself), and to impart my knowledge in a way that holds a visitor's interest and attention. Problems remain in abiding by the schedule and making it to the bus on time, but the other guides know I have this tendency, and they hurry me along.

When talking about career success, if you're referring to fame and fortune, a fat paycheck, a position of power, or a world-shattering discovery, I have nothing to offer. However, what I am able to impart is a story about a low-paying, seasonal, offbeat job that has made me very happy, provided me with a touchstone through years of loss and personal tragedy, and given me an opportunity to develop many interpersonal and social skills that I never dreamed I could possess.

Mid-40s Subsistence Living

Although I have several advanced degrees, I have spent most of my adult life either unemployed or underemployed. By my mid-40s, I had learned to eke out a subsistence living by putting together a patchwork of part-time, low-paying jobs, all of which I was overqualified for. I understand this is a common pattern with Aspies. At the time, however, I had not received a formal diagnosis. To my mind—and the minds of others around me—I was simply a disappointment, a failure, and an underachiever—a "no-good, lazy bum" who did not try hard enough. As a child in the 1960s, I had been tagged as being "emotionally immature," and that label stuck well into midlife. Then I saw an ad for tour guides at Kykuit. I've had this job for 10 years now, and it has quite literally saved my life during my darkest days.

Feeling of Empowerment from Diagnosis

Three years after losing my mother, my dad also passed away. Two years ago, I lost the elderly aunt who had rescued me when I was a totally dysfunctional person in my early 20s. She had given me a home for 30 years, and when she died, I was so paralyzed with depression and anxiety that I contemplated suicide. In the end, I sought therapy and received a diagnosis of Asperger's syndrome with anxiety and depression. My diagnosis has given me a feeling of empowerment. Finally knowing what was "wrong" with me allowed me to embark on a belated but liberating journey of self-discovery. Through it all, my job as a tour guide at Kykuit has provided me with solace, purpose, and, at times, the only social life I had. It has also given me the chance to shine. Today, guests often compliment me—sometimes to management—on what a knowledgeable, funny, and articulate tour guide I am. Although few people in the neutorypical world would consider my story indicative of professional success, the personal level of success and fulfillment I have found is invaluable.

MY STORY

To look at me now, you might never know I have spent my life living in a world of strangers.

Until the summer I turned 13, I was a rather high-functioning child in the small riverside village of Croton-on-Hudson, New York. My mother was beautiful, intelligent, glamorous, and aloof. I adored her. She had difficulty displaying her emotions, but it was probably not her fault. Her own father, for whom I am named, was just like her—handsome, taciturn, and remote—a "refrigerator grandpa." I adored him, too, but he never let me get close. My mother's name was Jacqueline, like the First Lady, whom she did indeed look like. In fact, the resemblance was so strong that when Jackie Onassis died, I felt pangs of grief, although my own mom was alive and well at the time.

My Parents

My mother claimed that, as a child, her family had been wealthy and lived in a big house on a hill, with a maid. I discovered later this was indeed true. Grandpa Charlie had once been a big wheel in the local restaurant business and probably a former bootlegger, as well. By the time I was born, however, my grandparents were anything but rich. They operated a bar and grill two blocks from Sing Sing Prison in the neighboring village of Ossining. We called it "The Saloon," but it was no honky-tonk—just an everyday bar and grill where the correctional officers hung out between shifts. Nevertheless, my mom always carried herself like a displaced aristocrat.

You would think that, given her obsession with lost wealth and status, she would have married "up," but the opposite was true. She wed her childhood sweetheart, the eighth of ten children of an Italian stonemason, all as poor as could be.

My dad was the polar opposite of my mom: warm, loving, easy-going, and thoroughly neurotypical. At the age of 17, he had quit high school and gone off to fight with the marines in World War II. He almost drowned at Okinawa, but fortunately he survived to return to his hometown and marry his childhood sweetheart, whom, like me, he regarded with absolute awe. Despite his good nature, my dad had very few parenting skills. Perhaps he was so disappointed I was not the daughter he had expected and longed for that he kept me at bay. Perhaps, as I began to suspect many years later, the horrendous events he had seen at places like Okinawa, Iwo Jima, and Nagasaki never really left him.

A Tomboy Best Friend

That my parents were not the best nurturers in the world mattered little at first. I had two sets of grandparents and a plethora of aunts and uncles within a few miles' radius to take up the slack. There were also plenty of other kids—our neighborhood was literally crawling with children my own age or near to it, as it was the height of the baby boom. I even had a best friend—golden-haired Alexis, who lived next door. She was a tomboy, like me, but she was built like a pixie. I spent a lot of time at her house, at the homes of other playmates, and out on the street in pickup games with the other kids. Sure, I was a bit of a misfit, but I was not lonely—at least, not then.

My mom knew I was different, but she believed I was different in the best of ways. She thought I was a near-genius. The evidence for this was not overwhelming, but I could read fairly well by the age of four, and shortly thereafter I came up with interesting but useless facts, such as the capital cities of every state, all the kings and queens of England, and the gods of Mount Olympus. My mother was certain she had a precocious little sage on her hands.

SCHOOL YEARS

Unkind Treatment by Teachers and Classmates

My troubles began when I started school, and I received unkind treatment by both teachers and classmates. I recall being sent to a speech therapist, but my teachers did not see me as being impaired—they viewed me as a gifted child with a behavioral problem, and they came down on me harshly. Such a bright child as myself should have known better than to misbehave so consistently. I did know better, and I misbehaved anyway. I did not mean to do so, and sometimes I didn't even realize I had misbehaved until I found myself cooling my heels in the principal's office. Especially in the early grades, the schoolwork did not engage me, which led to trouble. In my view, my mom had done me no favors by teaching me to read as a toddler. What was I supposed to do in the 1st grade, when the rest of the class struggled to learn the letters of the alphabet? What could I do but goof off, cut up, and act out to relieve my boredom? It was the practice of the time for scholastically advanced students to be allowed to skip a grade, but I was never permitted that option because I was "emotionally immature."

The difficulties I had with other kids were even more worrisome. At least I knew what the teachers expected of me. Although I did have friends of my own, most of my classmates treated me like a misfit. Some of them were schoolyard bullies, who seem to have an unwavering instinct for targeting children who fall short of societal norms. They chased me down the street and tried to steal my books and throw them in the mud. Others mocked and made fun of me, and I was never really sure why. Perhaps I talked a bit funny, and perhaps I really did walk like a swaying ship, as my classmates said. Perhaps it was my many food aversions, which made me an extremely picky eater—a circumstance which some found amusing.

I consulted my mother. She advised me that the other children were all jealous of me because I was so highly intelligent. I doubted the soundness of her opinion. In my eyes, I was not particularly bright or gifted. Anyone could open up a book or study a map and learn things. Where was the magic in that? I admired children who possessed skills that I coveted but entirely lacked—those who could turn perfect cartwheels, keep a Hula-Hoop up on their waist, or make sculptures with papier-mâché. At the age of 7, I was the last kid on the block to take the training wheels off my bike and learn to keep my balance. In many ways, I felt like a first-class *dummy.*

Life Is Not Meant to Be a Bowl of Cherries

Despite these challenges, I rather enjoyed elementary school. Back then, kids seemed to understand that life was not meant to be a bowl of cherries. All of us expected to get some bruised knees and hurt feelings at times, and we all had battles to fight. Some students could not keep up their grades, and others could not play sports. Some were called names because they were too fat or too skinny. Some were Jewish and got no presents at Christmas. Eventually, I learned to stand my ground and ward off the bullies. I tamped down my urge to misbehave, which appeased my teachers.

I also benefited from the freedom that was granted to youngsters back then. Our parents did not expect to know where we were every hour of the day. We left in the morning and came home for dinner. If I was on the outs with the other kids, I did not have to stick around, nor did I have to run home and hide. I could hop on my bike and pedal across town to the home of a relative who would listen sympathetically. Or, I could go to the public library, where I could lose myself in stacks of tantalizingly unread books. I could go to the sweet shop, get a soda, and read the comics—or, I could simply ride down an unfamiliar street and explore.

My favorite subjects in school were history, geography, and social studies. The other kids hated history, and I wondered why. To me, history was full of wonderful stories, and I could easily recall names, dates, and places.

I also had a bent toward theology. My parents did one good thing for me—they made sure I had a religious background. Both my parents had been raised Roman Catholic. Dad had lost his faith somewhere along the way, probably during the war in Japan, but Mom was more steadfast. She rarely went to church herself. However, she made sure I went and attended catechism class on Thursday afternoons at the local catholic school.

When I was small, I became aware that having no siblings made me different. One day in 1st-grade art class, the teacher told us to draw pictures of our siblings. The other two "only children" in the class submitted pictures of their pets. I had neither sibling nor pet and had nothing to draw. After school, I ran home and angrily confronted my mother. Why had she made me such a weirdo? Why didn't I have a brother or sister, like "normal" kids did? To my surprise and delight, she replied that it was indeed a good idea and that she would think about it.

As it happened, a few months later, my mother presented me with my very own brother. I was ecstatic. A little pal! A second in my corner! Someone to talk to when everyone else deserted me! I proudly took his baby pictures to school for "show and tell" and declared that I now had a "real" family, just like everyone else.

My Younger Brother Was Unlike Me

Unfortunately, the promise of a baby brother turned out differently than I'd hoped. At first, all went according to plan. He dutifully toddled around the house after me, calling me "Yar-Yar" in an attempt to say my name, "Charli." As he grew older, however, he treated me with complete indifference. All my life, I have grieved the loss of the brother and pal I wanted and expected. In his place stood the perfect stranger.

My brother could not be more unlike me. He is quiet and shy, sensitive and withdrawn—a natural introvert. His one lifelong obsession has been music. As a tot, he drove us all crazy with his constant repetition of television commercials. As a child, he raided my record collection with seeming impunity. I cannot recall whether he had friends in school, but by college, he had fallen in with some musically inclined students, and his life improved. All his friends are musicians. As an adult, he became a music writer and even published two books on rock music. Like me, he has never married, but he has had a proper series of live-in girlfriends. If fame and fortune are the standards by which to judge "success," then my brother had the career success in the family. However, I do not believe it brought him much long-lasting happiness or self-fulfillment. He has been out of work for some time now and fears that, at 50, he is washed up.

My brother is so dissimilar from me that, even when I began to suspect that I might be on the autism spectrum, it never occurred to me that he may be, as well. Two years ago, when I received a formal diagnosis, my psychiatrist gave me books on Asperger's syndrome. One of the books indicated that autism runs in families. A light went on in my head, and I immediately telephoned my brother. However, a lifetime of misunderstanding is not easily overcome.

Seventh grade was the best year of my life. Junior high brought a greater variety of class work, and advanced courses were available in my favorite subjects. I took violin and played in the school orchestra. I played sports the other girls played—floor hockey and softball. I was fairly good, despite some deficits in motor skills.

Both the disciplinary problems and the bullies were behind me. I even went to dances and began looking at boys. It seemed that I had finally conquered whatever-it-was that had kept me from fitting in. Just to be certain, I consulted my guidance counselor. "Do you think there is anything wrong with me?" I asked him. "Not at all," he replied. "You seem like a typical 12-year-old to me." I beamed in satisfaction.

My World Came Crashing Down When I Was Uprooted from My School and Friends

Unfortunately, my world soon came crashing down. The summer I turned 13, my parents purchased a crumbling old estate further up the Hudson, in the middle of nowhere. I was uprooted from my home, my school, and my friends—life as I knew it was over. I had no one to talk to, nothing to do, and no place to go. I mean *no one.* There were no neighbors. There were no kids my age around, nor even any grown-ups. My brother had already locked me out of his world. Aunts and uncles came up to see us at first, but my mother did not encourage visitors, and gradually I lost touch with my relatives. The nearest village was 3 miles away, and although I soon learned to bike there and haunt the small public library, the icy fingers of deep loneliness reached into my heart and paralyzed me. I foundered. I regressed and fell apart. As B.J. Thomas sang, "I'm so lonesome, I could die." He could have been singing about me.

For the most part, my parents did not understand what was happening as their little savant shattered into pieces. My mother believed that it was all make-believe and that I was pretending to be abnormal to punish my parents for tearing me away from my friends and my hometown. My father was convinced that my breakdown was physical in nature, and indeed I showed physical signs of distress. I had begun my menses 6 months before we left Croton. Once we moved, they stopped entirely. As a child, I had always been one of the tallest kids in my class. By 7th grade, I had attained my full height of 5 feet 4 inches and never grew a smidgeon more. My dad believed it was an indication of some unspecified illness.

Unbearable Loneliness in a Big High School

Eventually, I was sent back to school, but that did nothing to alleviate my unbearable loneliness. The high school I attended was a modern, sterile, overcrowded facility to which teenagers were bussed from surrounding towns. The teachers were too busy to devote personal attention to any one student. I made no new friends to replace those I had left behind. The necessity of riding the school bus seemed a humiliation. In Croton, school buses were associated only with the very youngest children and those who lived out in the sticks. After 3rd grade, you walked or biked to school. Bullies reappeared in my life. These bullies did not chase me around the schoolyard. They walked right through me, refused to move when I walked by them, and generally acted as though I was not there—which, in a way, I was not.

For a while I had a horse named Perhaps, who brought me some solace, although he could never replace Alexis. We cleared out a dusty stall in one of the old barns on the estate for him. Since we lived in such a remote area, I could ride him up and down the road without any danger. I had Perhaps for a year and a half. The second winter, it was extremely cold and I could not ride. By then I was battling not only loneliness, but what would now be called depression and anorexia. My mother quietly gave Perhaps away to a local horse farm. As a teenager going through a tailspin, I had neither the maturity nor the energy to care for a horse.

It was when I stopped eating that my father finally took action. With no notice and against my will, I was admitted to the local hospital. I was terrified. For a week, my blood was drawn and tests were run to check for every conceivable affliction. All the doctors could find was an underactive metabolism, for which thyroid supplements were prescribed. I was also given a psychotropic medication—I believe it was Ritalin. However, it had no beneficial effects; it certainly did not make me less lonely. I told my mother that I did not believe I needed it, and she agreed. The prescription was not renewed. The thyroid supplements, on the other hand, did seem to work. My menses came back, and so did my appetite. This satisfied my dad.

The only thing that ever did me any good in high school was my participation in the movement opposing the Vietnam War. I have read that Aspies have a keen sense of social justice. I would like to say that this was what finally motivated me to stand up for myself. The truth was, I was spurred on by an intense identification with the innocent Vietnamese peasantry, who, through no wrongdoing, saw their huts burned, their villages strafed, and their kinfolk decimated. Wasn't that similar to what had happened to me? While I was undergoing tests in the hospital, I pored over news magazines to ease the boredom, and the articles I read instilled in me a renewed sense of purpose. Shortly after my release, I began hiking a mile to the bus stop, taking the bus to Poughkeepsie, and holding candles against the wind, marching with signs to demand peace and volunteering for antiwar candidates. I wrote letters to the editor of the school newspaper and spoke up in class. Many of my teachers were likewise opposed to the war and looked upon me with favor. With their help, a political science club was organized, and at last I found classmates with whom I shared an interest. While I never made *friends,* as Alexis had been, I finally had people to talk to every now and then.

College Was a Disaster

If high school had been tough, college was an utter disaster. At first, I resisted the whole idea, but there did not seem to be a feasible alternative. I had very little guidance in choosing a career path. A large IBM headquarters had been built in a nearby town, and the people who worked there were paid a much higher salary than anyone else around. I never learned what it was the IBM folks *did*, but it was assumed that all the "bright" kids would try to get such a job, if not at IBM then in a similar firm. In preparation for such a position, one had to go to college. The entire prospect scared the living daylights out of me, but I was completely unaware that there were other options.

If a young Aspie came to me today and asked for advice, I would say, "Above all, choose a work environment in which you can thrive and be productive." Not everyone is cut out for the corporate life. Would you be happier working on a ranch? In a zoo? Designing sets in a theater? Punching tickets on a train? As for me, it took many years—and many false starts—before I realized that work does not have to entail a windowless cubicle or a forbidding high-rise.

In the end, I selected Catholic University in Washington, DC. I selected it for no legitimate reason other than I thought it would be exciting to live in the nation's capital.

It was a bad fit from the beginning. The student body was homogenous to the extreme—all white and middle- to upper-middle class, all perfectly attired and perfectly behaved. I found no diversity of thought, either. Somehow, it seemed I had chosen the only university in the 1970s without its share of hippies, counter-culturalists, or freethinkers.

I Wanted to Be Social but Was Rebuffed

I wanted very much to be social. I tried very hard to make friends, but I was constantly rebuffed. I tried to establish relationships with young men, to no avail. Unable to find a warm welcome on campus, I spent a lot of my time in the downtown area, running wild in the streets and attempting to latch onto the radical groups who eventually rejected me, as well.

In truth, I was not an attractive person when I was in college. My parents, for all their poor nurturing skills, had at least provided me with some structure. They cooked my meals, did my laundry, saw to it that I went to bed at a reasonable hour, and got me off to school the next day, adequately dressed and groomed. Without their guidance, I did what was right in my own eyes. I bought an oversized khaki jacket from the army supply store and wore it day in and day out. What had begun as innocent idealism had devolved into full-blown anarchism. I was so full of resentment that I wanted to bring the world crashing down with me. I walked around campus muttering about the coming revolution and the "military industrial complex." My hair was uncombed and uncut. Showers grew more and more infrequent. I plastered my dorm room with controversial posters.

The school administration attributed my weird behavior to drugs, which was a fair assumption. Illegal drugs were rampant on college campuses in those days, and it was known that students who abused drugs acted in strange ways. In truth, I never really took drugs, but the college officials searched my dorm room regularly anyway.

Things came to a head at the end of my third year, when rumors swirled around campus that I had attempted to do someone an injury. Although the rumors were completely false, no one came to my defense. I was subjected to a psychiatric examination. I must have passed the exam, because I was readmitted to the university. It was too late, however, to salvage my college career or my faith in humanity. I spent the next 2 years holed up in an off-campus apartment, gorging myself on my favorite foods and rarely attending classes.

Once I graduated, then I had a *real* problem—what was I supposed to do next? I was in my early 20s and had absolutely no clue as to how to live an adult life. If I had not been rescued, I do not know what would have become of me.

EMPLOYMENT

A Kind Aunt Helped Me Get My Life Together

My dad's older sister, Aunt Rose, graciously took me in. She cleaned me up, gave me a bit of a polish, and provided me with some minimal social skills. I returned to the village in which I had lived as a child, and she taught me to bake bread and drive a car. It was far from easy. When I first went to live with her, I had the social graces of one of those jungle boys in the old movies, "Raised by Wolves." I may as well have been.

Up until this time, I had never worked a day in my life. I hadn't done any babysitting as a teenager, presumably because I had fallen to pieces and my parents wanted to keep me at home. In high school I did do some volunteer work for antiwar political candidates, but by the time I went to college, I really was in no condition to work.

Aunt Rose helped me look for work. She called up her friends and neighbors and lined up job interviews. She dragged me to career counselors. She found me temporary positions as a lunchroom monitor for the school district, an election registrar, a dog walker, and an office clerk. However, nothing really panned out long-term, so when my parents offered me the opportunity to go back to school, I jumped at it. Reading books and taking tests had never been a problem for me. I earned my master of arts degree, and then I went to law school. Aunt Rose inquired whether I would not be more comfortable with some "quirky, offbeat job" (her words). She was unaware that I was an Aspie, of course, but she was a keen judge of character. Unfortunately, it would be another few years before I listened to her.

Getting and Losing Jobs

I was 30 years old when I got my first "real" job, working for a lawyer in Atlantic City, New Jersey. The year I spent working in Atlantic City was the happiest of my life since junior high. I had gotten the job entirely on my own merits—no one had called up a friend of a friend. No agency sent me. I had not even responded to an ad. I had just knocked on the door of an attorney who happened to have an important brief due the next day, which he had not even started to compose. I was so proud to be employed. I felt authentic, legitimate, and grown-up. People no longer walked through me. They talked to me with respect. Atlantic City was a good fit for me, too; it almost felt like home. In those days, the city was transitioning from a quaint, rundown, seaside resort to the bustling "Las Vegas of the East" that it is today. There was enough of the quirky old town left to make me feel that I belonged, while I could enjoy the adventure and excitement of venturing into the sparkling new casinos that sprung up at an amazing rate. For the first time, I had money of my own; I no longer had to beg my parents for every dollar. My boss's secretary and I developed a friendly working relationship. I located an apartment with a landlady who was sympathetic and kind. I made up my mind to stay and practice law in South Jersey for the rest of my life. That summer, I took the New Jersey bar exam. When I passed, my boss threw me a little party. My commitment to my new career was so strong that I put down 2 months' salary on a secondhand Chevette, which I could drive to the courthouse on the mainland.

I Never Saw the Social Warning Signs

Like many Aspies, I never saw the warning signs, which, in retrospect, I am certain were there. Perhaps my boss was growing irritated with my quirky behavior. Perhaps I was tardy once too often. Perhaps I dressed too casually in his eyes. Maybe it was not all my fault. My boss was a lone wolf himself and simply may have had no desire for a permanent associate that he had to pay week in, week out, no matter what the workload. One Friday afternoon, my boss handed me my paycheck and announced, "This isn't working out." I was stunned and completely blindsided.

A Kick in the Pants

Losing that first job sent me into another tailspin. I hopped in my Chevette and headed west, looking for another place where I might feel that I belonged. I spent the next year on the road, sometimes picking up work along the way. For 6 months, I worked for a small-town lawyer in Colorado. He asked me to stay, but the twin demons of loneliness and homesickness landed me back on Aunt Rose's front porch, begging her to take me in again. She agreed, but on one condition. Aunt Rose gave me what she called "a kick in the pants." This time, there would be no "moping around." I would have to work. Even though I experienced depression and anxiety, when I was working steadily, the depression receded. I am glad I found work and actively developed the skills that steady employment requires.

My first job upon returning to Aunt Rose was my worst. I was hired by the collections department of a magazine in lower Westchester County. The work was borderline scummy—extracting money from struggling start-up businesses who could not afford to pay their advertising bill. The owner of the magazine treated everyone very unkindly. She ranted and raved and made demands that could not be satisfied. She spread stress around like butter on toast. No one lasted very long in that office; the turnover was phenomenal. She hounded people until they quit. I gritted my teeth and hung on for a year and a half, until I too could take it no more.

Two weeks after I left the magazine, I ran into a local attorney who said he might have some work for me. He did not mean putting me on the payroll or giving me a regular job. He wanted me to help him on a per diem basis, whenever his workload became overwhelming. This finally opened my eyes. I did not have to squeeze myself into that "windowless cubicle," corporate-type job after all. I had marketable skills. I could freelance. In every small town, there is at least one solo practitioner who has neither the money nor the inclination to hire another full-time employee but who will invariably have special projects from time to time for which assistance is required: filing papers, serving process, answering the court calendar, conducting legal research (my specialty), and drafting briefs. I even helped one attorney supplement a legal treatise. I had a business card printed up, and, before I knew it, my phone was ringing.

Now, this was not "career success" in any conventional sense of the word. My income was erratic and modest at best. I did not have benefits. However, at long last, I was being productive, exercising my skills, and performing tasks at which I excelled, while avoiding undue stress and office politics. I had found my own comfort level, midway between the prestigious, high-salaried law-firm job that my father desired for me and the "no-good lazy bum" that I had been on the road to becoming.

A Strong Attachment to Familiar Places

I did not yet know what was "wrong" with me, but over the years, I came to recognize and accept certain autistic traits in myself, chief among which was a strong attachment to familiar people, places, and things. I felt safe and secure living back in my hometown, even though my childhood friends had long since grown up and moved away. Walking down streets on which I had biked as a child and shopping at stores where I had shopped for years kept my inner chaos at bay. When people asked me why I did not go back to the city to look for a "real" job, I replied that I was needed here to care for an elderly aunt. In truth, it was the other way around. My elderly aunt was taking care of me.

I supplemented my income with colorful, quirky part-time jobs. I was a night clerk in a motel. I handed out coupons in the supermarket. I worked on village elections. My all-time favorite job, prior to my present one at Kykuit, was as a photographer's assistant and order taker for a studio that photographed high-school proms. For 20 years, until the company folded, I worked at the proms from April to June. For those 20 years, I lived for the spring. This job provided me with the opportunity to dress up and visit places I otherwise would never have seen—country clubs, fancy hotels, and catering houses—while listening to music and watching the young folks in their gowns and tuxedos. Best of all, it had *social* benefits. I met people, and I fraternized with other crew members.

Work Filled a Void in My Heart

Work filled the void in my heart where a social life should have been. After moving away from Alexis, I never made any close friends, with one exception. One of the small advertisers that I had to visit for the magazine collections department was a young attorney who had recently opened her own law office. We got to talking, and we ended up working together for more than 12 years. She acted as a public defender—the court would assign her as appellate counsel for persons convicted of crimes, and I did the legal research and drafted the briefs.

Attempting to free someone from jail seemed a worthwhile goal. I liked the moral purpose of it. The attorney and I went to visit our clients in prison, and we had "power lunches" at a diner, where we would spread the case record out on the table and hash it out over a burger. We also got together socially on occasion, visiting each other's homes or going shopping or to the beach. Eventually, she moved on with her career, and as a result, I found my present job at Kykuit.

RELATIONSHIPS

My Relationships with Men

My relationships with the opposite sex have been strange to say the least. I rarely dated in the conventional sense. Instead, in my younger days, I often engaged in an activity that today would be called "stalking." While I truly intended no harm, I experienced un-bearable loneliness, and if a handsome young man appeared on the periphery of my solitary life, my better judgment deserted me. I was drawn toward men who seemed to possess all the attributes I would have wished for myself—charm and popularity or a talent for singing, acting, or athletic ability. There were men who asked me out and tried to form relationships with me, but they held no attraction for me at all. I would rather chase what I could not capture. I only wanted what was unattainable and scorned every man that was actually available to me.

Learning about Asperger's

It has always been a mystery to me why I engaged in "stalking" types of behavior. I have analyzed it as I would a legal problem and still come up empty-handed. It even puzzled my therapist. She suggested that I write to Dr Tony Attwood, a world-famous expert in Asperger's syndrome. I did, and he actually wrote back. Dr Attwood replied that many Aspies engage in stalking-type activity and likened it to a special interest. Another person becomes the object of fascination, rather than an academic subject or a set of facts.

About 12 years ago, one of the attorneys I worked for sent me to the library to research Asperger's syndrome. He represented a local couple whose 18-year-old son had received a diagnosis of Asperger's. The attorney wanted to know if an adult Aspie would be considered legally competent to handle his own affairs. I asked my boss what Asperger's was. He said, "It's a little bit autistic." I had not read much before I realized that all the symptoms described in the literature applied to me. At that time, however, it was just a label. It was good to know that there were people like myself out there, but the information seemed of no practical value. It was just another obscure fact I had collected. After all, I was already over 40, and I thought any opportunity for a better life was far behind me.

Finding My Tour Guide Job

Then, in the winter of 2002, I came across an ad for part-time tour guides at Kykuit, the Rockefeller Estate. I had grown up when Nelson Rockefeller was the governor of New York, and, history and politics being special interests of mine, I knew something about the Rockefeller family. However, Nelson had died some years before, and since then I had not given him a passing thought. I did need a new part-time job, though. My attorney-friend in Connecticut was closing her practice, and that source of income had to be replaced. Kykuit sounded like fun—just the kind of quirky, offbeat work that Aunt Rose had wisely suggested I might be most suited for (like my job working at the proms, which I loved). I sent in my application, and it was the best thing that ever happened to me in my adult life.

To this day, I wonder how I passed the screening process. I persuaded one of my attorney-bosses to write me a recommendation, and I was hired. Everyone I work with at Kykuit is ten times more poised, graceful, self-assured, and sophisticated than I could ever be. That was the glamour that drew me to them. I wanted to be one of them.

I Love My Tour Guide Job and Learned How to Keep It

I loved the job from the start. The subject matter was right up my alley. Soon I could spout off the names and dates of Chinese dynasties and modern art movements as though it was second nature. The site itself was beautiful, wondrous, and a natural haven for a troubled mind. That is why the first John D. Rockefeller built it—as a refuge from a world that had provided him with amazing financial success but hated him for it. Best of all, the other guides did not automatically shun me or call me 'weird.' Many of them were older women, and when my mother died, they comforted me and got me through it. The job provided me with the structure I needed in my life. When you are writing a freelance legal brief, you can get out of bed or not; there is no one standing over you. However, when you are scheduled to conduct a tour at 10 o'clock in the morning, you'd better be there, or else. I was so desperate to keep this job that I forced myself to look visitors in the eye, even when I didn't want to. I looked at my watch and hurried my groups along so I wouldn't run late; I concentrated on speaking with inflection and projecting my voice. Talking for 2 hours was not the part that was difficult; like many Aspies, I can talk a blue streak on a subject in which I am interested. The trick was talking in a way that made people want to listen. All through the winter between my first and second seasons, I practiced before the mirror, like a trial lawyer preparing his closing argument. I tried out my new techniques with Aunt Rose. I knew I had finally found a place where I felt I belonged.

By dint of sheer self-will, I developed enough skills to hang on to my job. I became an adequate guide, and then, over the years, I became a very good guide. The job became my anchor through all the rough patches to come, such as the death of my father and Aunt Rose. In the case of Aunt Rose, not only had I lost my caregiver, but I had lost the last person in the world who really cared about me.

Losing My Family Was Very Traumatic

I imagine that losing one's family is traumatic for anyone, but to an autistic person it can seem like the worst thing that could happen. Many of us lack the ability to form strong friendships or relationships, and when we lose our family of origin, there is no one to fill the void. After Aunt Rose died, I had to vacate her home, and this increased my stress levels. Depression and anxiety overwhelmed me.

However, the Kykuit season was about to start, and I liked guiding so much that I decided to seek therapy and find out, once and for all, what was "wrong" with me. In this manner, I came to receive a diagnosis of Asperger's at the age of 54. I delved into learning about my diagnosis. I read books and scoured the Internet for information on the autism spectrum. I met other adult Aspies, both online and in person. I was pleased to find that, although my autism would not go away, my symptoms could be alleviated with small doses of an antidepressant (buproprion) and an antianxiety medication (klonopin).

Diagnosis Gave Me a New Perspective

A wise Frenchwoman once said that to understand all is to forgive all. Once I began to understand myself, I looked at the pattern of my past through a new perspective and began to forgive myself for all the repeated mess-ups in my life. I felt that I was finally able to move on.

At Kykuit, I had rediscovered the Real Me—the brave, spunky child that I was before I sank down into despair. My job as a tour guide has at last offered me an opportunity to shine and to develop skills I always wanted to possess. My self-confidence has grown, and I have actually been able to make friends.

I have added my own unique spin to the tour, which visitors seem to love. While my colleagues focus on the more dynamic characters of the Rockefeller family—John D. Rockefeller, Sr, or Nelson Rockefeller—I often talk about the generation in between. John D. Rockefeller, Jr, and I have a lot of traits in common. Like me, he had a hard time fitting in. He was fascinated by history and classical art. He felt so out of place in the 20th century that he built Colonial Williamsburg and spent a portion of each year at his home there. Just as the image of the IBM cubicle was impressed upon me in my youth as the archetypal job, "Junior" was always expected to follow in his father's footsteps and take over the Standard Oil Company. Like me, he had a lot of false starts, disappointments, and inner struggles before he realized he was simply not cut out to be a corporate executive. He knew he had to chart his own course in life.

Reconnection with My Childhood Friend

Last summer, a Christian tour group visited Kykuit, and I was their guide. One of the ladies had an identification tag with the name of the small town in North Carolina to which Alexis had moved 30 years before—the last time I had heard from her. As a lark, I asked the lady whether she knew Alexis. To my stunned delight, another visitor suddenly exclaimed, "Alexis? I work with her!" As it turned out, the visitor was a nurse at a hospital where Alexis is the chaplain. I gave her my e-mail address, and now I have reconnected with my childhood best friend. This is the kind of intangible treasure I have found through my work at Kykuit.

I have never become exactly like the other guides here, but in my eyes I've managed to become something even more meaningful. I've finally become myself.

CHAPTER 2

STEPHEN SHORE

Special-Education Professor and Autism Advocate

STEPHEN M. SHORE, BA, MA, EdD

Age: 50

Resides in: Newton, MA

Occupation: Assistant professor of special education,
Adelphi University, Garden City, NY

Marital status: Married 21 years

FROM TEMPLE:

Stephen worked hard and achieved success by becoming a professor at a university. He was very resourceful and set up a bike repair shop in his dorm room to pay his way through school. Stephen has authored several well-known books, and I love his overall positive view on life. Dr Shore still experiences some sensory difficulties, and when there is too much noise and commotion, he has to get away. Despite these challenges, Dr Shore's story illustrates how hard work and ingenuity can lead to success.

STEPHEN'S INTRODUCTION

At this time, I have been an assistant professor of special education at Adelphi University for 2½ years. In addition to my teaching duties, I develop curriculum and teach courses on autism and special education. I work with students who are preparing to become teachers, as well as those who want to update and increase their knowledge about autism and/or special education. I also teach students from the schools of psychology and social work. With committees, projects, collaborations with others to develop programs, and outreach to area schools, I find this career very rewarding. My research focuses on comparing different approaches, such as applied behavior analysis (ABA), Treatment and Education of Autistic and Communication related handicapped Children (TEACCH), Daily Life Therapy, the Miller Method, and Floortime, with the goal of applying the best practice to the needs of individual children on the autism spectrum. Because of the great diversity of the spectrum, it makes no sense to me to try to prove which approach is the best one overall.

The things I like most about my job are preparing for classes and teaching students about autism and special education. I also enjoy collaborating with my colleagues on instruction, curriculum building, and research. I tend to get very good teaching evaluations, averaging in the low-to-mid "1's" on a 4-point Likert scale, where 1 is the best score possible. Knowing that I am contributing to the field of education is very important to me. And that is verified every time students tell me in an unprompted way that they enjoyed my courses, when they reconnect to report that they have found teaching jobs, or when they reach out to ask for advice as they go on to educate students with autism and other special needs.

One dislike about my position relates to the sometimes long meetings that seem to consist of "data dumps" of information that could be read online, when a lot of time is spent between two or more people bickering about something, or when the gathering drifts off the agenda and runs overtime. However, I realize that, in addition to the things that do get accomplished at these meetings, in some ways they also contribute to the social cohesiveness of the various departments, as well as the various schools and the university at large.

One challenge I have overcome to some extent is managing subtle social situations and office politics. I continue to work on this. To help in this area, I make liberal use of mentors I can trust to help translate what is happening, decode the "hidden curriculum" of the workplace, and help prepare for when I do have to get into situations that require me to read "between the lines." That said, having good mentorship can be vital to achieving success in the workplace.

In all, I find my position serving as an assistant professor at Adelphi University very meaningful, and I plan to continue teaching there as long as possible.

EARLY YEARS

I am the youngest of three children. My brother, Martin, is 2 years older. It was clear that he had difficulties at birth and later received a diagnosis of mild to moderate retardation. He has certain skills that make me wonder if he has some autistic characteristics, as well. Most of the time, we got along fine and had the usual sibling rivalry. Here's an example of a misunderstood sensory event. One day, while we were playing on a swing set, I was sensorially overloaded by contacting the cold bars of the gym set with the underside of my knees. This caused a meltdown, and I banged my head against some flagstones and had to get stitches. It was many years before I told my parents that it was in fact the sensory overload that had caused the incident, and not anything my brother had done. On the whole, we were expected to treat each other civilly and help each other when needed.

My sister, Robin, is 4 years older. I used to think she got all the "neurologically typical" genes, but I am finding out that's not entirely true. For example, as a child, my sister used to yell at me for making too much noise as I walked around my bedroom, which adjoined to hers. In a recent conversation with her, I found out that she has significant hearing sensitivity.

After my first 18 months of otherwise typical development, I lost functional communication, had meltdowns, spun in circles, and demonstrated several other autistic characteristics. Because my brother had received a diagnosis of mild to moderate mental retardation, my parents knew it was not that. They suspected I was intelligent, and upon the urging of their pediatrician, at the age of 2½ I received a diagnosis of "strong autistic tendencies, childhood psychosis, and atypical development."

My Parents Kept Me Out of an Institution

Fortunately, my parents refuted the recommendation to have me institutionalized (thought to be warranted for such a diagnosis in 1964) and advocated for my admittance to the James Jackson Putnam Children's Center after a delay of a year and a half. In the interim, my parents provided what we would today refer to as an intensive, home-based early-intervention program that emphasized movement, sensory integration, music, narration, and imitation.

At first, my parents tried to get me to imitate them—especially my mother. When that failed, they started imitating *my* sounds and movements, which made me aware of them in my environment. Only then were they able to pull me out of my own world and into theirs. In my experience, the most important educational implication has been that before any significant teaching can happen, a trusting relationship has to be developed between teacher and student.

I Took Watches Apart and Put Them Back Together

At age 4, I started dismantling watches with a sharp kitchen knife. When my mother saw me demonstrating this skill, she began to provide me with additional watches, radios, and other things to take apart. Also, my parents both sat with me to make sure I got these things back together again in good working order! It was not hard for me to reassemble these mechanical devices. However, it was an important lesson my parents imparted—that if I took something apart, I should be able to put it back together again.

My mother did most of the caretaking and "early intervention," because in those days, it was the father's responsibility to work and earn money. Additionally, I think my father was pretty confused in terms of what to do with me. However, he still loved and supported me the best way he knew how.

My Parents Expected Proper Behavior

My parents expected me to show proper behavior at mealtimes, chew with my mouth closed, ask to be excused at the end of the meal, push in my chair when leaving the table, and participate in family chores, such as clearing dishes, taking out the trash, walking and feeding the dog, taking care of the cat, mowing the lawn, keeping my room clean, shoveling snow out of the driveway, and doing laundry when I was older.

Being Jewish, I was expected to go to religious services on Sundays and to attend Sunday school, just like my sister. My brother, who had more cognitive difficulties, did not have to go to Sunday school but still had to sit through the Sunday services, most likely because there was no special education version of religious school at that time. Sunday services and school also meant changing into nice but scratchy clothes, which I took off immediately upon returning home.

My brother and I both had bar mitzvah ceremonies at age 13, as is customary. Again, because of my brother's cognitive challenges, his requirements for reading and reciting Hebrew were limited to repeating another person as they recited short phrases in Hebrew. However, I was expected to do everything the others did, which I found exceedingly challenging. When I failed to improve with private tutoring in Hebrew, my parents made a recording of one of the elders at the temple, who recited the entire passage from the Torah that I needed to learn, plus all of the important prayers. Because the words were chanted in a singsong voice, they were easier to remember.

I put on a good show at the bar mitzvah, reciting everything in a sort of echolalic fashion, right down to the gravelly old voice of the elder who had recorded what to say. I had no idea *what* I was saying, other than knowing in a general way that I was talking about the first three days of creation, which I had read about in an old bible we had at home. However, it worked!

I Had to Earn Money for Things I Wanted

My parents addressed whatever basic needs we had. But if I wanted something extra, I had to earn the money to pay for it. For example, I wanted a new, "grown-up" bicycle that cost $50. I was expected to earn that money by doing a series of odd jobs around the house, mowing neighbors' lawns, and shoveling snow. It took about 6 months to earn enough money to pay for it, but I did it.

When I was given my grandfather's car after he could no longer drive it, I was expected to pay for my own gas, insurance, and maintenance. During the summertime when I was home from college, I was expected to contribute $25 a week toward paying the family expenses.

ELEMENTARY SCHOOL YEARS

By the time I entered the Putnam school as a child, after the "early intervention" provided by my parents and some speech therapy, my speech was beginning to return. I was reevaluated, and my diagnosis was upgraded from "psychosis" to "neurosis," so things were looking up for me.

I was in a class with three other boys in what seemed like more of a play-based intervention, which was focused on developing social interaction rather than ABA. To me, the most important variable of that program in terms of its successful outcome was its intensity.

I saw psychotherapists once a week for about 10 years, beginning at age 5. Some were better than others. What I hated most about these sessions was when a doctor decided I should play with either play dough or puppets. Both of them smelled terrible, and the play dough also left a residue on my hands.

Dr Martin Miller is one therapist who particularly stands out in a positive sense. He was ahead of his time in that, rather than trying to analyze me in an attempt to "cure me" of my autism, he helped me deal with the issues that stemmed from my condition.

A Social and Academic Catastrophe

In elementary school, I was a social and academic catastrophe. I did not know how to interact with my classmates in a way they could understand or expect, which resulted in a lot of bullying and teasing. For example, I remember walking around in kindergarten, repeating the letter "B" over and over. Even though I thought it was an ugly sound, I was compelled to repeat it. Around that time I realized there was something different about me, as I was the only one I knew who went to a special clinic and saw a special doctor (the psychiatrist) every week.

Instead of talking *with* my classmates, I had a repertoire of sounds and actions that I would make *at* them. I actually hoped I would get them to repeat these sounds and actions back at me. For me, that was a more predictable type of interaction than attempting to enter into a conversation.

I Loved to Read Books about Special Interests

Academically, I was almost a grade behind in most subjects and was often surprised when I got promoted to the next grade. However, I still had my special interests, in areas such as astronomy, airplanes, electricity, natural history, weather, cats, music, and the like. I spent hours at my desk, reading stacks of books on my favorite subjects. One day in the 3rd grade, I was busy taking notes and copying diagrams from a stack of astronomy books on my desk during a math lesson. My teacher told me that I'd never learn how to do math. Yet somehow, I've learned enough math to teach statistics at the university level! The good news is that today, an educator would likely notice such a special interest and find a way to incorporate it into a child's curriculum.

Sometimes I wondered if there was more to school than sitting at my desk, reading my favorite books. Often, just figuring out what teachers wanted was a perpetual challenge. Until I went to college, school always seemed like a bit of a game, as I tried to guess what the teachers wanted me to do. I think my teachers did not know how to reach me, and since I was not a behavioral problem, they just left me to my own devices. In those days, before there was special education law, it was probably for the best.

My Parents Supported My Special Interests

My parents supported my special interests. When I was focused on collecting seashells, my mother and I spent hours sorting and gluing shells onto a cover of a cardboard box. We also wrote the English and Latin names for the shells below them. When I was interested in astronomy, a telescope appeared, and we would stay up late at night, looking at the moon, stars, and constellations. My parents supported my interest in chemistry by providing me with a chemistry set and eventually a lab bench in my room.

I followed the Apollo space program closely and had a model of the lunar module at home. I read every book I could get my hands on that related to aviation, space exploration, and astronomy. At the time, I desperately wanted to fly on an airplane and thought about becoming a pilot. One of the highlights of my life was my first flight from Boston, MA, to Tampa, FL, to visit my grandparents. The feeling of takeoff was pure nirvana. Knowing what I know today about sensory integration, I was underresponsive in the vestibular and proprioceptive senses, and I was a sensory seeker. This may explain why I was and continue to be attracted to airplanes.

Some of my favorite sensory-seeking activities as a child were riding my bicycle into a snow bank as fast as possible to launch myself over the handlebars, climbing a tree about 20 feet in height and jumping to the ground, and swinging high on a swing set to find the perfect launching-off point, so I could sail through the air and land softly on my feet. To this day, I still enjoy take-offs on airplanes, as well as when the ride gets turbulent.

MIDDLE- AND HIGH-SCHOOL YEARS

In contrast to many, if not most people, middle and high school were better for me, probably for the following two reasons: *(1)* I started using words as my primary means of interaction with my classmates, instead of sound effects from the environment, and *(2)* I was able to engage in my special interests. The middle- and high-school years are when courses, clubs, and activities begin to form around particular interests. At first, I took a shop class in electronics and finished the material in about 3 weeks, when there were 9 more to go. However, the shop classes at my school contained bullies. My teacher saw that bullying was beginning to be a problem, so I was transferred into band.

In the band, I now had a structured activity in which to mediate my interactions with other students. Music was a place I could be successful and "geek out" with other like-minded students. My interest in music may have stemmed from the music my parents used for our home-based "early-intervention" program when I was young.

When I was 6 years old, my parents had found a teacher to give me music lessons. However, the lessons went badly. I think the most important thing I learned from these lessons was how *not* to teach children with autism how to play musical instruments. While I was taking those lessons, however, my parents remained very strict about having me practice 30 minutes a day to prepare for my time with the teacher.

I Learned to Play Most Musical Instruments

I became so taken with music that I would spend hours in the instrument closet with introductory music lesson books, such as *A Tune a Day,* to learn how to play most of the instruments. A leading factor in my choosing music education as an undergraduate college major was that one of the requirements *was* to *learn all of the instruments!*

How I Coped with Physical Education

Physical education was often problematic to me, owing to the challenges I had with motor control, and, later, bullying in the locker room. One day in middle school, I noticed a chart on the wall of the locker room that read "100-Mile Club," with a bunch of names on it. I asked the gym teacher what it was, and he said that anyone who walked or ran around a track 100 times during the semester got their name on the board. I requested to use my gym period to work on that very task. Upon his agreement, I queried as to whether I could walk or run in my "civilian" clothes, to which he assented. This was great, because now there was no more dealing with locker-room bullies, and I didn't have to engage in all of those ball-oriented sports I was so bad at. Rather, I could work on something that was a strength for me—running around a track.

In those days, there was no Individualized Education Program (IEP) and no special services for kids with autism. I was lucky to have a sensitive gym teacher who must have agreed I needed to get my physical education in an alternative way.

In high school, I had an opportunity to design an independent-study curriculum for myself in physical education. Bicycling was a special interest of mine, and I developed a weekly training schedule to prepare for long rides of 100 miles a day, as well as bicycle races.

I never had a problem with physical fitness, per se, but rather the social aspects and coordination needed to play team sports. Additionally, I had great difficulty with catching a ball because I always thought it was going to hit me, and I'd run away or duck. This was probably due to my visual perception issues.

Other enjoyable middle- and high-school activities included joining a rock-climbing club, where we went climbing with ropes and carabiners (a metal ring used to hold the ropes when climbing). I also convinced one of the teachers to sponsor the bicycle club I wanted to start, where I'd lead rides of up to 25 miles. It was great fun drawing up maps for the ride by hand, as there were no Google Maps at the time.

EXPERIENCES IN COLLEGE

As an undergraduate in college, rhetoric class was especially hard. It was essentially a freshman course to develop writing skills. Analyzing music from the romantic era posed a real challenge, as I found the forms to be less structured than compositions from other periods. I also found physics of music to be incredibly tedious. The subject interested me, but I found the teacher to be horribly boring—possibly owing to a lack of structure in the class. And, I was still afraid of doing math—statistics class was particularly daunting, until I took it as a summer course. The grade-school teacher who had told me I would never be able to learn math years before had succeeded in scaring me away from all math-oriented subjects. However, in college, when I decided to pursue an accounting degree in addition to my music degree, I faced the sizeable hurdle of required courses in mathematics.

With much trepidation, I took the first two required courses during the summer, when they would not interfere with my other coursework. Those courses went well. Emboldened, I started a statistics class that had the reputation of being incredibly difficult. That class was notoriously a good way to bring down your cumulative average, because poor grades were commonplace and it drained away study time from other coursework. After 2 weeks, I found this to be true, and I dropped the class.

Conquering the Dreaded Statistics Class

The following summer, I took the same statistics course again, all by itself, figuring it would be my lone "D" (and hopefully not an "F"), but at least it would not interfere with my other studies during the semester. To my surprise, my hard work, in combination with the support of an effective and helpful teacher, resulted in an "A!"

Doing well in that class made me realize the following: First, math was no longer to be feared—I could do well and even enjoy it! Second, I could use my newfound math abilities to make money by tutoring other students. And third, it became my impression that many people found statistics difficult because it was taught badly. Therefore, it became a personal goal of mine to teach statistics at the college level and do it well. That is how I came to teach statistics at various colleges as an adjunct professor, until 2008. Once I get tenure at Adelphi University, I may return to teaching statistics, in addition to courses in autism and special education.

In school, I remember struggling mightily to understand the concept of going from broad descriptions to honing in on a specific subject and then expanding upon that subject. This became pronounced when I was doing qualitative research as part of my graduate and doctoral work. It was only about halfway through a doctoral-level course in qualitative research, after drawing a funnel-shaped diagram, that I was able to grasp this concept more fully as I studied the way the broad end narrowed down to a more pointed tip. It would have been easier for me if my professor had included such a graphic in her lecture.

THE IMPORTANCE OF MENTORS

For me, mentors have played a valuable role throughout my school and teaching years. For instance, the orchestra conductor at my high school took a special interest in my musical curiosity and gave me free music lessons during his break time. When I was a professor of music in the Boston area, the dean of business became a mentor of mine. Although we did not share much in terms of common interests, he was very helpful in guiding me through the political maze that academic institutions can often be. Arnold Miller, the developer of the Miller Method, took a keen interest in my career, as well as in special education and autism. It was he who encouraged me to write my first book, *Beyond the Wall: Personal Experiences with Autism and Asperger Syndrome,* for which he wrote the foreword in the first edition. Dr Miller's guidance was invaluable in getting me through my doctoral program at Boston University, right through my dissertation and beyond.

EMPLOYMENT

Working as a Youth

My first taste of work came at age 8, when I began shoveling my neighbors' driveways after snowstorms. By middle school, I had teamed up with a friend, and the two of us had regular customers we shoveled for when needed. On a good day, we could make more than $50 each, which was a lot of money to a young kid in the late 1960s and early 1970s.

Toward the end of elementary school, I had a paper route, which I maintained through middle school. A paper route was a great thing for a child to have, because it contained all the aspects of a business enterprise at a small enough level for a young person to handle. Part of differentiating my service from other paperboys was placing the newspaper between the storm and main front doors of each house, so my customers could get their paper while remaining indoors— especially in bad weather. After a while, I had both a morning and afternoon route, with nearly 100 customers in all. Weekly collections for the papers got to be onerous, so I converted to a monthly system, where I collected customer payments a month in advance and reduced my time knocking on doors by 75%.

I Won a Trip to Disney World from My Paper Route

Sometimes there were contests, whereupon getting a certain number of "starts" (new customers), a paperboy could win a prize, such as a free trip to Disney World. A free trip to Disney World for finding only 20 new customers seemed like a great deal. After exhausting possibilities for new customers within my paper route territory, I reached out to other parts of my neighborhood and soon had almost twice the number of "starts" required. I gave some of my starts to a friend of mine, who was also a paperboy, and we went to Disney World together and had a great time. I also got my brother involved in the newspaper route, and he helped to deliver papers, as well. Currently, I know that newspaper delivery jobs for youth are becoming rare. However, possible employment substitutes that combine the need to do a job well on a regular basis and other aspects of running a business on a child-sized scale include dog walking, babysitting, and lawn care.

Bicycles had become a very strong interest for me at this time, so I began repairing bicycles at an hourly rate of a dollar above minimum wage. As described earlier, my parents insisted that if I wanted a "grown-up" bicycle, I would have to earn my own money to pay for it.

Working in a Restaurant Was Sensorially Overwhelming

My first "real" job was working as a busboy at a steakhouse when I was about 15 years old. This was a horrible job. Back then, it did not occur to me that autism had anything to do with the problems I faced. However, now I realize that the conditions of a noisy, busy restaurant were sensorially overwhelming, causing me to shut down and work slowly. The managers certainly did not like that. As a result, I realized that I needed to find a different job. However, I would not leave even a bad job before finding another one first. Fortunately, I saw situations like this one as learning experiences that drove me to find more suitable employment, rather than wallowing in self-pity and remaining in ill-fitting jobs. In this case, I decided to look for a position as a bicycle mechanic.

Being a bicycle mechanic was a dream job to me, since fixing, designing, and assembling bicycles was my passion. My interest and skill with bicycles got to a point where I was able to disassemble a bike down to the ball bearings and build it back up again. I also taught myself how to lace together a bicycle wheel from a hub, a collection of spokes, and a rim. This was a valued skill in a bicycle mechanic, and demonstrating that I could build a wheel got me at least one job.

Dorm-Room Bike Repair and Tutoring Business

To get a bicycle repair job, I would ride my custom-made bicycle to a bike shop and strike up a conversation with one of the mechanics or the manager himself. After talking with the manager, I would ask if he needed a mechanic. My bicycle was my portfolio. By having something concrete to talk about, instead of making small talk, I was able to gain the manager's attention and get a job.

I was employed at a number of shops and eventually worked my way up to managing these shops. In my late teens and early 20s, my grandfather offered to help set me up with my own bicycle shop. However, I already had a sense of what was needed to run a successful shop, and I preferred to focus my energies on higher education.

Knowing what I know about autism and sensory issues, I realize now that fixing bicycles in the back of the shop allowed me to better regulate my interactions with others in a way that suited me. Additionally, my interactions with other shop employees and customers related to my special interest in bicycles.

I received my two undergraduate degrees in *(a)* music education and *(b)* accounting and information systems at the University of Massachusetts in Amherst. In looking for employment to raise money for tuition and other expenses, it made much more sense to use my bicycle repair skills rather than work in a minimum-wage work-study job in the noisy dining commons or in another position at the university.

My solution was to open my own bicycle shop…right in my dorm room. I set my repair prices at two-thirds what the local bicycle shop charged, and I plastered the campus with simple, hand-written signs photocopied onto orange Day-Glo card stock. Soon, I had a dozen or more bicycles to fix on any given Saturday. I could spend half a day repairing bicycles and make more than I would have during a week of employment in a work-study position.

My dorm room was perfect for bicycle repair. The cinderblock walls had a metal lip at the top for hanging pictures. I used that lip to hang a bicycle rack that was designed to be strapped to a car trunk. Then I placed a 4-foot length of wood across the "legs" of the bicycle rack and had a great shelf on which to place my tools while I worked.

One day, one of the bicyclists I hung around with at the university mentioned that there was a bicycle trade show in New York— bicycle nerd heaven! In finding out more about the trade show, I learned that only owners of bicycle shops were allowed to attend, as opposed to customers or interested people. As a result, I generated business cards and stationery and gave five of my friends "positions," such as repair manager, sales manager, and chief mechanic. Properly credentialed, we piled into the car I got from my grandfather, drove to New York City, and got into the show.

All was well and good with repairing bicycles in my dorm room, and at least I didn't *think* my roommate had a problem with all the bicycles I kept in our room. However, my older (wiser) sister thought differently and made me promise to have no more than one bicycle on my side of the room at a time.

I found that tutoring was another good way to make money in college. After learning that I could do well in statistics, I decided to help other students who had difficulty in this area. I tutored in other subjects, as well, including accounting, computers, and music theory. Because I was an accounting major and had an interest in taxes, I began doing simple tax returns in undergraduate school.

After graduating with my bachelor degrees, I interviewed for jobs in accounting firms without success. Finally, the school career counselor referred me to an outside placement consultant, who found me a position in a medium-sized accounting firm where they audited mutual funds. Since I had an interest in mutual funds, this seemed to be a good idea.

A Sensory Nightmare at an Accounting Firm

Getting to work on the first day was a sensory nightmare. Again, this came at a time when I knew nothing about how autism affected me in any way. It took getting up at 5:15 in the morning to arrive at work on time at 8 o'clock. Returning home meant reversing the process and having dinner at about 8 or 9 in the evening. This was way too much travel time.

The second day on the job, I neatly folded up my suit (which was another sensory violation with the binding jacket and tie), rode my bicycle, and got to work in less than 45 minutes! Within days, I had arranged with the superintendent of the building to store my bicycle. I kept a selection of business clothes in the basement, where I changed into appropriate work attire before taking the elevator up to the office.

Shortly thereafter, the personnel director pulled me aside and indicated that I was seen entering the building without a suit and that it would be better if I took public transportation. I also had difficulties blending in with the other accountants.

After 3 months, I was let go from that position. The director of personnel said, "Perhaps you have a disability you have not disclosed. It's just not working out." It never occurred to me at that point that difficulties I'd had with autism as a child played any role.

Within another 3 months, I found another job at a bank, working as a portfolio accountant. Because the organization was so large (with 5,000 employees), I could ride my bicycle to the far end of the office building, do my Superman routine to change into business clothes, and walk across the expansive building to my desk without anyone being the wiser.

Although I performed my job in a satisfactory way, I still did not seem to fit in with the people working there, and I soon grew bored of the routine. I managed to locate a position at a vocational school, teaching computers, mathematics, and other business-related courses, before leaving my job at the bank.

I Like Teaching

I found that teaching worked well for me. My colleagues were intrigued that I rode my bicycle to work and didn't see it as a negative at all. About a year into that job, I realized that I preferred to teach music rather than business, so I negotiated my hours down by a third and started working toward a master's in music education at Boston University.

The vocational school shut down after about a year, and I began teaching as an adjunct faculty member in several colleges and universities in the Boston area. At first, I taught business and computer classes, and then music. I even taught classes in both accounting and music at Boston University while I worked on my master's and doctoral degrees. I began a doctorate in music education but switched to special education instead.

Academically, I thrived. Most of the work I did to support myself came from teaching adjunct courses. I even managed to get a full-time teaching position at a secretarial finishing school, and then later as a professor of music at a community college in Boston.

Unfortunately I lost that job, most likely because of a failure on my part to pay careful attention to office politics. When I started the position, I proposed a restructuring of the course offerings in the music department. While I had the support of my dean, I neglected to get an official "OK" from a long-term faculty member from another department, who taught a single course in the music program. From that point forward, he was always at the ready to oppose future proposals of mine and eventually convinced the school to close the music department.

RELATIONSHIPS

Making Friends

As a young child, making friends in elementary school was difficult. Sometimes I had one or two friends, but the school seemed mostly full of bullies. Sometimes I'd make friends with someone who seemed different than the other students. Additionally, the friends

I had were all older—they were either my sister's friends or adults. Thinking back, they may not have really been true friends, but since they were nice to me and listened to what I had to say, I considered them friends.

As a teenager, again I was friends with older people. I still had very little in common with my classmates, and there was some bullying, but less so than in elementary school.

Finding Friends with Common Interests

In college, I built more friendships with my peers. This is probably because classmates seemed more interested in who a person was, rather than how much they were like someone else. Also, since my school had 25,000 students, it was much easier to find people with common interests. For example, if I wanted to ride my bicycle at midnight, I could find someone just as strange as I was to ride with me.

In my first adult job as an accountant, I had no friends there. I did make some friends at the job that followed, at the bank. However, all of my friends were from other countries, such as India, Eritrea, and China.

Even now, I find that most of my friends are from other countries. My theory on this is that people of a given culture intimately know how another person from their culture is supposed to behave. Deviances from these behaviors are disliked. In grade school, these differences are met with teasing and bullying. In the adult world, the more likely outcome is being shunned. Additionally, people in other cultures don't pick up on differences as much, owing to their relative lack of familiarity with your own culture. Differences that they do notice may be misattributed to your culture instead of your individuality. I have also found that people in other cultures have their own challenges with integration and may be more tolerant or even appreciative of differences in others. This may explain in part why I married a Chinese woman. I still feel more comfortable with people of different ages and cultures than my own.

Dating was always confusing to me. There was too much non-verbal communication and hidden curriculum. There were times when someone told me that a woman was interested in me, but I never picked up on the signs. I just considered myself hopelessly clueless in this arena.

In undergraduate school, after spending a lot of time with a particular woman, she suddenly told me that she really liked hugs and backrubs. My interpretation of that was, "Great! I have a new friend, and not only that, but now I can get the deep-pressure hugs I've always craved!" However, she evidently had a very different idea of what our relationship was, and after a lot of conversation, I realized that in addition to wanting to be my girlfriend, she thought she had been dating me for a month! Because the feeling was not mutual, the encounter does not qualify as a dating experience or having an intimate relationship. It goes beyond the typical male cluelessness that is often espoused to my gender.

What this experience did do was inform me that there was a "secret channel" of communication, consisting of eye and body movements and postures, which led me to spend hours in book-stores, reading up on body language and nonverbal communication in general. I got so interested in this subject that I even did a paper on nonverbal communication for a psychology class.

Doing Homework Together Morphed into Marriage

In total, I've had three intimate relationships in my life—all of which resulted from a woman making it clear to me that she wanted to date. In the case of my wife, our relationship eventually turned into a romantic one, but it may not have, had she had not made her sentiments clear. After playing the harp for 9 years in the Beijing Symphony, she arrived in the United States from China to further her education. She had been in the U.S. for about 18 months when we met as graduate students in a music class. Reviewing each other's homework morphed into doing things socially. Then, one day at a beach, she suddenly gave me a big hug and kiss, and she held my hand. On the basis of my readings, this made me realize that she probably wanted to be my girlfriend. We have now been married for more than 21 years.

Forming platonic relationships or simple friendships with the opposite sex is not too difficult for me. However, forming an intimate relationship with a person of the opposite sex was always very difficult or impossible for me to initiate. I was just lucky that the three women I dated (especially my wife) made their intentions so clear that their wishes could not be misunderstood. Without these women making their intentions known, I would likely remain single to this day.

ROLE MODELS

My grandfather was the smartest person I knew and had great mechanical abilities. Initially very poor, he educated himself, became a lawyer, had his own business selling plastic shades all over the world, and could plan and build a house from the ground up. He had little tolerance for stupidity and changes in routine, even as simple as dinner being 10 minutes late. Thinking back, he probably had some Asperger's tendencies.

As I moved into high school, Bernard Thévenet, two-time winner of the Tour de France bicycle race, became a role model of mine. I had a big poster of him in my bedroom, and I wanted to be like him. Tullio Campagnolo was an Italian bicycle racing component maker. I didn't want to become Tullio. However, I thought Campagnolo bicycle components were just the most beautiful and functional components that could ever be made for a bicycle.

I always admired musical composers, such as Tschaikovsky, Beethoven, Mozart, Berlioz, Mahler, Richard Strauss, Schubert, and Stravinsky. I didn't want to *be* like them, but I was inspired by their music and wanted to compose like they did. I spent a lot of time burrowing into musical scores and rearranging the instrumentation for different ensembles. I thought the most honorable thing one could do was to become a music major at a conservatory or university— which I eventually did.

During my graduate work, a music history professor by the name of Joel Sheveloff impressed me. He had immense knowledge of both music history and theory, and his history courses often seemed to be taught through a music theory lens. He is just a good, all-around ethical and moral person.

Last but not least, I received much support from Arnold Miller, who developed the "Miller Method," a cognitive–developmental systems approach for working with children on the autism spectrum. From my initial observations, it seemed like what he was doing with autistic children was…right. Later on, I found that one important aspect of his developmental-cognitive approach focuses on determining how a child with autism perceives his environment. In other words, figuring out how people with autism *think*. Arnold was very helpful and instrumental to me throughout my doctoral study in special education and remains so to this day.

ON AUTISM

My Autism Is Never "All Done"

One life-changing event for me was when I realized that my autism was not something of the past. What I mean by that is, by the time I got out of grade school and finished my sessions with the psychiatrists, I thought autism was "all done." In fact, up until my mid-30s, had someone asked if I was or am autistic, I would have said, "Well, that's something of the past, when I was a young child…but not anymore."

It was not until I experienced difficulties with some relatively unstructured information on a doctoral qualifier examination that it occurred to me that this "autism" diagnosis of the past was "haunting" me now, in this very subtle but perhaps very significant way. I underwent a neuropsychological examination and found out that the childhood diagnosis and condition were indeed still with me. However, with intervention, maturation, and intense curiosity about the way things work, I was able to work around most of the challenges. I did receive some suggestions for mild accommodations to enable me to take the doctoral qualifier examination, but the school refused to make them. Rather than spending a lot of time with lawyers and a potential court hearing, I decided it best to refocus my doctoral studies on special education and the autism spectrum. However, I never thought of autism as being an excuse not to do something. Rather, understanding the characteristics of the condition as they affect me serve as a guide to help me do things better.

Leading a Fulfilling Life

From my initial presentation on autism in 1997 to my first book, *Beyond the Wall: Personal Experiences with Autism and Asperger Syndrome,* it has been my goal to combine academic, professional, and personal experiences on the autism spectrum, instead of touting the experience of "being autistic." In other words, how can I employ my autistic characteristics—just as anyone on or off the spectrum should do with their own traits—to lead a fulfilling and productive life and help others realize they can do the same?

I like to think of *Beyond the Wall* as employing an autobiographical structure in which to address the issues of education, accommodations, sensory issues, and a successful transition to adulthood in the areas of self-advocacy, relationships, continuing education, employment, and, in short, having a real life, working and doing things just like everyone else. One can *be* autistic rather than *living a life* of autism.

Rather than attempting to make a career of talking about autism at conferences, I do the following. First, I serve as a professor of special education, developing and teaching a number of courses on a variety of subjects. Second, I write books about autism. The goal behind my books is to provide practical information about supporting individuals with autism in meeting and overcoming challenges. The same holds true for articles I write and for when I consult and do workshops and presentations about it. And third, I teach music lessons to children with autism. Engaging children in music therapy has many benefits. It provides them with an important avenue for developing interactions with others, as a musician and in the community (such as being a member of a local ensemble). Plus, music is just plain old fun, and fun is always a worthwhile pursuit.

I believe I have made a career in autism and special education on the basis of hard work and conducting research in the field, combined with my own experiences of being on the autism spectrum. This is in contrast to what I see some people doing when they want to make a career out of being autistic. It may be a subtle distinction, but I think an important one to emphasize.

CHAPTER 3

ANNA MAGDALENA CHRISTIANSON

Psychiatric Rehabilitation Practitioner

ANNA MAGDALENA CHRISTIANSON, MS, CPSS, ETS, CPRP

Age: 60
Resides in: Berrien Springs, MI
Occupation: Psychiatric rehabilitation practitioner and peer-support
specialist at Riverwood Center, Berrien County
Mental Health Authority
Marital status: Married 38 years, with two children

FROM TEMPLE:

Anna feels that her life really began in her 50s, when she began working as a rehabilitation specialist. She largely deals with clients who have severe mental illness. Fortunately for Anna, she has a boss who is aware of her Asperger's syndrome and who coaches her when she needs it. Anna draws inspiration from classical music more than from other people. She feels music at the core of her being, and it inspires emotions within her she would not be able to experience otherwise. At the end of her chapter, Anna writes that some people might consider her job to be a "dead-end job" but that it has been perfect for her. It has allowed her to grow and "blossom" at an amazing rate.

ANNA'S INTRODUCTION

Since July 2008, I have worked for the Berrien County Mental Health Authority as a psychiatric rehabilitation practitioner and certified peer-support specialist at the Riverwood Center. I work both one on one and in group settings with individuals with severe mental illness, facilitating their recovery. I oversee a number of recovery- and wellness-orientated workshops and classes. I do benefits counseling, housing, and sometimes employment. I am also an advocate for the mentally ill and sometimes speak publicly on mental illness and my own experience with a severe mental illness.

I consider myself fortunate to work where I do and to have an understanding supervisor, who gives me the freedom to be myself. I work on a number of committees, both at work and on the state level, and I have grown both professionally and personally as a result. I am able to incorporate several of my likes into the work I do, namely literature research and review and curriculum development. One aspect of work I am not fond of is documentation, because I find writing so difficult and intimidating. I feel awkward and sometimes have trouble finding the right words.

I have experienced some interpersonal problems at work. In the past, I had difficulty understanding the role of a coworker and made some terrific blunders. I have said things I ought not to and misunderstood what was said to me. The social aspects of life have always presented a problem, but I am working hard to "be nice."

I've been such a free, stubborn spirit for so long, that I have had some difficulty at work adjusting to supervision. After 3 years of employment, I just learned that one *asks* one's supervisor if one may take time off. I thought one just *told.* This has been a struggle to learn and remember.

Lars, my son, lives in Napa Valley and is pursuing a degree in computer science. He's researching topics such as augmented reality and human-machine interfaces. He would like to bring cutting-edge technology, such as head-up (transparent) displays and intuitive input interfaces, into everyday use. He supports himself and his education by working as a janitor. He's a union steward and a classified senate vice president at the college at which he works. (As he explained it to me, the union is the negotiating body at the school. The senate is a governance body. He represents the nonteaching staff.)

Else, my daughter, is an artist and an integral part of the Sebastopol alternative art community in California. She is currently working with colored pencil on birch panels. Else is also a costume designer and art director for an indie rock band called Baby Seal Club. With a group of friends, she formed a large community garden, which provides her with quite a bit of her own food.

Growing up, Else took it upon herself to teach me about social cues. "You didn't have special ed," she quipped. "You had children." She used to tell me in the grocery store, "Mom, don't point—it's rude!"

It is important to note that both of my children believe they were profoundly affected by my experience with bipolar disorder, anxiety, and an autism spectrum disorder. Lars has told me that he is now in the finishing stages of working through childhood issues. He believes that the biggest impediment to a more healthy childhood was the almost complete lack of information on how to deal with both his and my symptoms and idiosyncrasies. He also has an autism spectrum disorder, although he feels he is now "without symptoms."

CHILDHOOD AND YOUNG ADULT YEARS

With the exception of Stanley, my twin brother, I am the eldest of five children. Becky and Barbara are 1½ and 2½ years younger. John is 10 years younger. I tended to play mostly with Becky. Stanley and Barbara played together, as I recollect. Since John was so much younger, he was like "an only child."

I remember playing with Stanley's trucks in the sandbox and in the dirt. I colored and painted, read books, put together puzzles, and played with dolls. I made rose petal perfume and covered myself in mud. I pretended to be a pioneer and an Indian. One magical Iowa day, I played all by myself with little rocks in the dirt by the side of the road. Every summer, I designed a new handwriting style to use during the coming school year. I rode my bike, executed insects with Becky (by hanging them or decapitating them), played in the haymow (piles of hay) in the barn, and made forts. I watched cartoons and Shirley Temple movies at the neighbor's house. I was fascinated with exploration.

But I was not a happy child.

I Was Taught Manners and Punctuality

I was brought up in a conservative Christian home. I attended the Seventh-day Adventist church, was baptized when I was 12 (and took it very seriously), and attended private Seventh-day Adventist schools. As kids, we were expected to obey and were taught manners and to say "please," "thank you," and "excuse me." I was taught to be neat and clean. While I did not always keep my room straight as a child—I shared it with my two sisters—my drawers were always ship-shape. I was taught to let my mother know where I would be and when I would be home. "How come you trust Anna?" Becky queried. Because I was always where I said I'd be, and I was punctual in returning home. I was given chores and was expected to help clean the house every Friday afternoon in preparation for the Sabbath. I played "sink the saucers" (washed the dishes), ironed, and was expected to keep my room clean. Every Friday, I dusted the living room. It was all I had time for on Friday, because I felt compelled to dust everything—every book, shelf, rung, furniture leg, figurine, and picture frame. I also had other irregular jobs, like sweeping the walk or helping my mother can fruit in the summertime.

Early on, I was taught to know the difference between right and wrong and to always tell the truth. I was also taught to respect adults and refer to them by title. My parents emphasized the importance of generosity. One winter, I gave my sister, Becky, my favorite coat as a nice gesture. Later on, I found out that the one I kept for myself was actually her favorite!

When I was 10, my little brother, John, was born. It was my responsibility to help my mother care for him. I protected him as best as I could from Becky, who used to try and bribe him to do things for her. When he was 2 years old, I saved his life by plucking him from a stream—he was sliding down toward a precipice and a waterfall. I saved my mother once, too. We were tubing in rough water, and she fell off into the rapids. I grabbed her and pulled her over to the riverbank, sputtering and thrashing. She had never learned to swim.

I Was Educated to Value Art and Music

I was raised to value art and music, the accoutrements of "culture." We were the only family I knew that attended classical music concerts and visited art museums. As a child, I once invited my friend, Suzanne, to accompany us to a Sunday afternoon concert at Redlands University. She declined. Growing up, the only music I listened to was on the classical music radio station out of Los Angeles. I remember lying on the carpet by the radio in the evening, listening to someone playing the piano. When I was 10, I started taking piano lessons. We all took music lessons, but the piano became my instrument. Sometimes, when I practiced, Becky would stand behind me with a paring knife at my back. She told me that if I moved, she'd stab me. While she may not have done it intentionally, she was clumsy enough to do so accidentally. I was afraid.

I was taught to value the natural world. Every Saturday afternoon, we went to the country. We often went camping—to the beach, the mountains, or the desert. We were free, then, or at least I was. We collected rocks, shells, insects, and flowers. I knew the names of things then. My father thought I would become an entomologist. Close. I did graduate work in entomology, I just didn't complete the thesis.

Teen and Young Adult Years

On the Sabbath, I went to work at the hospital with my dad. Sometimes I was scared of my mother's driving. Going to summer camp was a source of discomfort. I was afraid of my cousins. I was also afraid of a girl named Ann, as well as older children. I lay awake for hours at night. My mother chewed too loud.

When I was 17, I discovered the lutenist Julian Bream and Elizabethan music on a record I got from Smiley Library. I played that record nonstop for a year. Becky hated it. Therefore, she hated me. My mother thought it was because Becky was jealous of me, because I was the eldest. That did not make any sense. Last year, Becky told me it was because of Julian Bream and the lute. I was very, very much "into" the Renaissance and Baroque periods then, particularly the arts. I also loved the Beatles.

I do not know if my parents suspected that I was different. My mother has only said, "You were all different." She did note, however, that I seemed "high-strung" and only relaxed when we spent the day in the mountains. I also seemed content when I was little to play by myself and would ignore the others around me. I did not act like I needed much attention and did not seek it; therefore, I did not get a whole lot. My mother had her hands full with my siblings. I had a temper, and my mother has told me how mortified she was when I'd throw myself on the ground and kick and scream.

When I was 17, we were seeing a family counselor for a problem with another sibling. It was this specialist who alerted my parents that I was the one who really needed help. I don't know what she saw, other than an extremely depressed, withdrawn adolescent. I began seeing a psychologist and, later, a psychiatrist. Neither one helped me, nor did the medications prescribed for me. I talked very little, and I had begun acting out, even though I had always been reasonably well behaved. One afternoon, while home alone, I smashed two-thirds of the windows in the house and then took off for the local cemetery. I don't know why I did it. My condition was diagnosed as an adjustment disorder.

Anxiety and Bipolar Disorder

I later received diagnoses of bipolar disorder and an anxiety disorder. My mother has asked me, "What could I have done differently?" And I've told her, quite honestly, "Nothing," for I know of nothing that could have changed my life. I was unhappy as a child. I had a suicide plan when I was 9. My mother has told me that I didn't seem happy at home. I preferred school. My only explanation is that perhaps school was more organized and predictable and less personal. Perhaps there were not as many emotions floating around.

I did not connect with people well. I do not remember ever doing so, actually, except for an isolated occasion when I was 20, when I was doing hashish with a girl named Jenny. I still do not connect. This lack of emotional reciprocity—if that is what it is—has been my greatest discomfort. I was loved as a child. I was my paternal grandfather's favorite grandchild. Yet, I never felt love.

SCHOOL EXPERIENCES

I was taught to value learning and education. My family was educated, and there was never any question that we would all continue on in school.

I attended morning kindergarten with Stanley. Apparently, I clung to him—that's what the grade card said at the end of the year. "Ann does not cling to Stanley as much." I don't think that was literal. I don't recall being comfortable in kindergarten, though. I was 5 and in a foreign place. One day, Stanley was sick and I had to go to school alone. Most of the way, I had to walk by myself because my mother had to stay with the other children. I was scared, and I cried. Ann, the girl I was afraid of, told me to rub spit on my eyes and then no one would be able to tell that I had been crying. It didn't work. The teacher immediately asked me what was wrong.

In 1st and 2nd grades, I was in a two-room school with four grades per room. I don't remember the number of students in my room, maybe a dozen. I absolutely adored my teacher, Mrs Addison. And she liked me—all my teachers liked me. I felt like a teacher's pet, and maybe I was. I was quiet, well behaved, and a natural student. I took school very seriously. On the first day of school in the 1st grade, I met Suzanne. She became my best friend until she went to Loma Linda Academy in the 10th grade. I think she and I were teacher's pets together. Maybe.

My favorite color was blue. "What's your favorite color?" "Blue." That's because Suzanne's favorite color was blue. In actuality, I really didn't have a favorite color, but everyone always thought it was blue. Suzanne and I, never, ever, once fought or argued or had the tiniest hint of a disagreement. I think I just went along with whatever she wanted. Or maybe she was just as agreeable as I was. I don't know. I was appalled at my sisters and their relationships. Suzanne's little sister Roxy was Barbara's off-and-on best friend. They alternately loved and hated each other. I never understood it. Becky was the same. They also had a lot more friends than I did. I really only had one. But, I also had no one who disliked me.

I don't recall ever inviting Suzanne over to my house. I went to hers maybe twice, and I was extremely uncomfortable. In the summertime, sometimes I'd go over to her grandmother's. We'd play Indians with stick spears in the tall grass. Sometimes we were animals—Suzanne's idea. Sometimes we played with little green World War II soldiers.

In 3rd grade, the school moved to a brand new location, and we only had two grades to a room. Well, 3rd grade actually had its own room, I think because the class was "large." After a time, the five smartest students were moved into the 4th/5th grade room, not sure why. It was Stanley, Mark, Albert, Suzanne, and me. We were still in the 3rd grade. But one afternoon before we were moved, I was copying something off of the blackboard before going out to recess. My teacher, Miss Biggs, was standing in the way. I very politely said, "Hey, kid. I can't see through you." She made me put my head down on my desk. I didn't understand. Other people said things like that. Even adults. They said, "You make a better door than a window." I said the very same thing. My mother told me Miss Biggs was shocked, and she made me go back after school to apologize. I didn't understand why.

In 6th grade, I came home from school every day and immediately sat at the wall-mounted desk my dad had made me and did homework. All evening, I would do homework. I loved it. I was in Mr Larsen's room. I liked him. Of course, I liked most of my teachers. All except Miss Biggs. She thought that if parents did their jobs right, children would come to school and be perfect little angels.

I Became a Stranger in a Strange Land in 11th Grade

In 11th grade, I moved to Loma Linda Academy, because Redlands Junior Academy only went to the 10th grade. I was lost. It was much bigger, and there were crowds of students I didn't know—and never would. I knew a few people, but not well. Of course, some of my classmates from Redlands also moved to Loma Linda. It didn't matter. I was still a stranger in a strange land. This was the year it really hit me that I was alien, that I didn't fit. I was a wallflower and was unable to connect with people. I was the island that John Donne said no man was. This is the year I really began falling apart, the year I began my descent into hell.

Academically, I did well at the academy. I was, in fact, one of the two brightest students, according to one of my teachers. The other was my friend, Joy. I was among the popular girls at school. I was quite nice looking and dressed very well. I was also very disturbed and "different," but "different" in a good way. It was, after all, the late 1960s. Perhaps my quirks even added to the intrigue that was me.

When I was 7 and asked what I wanted to be when I grew up (not that the thought had ever crossed my mind), I said, "an artist." I was very good. I could look at something and draw it. Reproduce it. I had an artistic gift. When I graduated from the Academy, I moved to the dorm at La Sierra College (now University) and became a music and art major. I didn't last the semester. I ended the year in the psychiatric unit of Loma Linda University Hospital. I was there 3 months. I'd pretty much stopped talking. And that's when the death of my music and my art began. Fortunately, I had never been more than a reluctant artist, anyway.

I Did Well Academically

In 1995, I finally graduated from Andrews University with a bachelor of science in zoology, with a biomedical emphasis. When Lars started school, I went back to school myself, first taking drawing and printmaking classes. Else accompanied me to class—she is now quite a fine artist. Once Else was in school and I was feeling more confident, I began taking more classes. My goal was to get into medical school. But I still was not "all right." I still talked little, and I kept ending up in the hospital. At one point, I had so many electroconvulsive treatments that I forgot everything except how to use the restroom. Else had to teach me everything I had lost.

I managed to get through school by sitting in the very front row, in the center, immediately before the teacher. This way I was, to my mind, virtually the only student in the class. I never offered any response, but then I had never responded in class. I took copious notes and did very well. I made no friends and rarely spoke to anyone.

I went to Michigan State University in 2000 to complete a master's in entomology. I was still having major difficulties, so after completing the class work and my research, I came home. I just wasn't able to complete the thesis, so I never graduated.

I have recently been accepted into the online master's program in psychiatric rehabilitation, leadership track, at the University of Medicine and Dentistry in New Jersey. I'm scheduled to begin classes soon.

Social Aspects of School Were Difficult

Calculus and physics—and classes with really uninteresting teachers—were my difficult subjects. But what was most difficult about school was the social aspect, particularly communication. Perhaps that's why I was so very quiet. It got so I just didn't have anything to say. Another great difficulty was creating—making something up. I have an extremely difficult time writing creatively. I'm best with literature reviews. There, the ideas are already present for me. I have difficulty putting things into my own words, so sometimes I find it almost impossible not to plagiarize. I shall never write a novel. I would never be able to think of a plot and then flesh it out. I have a similar difficulty with art. I have to have something concrete in front of me. I have trouble just "drawing from my head"—drawing something imaginary. If I do, the quality is inevitably very poor and quite juvenile. The same was true with music, back when I played. I had to have music in front of me. I couldn't play "by ear."

Just about everything else came to me easily. I particularly liked diagramming sentences, algebra, geometry, aesthetics, biochemistry, and neurochemistry.

MENTORS

Nancy Magi showed up in my life as my 11th-grade English teacher at Loma Linda Academy. She was young and pretty, and she took an interest in me. I liked her. I think all the students did. In 12th grade, I was her "reader." Somehow, she became my friend. I remember accompanying her to the beach one sweltering summer day, wearing my navy blue wool pea jacket. Sometimes I went on picnics in the mountains with her and her husband, Enn. Even though she was my friend, I remember feeling very, very awkward and alien. When I moved away, she kept in touch.

Shirley Macaulay came along when I was at college in La Sierra. Her son, Doug, was in one of my music classes, and somehow I ended up at her house for dinner occasionally. Shirley took an interest in me. She probably took an interest in everyone, but she was very kind to me. She's remained a very dear friend. Often, when she visited her daughter, Diane, in Ann Arbor, we would get together. I remember when I was living in a house in downtown Riverside, and life was very black, I sat in a booth at a diner one night with Shirley. She talked to me and tried to understand me. She was very supportive.

I was quite disturbed at the times when I met Nancy and Shirley. Enn was a child psychiatrist, in residency, when I first met Nancy. Shirley was, I think, a school psychologist. Maybe this helps explain why they took an interest in me.

Employment as a Teenager

When I was 14, I volunteered as a candy striper at the old Loma Linda University Hospital. I remember delivering mail to the patients and taking stool samples to the lab. I liked the work. I was with Debbie Picard, a friend, so she was the one who spoke with the patients. I just ran errands.

When I was 16, I assisted the accountant, Mr Dale, in the business office at Loma Linda Academy. I helped with the bookkeeping, particularly the entry of the accounts receivable. I had studied bookkeeping in school the previous year, and I worked alone.

Babysitting as a teenager was awkward for me and rather traumatic. I hated it. I didn't have a clue as to what to do with children, much less their parents. One summer, I babysat for the Liu family up the street. There were two little girls. They were cute, but alien. One day, Dr Liu was home in his study while I watched the girls. I was so, so uncomfortable. The girls ran through the house, and I didn't stop them. I just watched. One little girl bumped a vase, and it fell to the floor and shattered. I stood and watched as Dr Liu came out and cleaned up the pieces. I have no idea why they didn't hire a more competent sitter.

Another summer, I watched two very homely children, a little boy and his baby brother. For some reason, I was boiling a pan of water—to heat up a bottle, perhaps? And I boiled the water dry. Confrontation has always been very difficult for me, and I was afraid to tell the mother what I'd done. So I stuck the pan in the very back corner of the cupboard and hoped nobody would notice.

During the summer between 11th and 12th grades, I worked in a lingerie department. This would classify as a "worst job," except it did not last as long as the babysitting did. I had no clue what to do in this job. I was no help to the few customers I encountered. I had no words and poor conversation skills.

I also worked in the back of a pharmacy, weighing and packaging medicinal herbs. I worked for my father, and I worked alone. My father told me to measure each package an ounce over the desired weight—rather like the "baker's dozen," which really appealed to me morally. I liked this job.

EMPLOYMENT AS AN ADULT

I Love My Present Job

My present job is the best job I've had. I am much older, at an entirely different place in my life, and I'm doing very well. My life basically began in my 50s, when I "woke up" from the long nightmare of severe mental illness. I talk and laugh and smile. I whistle when I work. And I like people, although I still do not connect. This, however, I see as an advantage. In my work, a risk is that one may become too emotionally involved. I do not run this risk. I do not take my clients home with me, so to speak.

In my work as a psychiatric rehabilitation practitioner and peer-support specialist I help individuals with severe mental illnesses. I facilitate workshops and teach classes on recovery, WRAP (Wellness Recovery Action Plan), PATH (Personal Action Toward Health), money basics, financial management, life issues, and stress management/relaxation, which I love. I connect people to needed resources, such as food, housing, and benefits. I work with individuals in crisis. I mentor. I advocate. I listen and share my recovery story.

The people I work for—the individuals with severe mental illnesses—really seem to like me. They miss me when I'm absent from work. I seem to be able to establish a good rapport and a positive relationship with them easily. This work is within my realm of expertise, and I am an expert in recovery, which is what this whole job is about.

I Was Helped by an Understanding Boss and Toastmasters

My job has allowed me to grow personally and has given me needed freedoms to do my work. Some time earlier, I had become a member of the public-speaking group Toastmasters, and there I became comfortable speaking in front of groups. This is a skill I use constantly in my work. My supervisor is aware of my autism spectrum disorder, has done reading on the disorder, and works with me when I encounter problems, such as saying or doing something inappropriate. I am very fortunate to have a very kind and understanding supervisor. She has added to the pleasure of the job.

It's interesting—I work with people and interact with them, often one on one, much of the day. And, I am comfortable doing so, unlike earlier in my life. I don't know what has happened to change this. It's like I've suddenly blossomed, the proverbial "late bloomer."

RELATIONSHIPS

My mother says that I was a cuddly baby and that I was extremely shy. She relates the story of how I came home from the first day of 1st grade, boasting that I'd made a new friend. However, despite the fact that Suzanne was my "best friend," I was remarkably unattached. I had no more reaction to her than I would have had if she had been a stranger. When we were 20, her entire family died, one by one. And while I was quite fond of her father—he used to take me and Suzanne to Catalina Island on his boat on the weekends—I felt nothing when they died.

I had other friends besides Suzanne, but they were just peripheral friends. They came and went, more like acquaintances.

Once Suzanne left for Loma Linda Academy, I made a new acquaintance: Myrta Rojas, from Chile. We became fast friends. But it was a short-lived friendship, as that summer she moved out of the country. This was 10th grade, the same year I met Jan, whom I would later marry.

Despite Many Acquaintances, I Was Still an Island

As an adult, I've had "acquaintances," perhaps mostly people Jan worked with, whom I would sometimes invite over for Saturday dinner. Those were very uncomfortable social occasions, but I ignored the discomfort and did it anyway. It never got any easier. Then there was Valerie. Jan recommended I befriend her. She was a coworker's wife, and she was quite depressed. Jan said, "Call her," and I did. She became my friend. Our children were similar in age. Neither of us was working, so we hung out. I don't think it was a healthy relationship or that it was particularly reciprocal. As an example, I would follow her around as she talked—literally follow her from room to room. I was, for the most part, very passive in the relationship.

There are a couple of people I have been acquainted with since 1977, when we moved to Michigan, namely Tom and Dianne Kimmel. We see each other just about every weekend for Saturday dinner. We'll often go with them to concerts on a Saturday night. They've become like family. But I feel very distant, as is too common for me with other people, even after all these years. I am still the island. But Dianne considers me a friend, which I have a hard time understanding.

I went on a hayride in 10th grade with Ron Robinson. Some of my friends were also on the ride. I turned my back on Ron and talked with my friends and really thought nothing of it. When I was in the 12th grade, I went with Ron Cardoza to see a performance of *Hamlet*. I enjoyed the play, but when Ron walked me to the front door afterward and asked if he could kiss me, I answered, "No." He was not happy. These are the only dates I can remember. I don't recall dating in college, although I was asked. I very transparently gave excuses why I couldn't go out. I remember one young man in particular because of his persistence. I really had trouble getting rid of him. But I was glad I did: He married the next girl he dated. In my mind, it could have been me—not a pleasant thought. I did have one good friend named John Sponenberg, but we never dated.

Isolation

I began to consciously realize that I was different when I was in 11th/12th grade and I went to a new school. I had attended Redlands Junior Academy from 1st through 10th grades. There was a core of students who I had gone to school with since the start. While I was not close to anyone, they were familiar. It was a small school, and I was acquainted with everyone in my class. I did not associate with any of the students in the other classes, even when I was in rooms with combined classes. My twin brother, Stanley, had always been in class with me, but in 11th grade he went away to boarding school. As my other siblings were younger, I alone went to Loma Linda Academy. Though still not a large school, it was larger than where I came from, and I never did become acquainted with everyone. I knew several of the students from Redlands. Suzanne was there, but I never did "hang out" with her. Besides, she had a steady boyfriend, which immediately put her "outside the circle." My second cousin Christine was there, too, but we were not well acquainted. I felt so removed, so alien, and for the first time became consciously and acutely aware of my isolation. It hit me full force. And yet, strangely, I was a member of the popular group in school.

Before I went to Loma Linda Academy, I thought my religion was what set me apart. I thought I was alien from everyone outside of school because they were not Seventh-day Adventist. I remember once standing on a downtown street corner in Redlands with my sister, Becky, and thinking how strange and foreign everyone was. I wondered what they were like, what it would be like to be one of them. I felt completely cut off from the world.

I Found a Husband Who Loved Classical Music

The "romantic relationship" I developed with Jan came about in an interesting way. I decided in December 1972 that it was time to marry. I was 21. I had only one criterion—my husband must love classical music. I immediately thought of two, and only two, people: Jan and my twin brother, Stanley. Naturally Stanley was out, and I forgot all about John Sponenberg. So, I decided I'd marry Jan. We had met in 10th grade, and I'd known for some time that Jan was in love with me. He'd written me as much. The one problem was that I did not love him—or even like him. So I prayed that I'd love him. And by February of 1973, I did. In July, he flew me out to see him—I lived in Southern California, and he was living in Tulsa, Oklahoma. The visit culminated in a proposal, just as I had planned it would. I flew back to California, and the following December Jan drove out for the wedding.

I have never been comfortable with "romance." I still remember a time early in our marriage when Jan hugged me. Or tried to hug me. I pushed him away, saying, "I have to protect myself." I did not know at that time what I had to protect myself from. During intimate moments, Jan used to tell me, "It's like you're not even here." He has said to me on a number of occasions, "You never touch me." So I try. But I have always had, and still do have, a terrible time with intimacy. I hate it. I would be most happy in a platonic relationship with Jan, which for the most part, after 38 years of marriage, it largely seems to be.

Why My Marriage Has Lasted

Since a relationship involves two people, and its success is dependent on the efforts of both, I thought it essential to get my husband's take on why our relationship has lasted.

According to Jan, our marriage has held together because he learned to get along by himself. I simply was not available to him emotionally. He ignored a lot of things I did and consciously learned to recognize and enjoy my good times. Even though I have a diagnosis of a mood disorder and an autism spectrum disorder, Jan says every woman has issues, whether or not she has autism. He chose to live with my particular set of issues. When we married, we made vows of faithfulness, and Jan took those vows very seriously. As he told me, he made a promise before God and before all those present at our wedding and had no intention of breaking that promise.

As for me, I made idle threats to divorce Jan on several occasions, but I've never really contemplated life without him. Being married to Jan is just how things are. Lars and Else are my children, and Jan is my husband. These are just indisputable, immutable facts. To me there is not life without Jan. He is all wrapped up in my reality.

Jan has respected me and my differences. He has given me the freedom to be myself and to pursue my interests. And that has entailed supporting me financially, as I have not worked for most of our life together. We share an appreciation of the natural world and a love of beauty, be it in nature or the arts. We have a compatible, though not identical, sense of beauty. We have very similar morals and values. We both love classical music and art. Our upbringing, religious heritage, and ethnic background are similar.

For much of our married life (and undoubtedly for most of my life in general), I have been "in the ozone"—in my own world—and perhaps not quite in touch with what was really going on. I am naive and take things as they present themselves, at face value. I have learned to ignore and block unpleasantness—like disturbing sights (a messy house) and unbearable sounds (my teenaged son's raucous music). I retreat into my head and only expose myself to what I want and to what I absolutely cannot "eliminate."

But, the sounds of chewing still grate on my nerves like fingernails scraping a blackboard. My ability to ignore and block is not absolute, nor is it always effective, but it has enabled me live in a marriage and to more or less function in a world with other people.

Parenting Was Difficult

I was 24 when my son Lars was born. I was totally possessed by him. I gave up everything, including my music, for him. Both he and Else were born "on my side of the glass." I felt an instantaneous connection with my children and a deep bond. I adored my children, but I had a very difficult time raising them. The mother-things tortured me: teaching in their Sabbath school classes, being room mother, and helping with field trips. I was out of my element, and I managed poorly. And then, Lars and Else slipped through the glass to join the rest of the world.

Inspiration and Feeling Emotion with Classical Music

I can't think of any one person who inspired me. Perhaps this is because I have been so unattached to people, so disconnected. I remember when I first learned—and it was a shocking revelation— that some people are *influenced by other people.* It was particularly startling because it came from my own twin brother. I was in college when I found out that he was *influenced in some of his decision-making by his friends.* This seemed to me to be a character weakness, which is why it was so disturbing that it was happening to my own brother. This, then, translated into a means of classifying people: There are people who are influenced by other people—Stanley—and people who are not—me.

What has inspired me, though, is music—classical music. When I was 10, I began taking piano lessons. Certain types of music said something to me, to the core of my being. Perhaps it transported me. It was another world. But it wasn't me. It didn't emanate *from me.* I was not able to sit down at the piano and just play. I had to read the music. But I did not sight-read easily, either. I could, however, memorize without any problems. I would be given a piece to learn, and by the next lesson, I had it memorized. That is, if I liked it. If I did, I played it over and over again. It was thought that I was gifted. I was not. I cannot figure out how I could have been. Perhaps what music—and art—is to me is an expression of emotion. I have a lot of trouble expressing emotions. For that matter, I have trouble even putting names to them. Certain music and art—to me what constitute beauty—express emotion for me. That's when I *feel.*

Curiously, perhaps, once I married, and particularly once Lars was born, I could no longer play the piano. Not that I could not *physically* play it, but my focus was elsewhere. To play the piano, it was an all-or-nothing thing. Either I put my whole being into it, or I couldn't play. So, I gave up the piano and have not played for 36 years.

Awakening

What has perhaps changed me and my outlook the most are my present job and receiving a diagnosis of an autism spectrum disorder. To understand my experience, I would suggest reading Oliver Sack's *Awakenings*, for it epitomizes what has happened to me. It is the difference between being alive and being dead. I was a zombie. I've never spoken much, and for most of my adult life, I spoke even less. For the first 17 years, my psychiatrist heard very little more than, "yes," "no," and "I don't know." There were more shrugs, headshakes, and silences than words. I did not converse, because I did not have the words. Even though I had received diagnoses of an anxiety disorder and bipolar disorder, I was skeptical. It just didn't add up. There was always, always something more that remained unidentified. Something deeper. Something at the core of my being. Now that I know I have Asperger's syndrome, it actually feels liberating.

My Job Was Instrumental to My Recovery

This job is different from all others I have held. It plays on my strengths and affords me a certain measure of freedom, which is something that is extremely important to me. It has also been very instrumental in my recovery. While in some ways it could be seen as a "dead-end" job, it's been perfect for me. It's allowed me to grow at an amazing rate, it's given me a purpose, and it introduced me to a new passion—psychiatric rehabilitation. I am working toward establishing and directing a psychiatric rehab center, something that will take some time and a lot of effort.

My husband asked me this evening when I think I might retire. "I'm not retiring," I responded. "I'll keep going until I can no longer function."

CHAPTER 4

KARLA FISHER

Senior Program Manager for Intel and Successful "Techie"

KARLA FISHER

Age: 48

Resides in: Portland, OR

Occupation: Senior technical program manager for Intel and general manager of a professional women's football team

Marital status: Divorced, with two children

FROM TEMPLE:

Karla is one of the lucky techies who fit in naturally when she "found her people" in the tech world. Not everybody on the spectrum has Karla's ability to do high-level computer work. Karla is a wonderful example of "techie" success, just as other individuals in the book have achieved in other ways. Karla has two kids, who have both found success in their own right. One received a degree in theater and education and is currently teaching theater. The other is married and is pursuing a PhD in historical languages. Karla received a diagnosis of Asperger's not long before writing this chapter, after her father died of a stroke. The diagnosis was initially very troubling to a generally happy techie who was struggling with her father's death. A supportive colleague made her wonder, if she had known earlier in life that she had a disorder, would she have been motivated to attain such a high level of achievement?

KARLA'S INTRODUCTION

I honestly have never suffered bullying in the high-tech world in the 21 years I have worked in it. Prior to this, I had to do a lot of "dancing" to keep my jobs, both in the military and in every other work environment. In the high-tech world, the way I am seems natural, and I am accepted. Of course, I am not accepted *exactly* as I am, but I'm mentored to be the best "me" I can be within the bounds of my stated goals.

My job at Intel is amazing and is adaptable to my own growth. There is an endless amount of data to learn and a never-ending number of jobs I can perform successfully. My entry into the high-tech world was telephone tech support. That was a challenging job for me, as I hate phones, but I gutted through it. Eventually it led me to software validation. What sort of autistic person would *not* like a job where she gets to point out flaws in other people's work? I actually *get paid* to do this, even today. When I did software engineering and architecture, my role was to bury myself deep in the details, find flaws, and fix them. As a program manager, my job consists of finding the flaws in the program flow (the bigger picture) and fixing them.

My review feedback has always included my autism-related "quirks." I had to learn to see more "gray" (as opposed to black and white), to network with others, and to see the bigger picture, and I was given plenty of instruction on these things through corporate training programs. Even with these areas of growth, I still habitually fall short of my neurotypical peers in many of these skills, so I must always seek out and use my strengths to advocate for myself. My recent decision to attempt program management was nearly catastrophic, as it requires a very "big-picture" approach. My approach has always been to start with the details. I know now that when I move into a new role, it may take longer for me to learn it initially. But, once I learn it, there will be no better person to do it. I make sure my boss knows this, as well, and buys into it beforehand. Even so, I still have to run very hard at the onset of any program to keep up with what's expected of me. Once I grasp the "big picture," however, I also grasp all the details and ultimately earn my keep.

A word about computers and autism. It makes complete sense if you think about it. At its core, each computer speaks by way of firmware and software that program the hardware with "1s" and "0s." The bits are all either "on" or "off." It is pure, unhampered, black-and-white logic. And, beyond that, think about just how *literal* computers are. If you want to execute a command and you make a mistake by just one letter, the computer is confused. It does not make the leap from the "attempted" command to the "right" one, even though this "should" be obvious to something as smart as a computer. Computers are just like us. I feel I have a "friend" in this group of "like" objects and in the people drawn to them. In fact, any autistic person I've met would be hard pressed to be the most unique individual in most of the high-tech lab environments I've been in for the past 21 years.

EARLY YEARS

One evening, a few years ago, in a quiet diner on the east coast, one of my dear friends and mentors, harp guitarist John Doan, turned and asked my mother and father what I was like as a child. John and I were traveling together, creating a movie/documentary ("In Search of the Harp Guitar") and attending a music festival in Virginia. My parents came down from Pennsylvania to join us for an evening.

They giggled a bit at this very open-ended question from a person they had never met before, and then finally my mother answered that she and Dad were never really sure where I came from, but they suspected Mars. Everyone had a good laugh about it, but she was actually not joking. I listened to her describe me as this weird, loner child who spent hour upon hour on the swing they installed for me in the basement. I remember that swing very fondly. If they had let me, I would have spent the whole day there, never even stopping to eat. Additionally, I spent hours watching a spider build a web or eat its catch, studying ant anthropology, lining up my extensive Breyer horse collection, passing grains of sand through my fingers in the sandbox, or studying dirt in the woods.

Playing Outside and Having My Brother's Protection

I grew up in a small industrial town on the east coast in the 1960s. My family was working class, very religious, and very large. My siblings and I always had cousins to play with, no matter where we were. I also had an older brother whom I was very close to, and he obviously loved me back because he allowed me to follow him everywhere, even though I was smaller and much slower. He was also furiously protective of me all during those early years. I remember him beating up anyone who tried to pick on me as I watched in amazement, not yet even registering what was going on. Boy or girl, it did not matter. He jumped in and beat them. As a result, I never really suffered from that much bullying, and his friends were always my friends. So even though I was different, I never felt excluded or unloved.

My brother and my cousins were very physical, and back then, children were always directed to play outside in nature. We ran and played "army," "tag," and any number of made-up games, and we settled things largely amongst ourselves. I had one female cousin whom I was fond of, but I was not very good at the things she liked or at playing house (a game she always wanted to play). I could be the "baby" if prompted, but I never really understood the purpose of this sort of play. In fact, one day, my brother and I completely destroyed a beautiful little playhouse my parents had proudly bought and given to me to encourage me to engage with dolls. (In those days, being a tomboy was not very acceptable.) I do not remember receiving it, but I do remember destroying it. I cannot remember if I came up with the idea or if it was my brother's, but we staged a tornado. I was the tornado, spinning, twisting, and crashing into the little house until it was a splintered mess on the floor. Boy, did we get into trouble.

I Was Fiercely Independent as a Child

My mother also says I was "fiercely independent" as a child. Today, I would be called a "wanderer" by autism specialists. I prefer to call myself an "avid explorer." As a very small child, I used to slip away from my family in stores to see the sights, and eventually I tried to find them again but wound up with a family that wasn't mine. I remember being laughed at by my folks for holding a complete stranger's hand. I was confused. I knew I was separated, so I looked for a connection—any connection. This person was close enough for me. Sometimes, when we went shopping, I hid in the middle of clothing racks or in any other dark, quiet place until my mother called me. When I played outside in my yard, I suddenly decided to "go exploring," only to be brought back to my house again by a neighbor. One day, I was on vacation with my family and I took off down the beach. I walked and walked and walked. I remember being fascinated by the fragments of information coming at me…I was lured by the ocean to keep walking. I wondered where it ended. It drew me in until I felt the coolness of the water on my legs. I looked out and saw myself way beyond the waves on a raft, and I was alone. I knew I was separated from my family, but I had no fear. I just kept walking. I remember getting very tired but being at peace. After many hours, someone grabbed me (a policeman) and held me in the air, shouting, "Is this her?" All of a sudden, I was surrounded by lots of people. They all made a commotion, and I received a lot of scolding and hugs, which I did not comprehend. My mother was so distraught that day, she had to be medicated. I did not understand what the big deal was. I continued to explore long into my 30s and still sometimes do so today (only without everybody worrying about me now).

The Environment I Grew Up in Was Less Ambiguous Than Today

Temple Grandin speaks of the TV shows during the late 1960s as having very black-and-white themes. In those shows, there were good guys and bad guys, which helped instill right-and-wrong values in the young people of the day. Temple rightly states that TV today doesn't teach values in those terms anymore and that this can contribute to confusion in many kids. I would add that it wasn't just the TV shows but our whole environment that was less ambiguous (more black and white). There really wasn't so much choice as a child growing up in that era, other than to obey your parents and other people of authority (teachers, policemen, and the like). An infraction in my home usually resulted in getting clobbered in some way. If you said something disrespectful or spoke out of turn, you would likely feel the back of Mom's hand across your face. Paddling at home and at school was a regular occurrence, and many times I got hit in school only to get home and get hit again because I got in trouble at school. As a result, I became very good at memorizing and following rules. I learned very early that to effectively break a rule, one must be intimately familiar with it. Even though this form of discipline had some effect, I do not advocate that we go back to those days, as I believe we should have more respect for our young people than I was offered. Still, I think there is a lot to be said for keeping the environment less ambiguous, with far fewer choices for young people—and especially for autistic young people.

The Moral Values I Was Taught Were Logical

My parents were exceedingly religious, and I grew up in and around the fundamental Baptist church culture. I hated church as a child. At first, I hated it because I had to wear scratchy clothing whenever I went, and, later, I hated it because I found it ridiculous. Besides the obvious hypocrisy displayed by the attendees, there really was very little actual logic in that religion. That said, some of the values espoused in the church are sound moral principles that I still live by today. For example, "doing unto others" had a logical ring to it, so I kept it around as a reminder to be nice to other people. After I grew up, these foundational principles that were instilled in me continued to have an effect. After earning more than I could spend for the first time in my life in my mid-30s, I heard one of my high-tech mentors (Bill Gates) say, "With great wealth comes great responsibility." And from that day forward, I put at least 10% of my salary and 10% of my time toward charity and community causes. This came directly from my youth, as the Bible teaches 10% tithing, so it just seemed right somehow. And you know what? I still think it is right.

SCHOOL YEARS

A Bored Student at the Top of my Class

If I had one word for my entire school experience, it would be "dull." The most difficult thing about school was fighting boredom. I spent most of my time in grade school daydreaming or plotting ways to draw horses or be with horses. I was so infatuated with horses in grade school that I could name any breed and all the body parts and could draw them fairly well, too. I dreamed of one day owning horses and a horse farm. I rarely ever paid attention in class, and I never found the work part of school hard. Reading turned out to be a strong subject for me, and I was always in the advanced reading groups. I read quite a bit on my own as a child but rarely read fiction, even then. I fared more poorly in group work and classes with less structure, such as music. Even so, I always had sufficiently high grades (a "B" or higher average), while my older brother always did poorly in school. As a result, he got all the attention and focus when it came to grades and extra schooling, while I was left alone—which was just fine by me.

A Top Student in Junior High

In junior high, I tested in the top percentile of my class and was put in one or two classes on the advanced track. This was a big break for me, as I was able to actually engage in the subjects a little more, and the kids in my class seemed friendlier than the ones in my other classes. The social dynamics got vastly more complicated in middle school, but I managed to avoid most of it. I fell in love with algebra, Latin, and physics and poured myself into the study of these subjects. Again, I did more poorly in unstructured classes, such as art, woodshop, and music, but I did not dislike any of it.

In High School I Grew Apathetic Toward Learning

In high school, there was no longer an advanced class concept, and Advanced Placement (AP) classes were still a few years away, so I was back in college prep courses with the general population again. I grew bored and spent most of the school day daydreaming or skipping class to hang out with my brother and his friends. My disinterest with life began to take a toll. I started to experiment in illegal substances with my brother and his gang. I grew apathetic toward learning, and my grades started to slip. I dropped below a 3.0 average for the first time. I was very restless during this time and felt like nothing was stimulating to me. I felt trapped in my life.

But all the grown-ups I knew had similar problems, and I had long ago stopped going to adults for help. They never seemed to be able to give me any real answers anyway. I remember feeling very alone, because I did not know who could help me. The image of being on a raft in the middle of the ocean was always in my mind. I was never sad or frightened on my raft, just alone. On this raft, I was exploring. I was seeking my island, and this "alone" feeling was somehow "right." I remember growing stronger with that image and spent many years of my life building my raft and seeking my island.

Becoming a Foreign-Exchange Student Was Life Changing

Finally, in 10th grade, I got a big break. I signed up for German class, and my whole life changed. I found that German was fairly easy for me to pick up and also very interesting. I was fascinated by the study of the culture and listened intently when my teacher spoke of her travels overseas. It occurred to me during that class that there was an entire world out there I had yet to see. I suddenly realized I did not have to stay in this small town, doing the same thing day in and day out. I told this teacher of my desires to travel to Germany, and she was thrilled to help me. She introduced me to the student exchange program. I applied and was accepted. While my parents could not afford this venture, my grandmother put up the money. I am indebted and grateful to her to this day for that gift of a lifetime.

I spent my entire 11th-grade year in Germany as an exchange student. This was the most powerful learning year of my life to date, despite the fact that I mostly did not attend school. The smells, sounds, and sights of this new world were so overwhelming in the first weeks that I slept 18 hours a day. My host family was actually worried for me and thought I might not be in good health. Finally, things started to come together, and I could navigate this strange country during more regular hours. School began, and it was in a completely new language. At first, this was fun. I picked up the language quickly enough and was able to pass exams within the first quarter. I also started team sports as a way to help me integrate with my peers. While I blended in all right with my sports teams, I never fully integrated at school. I actually suffered my worst bullying ever at that school in Germany, and as a result, I stopped going.

Someone with an "expert" knowledge of rules can also break them without being noticed. I traveled around Germany and Europe alone (either by train or via hitchhiking) for most of the school year, coming back to my host family just enough to keep them from worrying. Again I was wandering (or rather exploring), only this time nobody was worried for me. I was all alone. I *was* "the raft," and it felt "right" and strong. Taking in all the new data around me was exhilarating, as well as exhausting. Of course, when I returned to the U.S., I had to forge my school records so I could go into my senior year and graduate. I hated all the dishonesty, but the alternative of taking the 11th grade over again was not acceptable.

In 1981, after a fairly noneventful senior year, I finally graduated from high school with honors. My social aloofness really hurt me in my senior year. I was vaguely aware of other kids taking the SAT test, and I was taking college prep and AP courses, but how one actually applied to and ultimately went to college was so far beyond my ability to comprehend that it never seriously entered my mind. When I raised my own kids, I made sure they knew no other path.

EMPLOYMENT

Childhood Jobs

As a child, I was required to do chores around the house with my brother. We did yard work and some housework. When we were old enough to wander the streets on our own, we invented ways to make money, such as doing yard work for our neighbors, selling newspapers, and even opening up lemonade stands. I am not sure that I ever really understood the connection with money and carelessly gave it to friends and my church, but I did know that working and making money was something that all people are expected to do.

My Dad Was a Role Model for Work Ethic

I had the very best role model in the world when it came to work ethic. My father was the hardest-working person I have ever known. He put himself physically and mentally into all his jobs around the house and worked overtime nearly every week, as a truck driver. Whenever my life got hard and the work I was doing seemed dull or tedious or just plain tough, I thought of him and pushed on.

When I landed at the airport after my year abroad, I was nearly 17 years old. My father and mother were there to meet me. They had not seen me for a full year, so they were happy to have me back, but my father was especially excited. He had a childlike grin on his face as he held up a set of car keys—to my new car. It wasn't brand new, of course—he had bought it from his sister. It was a 1963 Dodge Dart, with a "slant six" engine. He paid $250 for it, and he told me I could keep it, provided I reimbursed him for the $250 in time. I immediately sought work to be able to have this car. I understood quite well the concept of "earning" something that I wanted, and with this car, I was able to explore more than I could without it.

As a Parent, I Learned to Give

My best job and worst job are one and the same—parenting my children. I was a single mom for much of the time I was raising my kids, and it nearly destroyed me, both physically and emotionally. I experienced several bouts of complete exhaustion. I felt continuously overwhelmed and had many panic attacks. I developed ulcers and high blood pressure during the years they were growing up. I found mothering incredibly tough and often even unrewarding. But, it taught me so much, and ultimately it gave me so much more than any other job I have ever had, either previously or since. I would not be the person I am today or nearly as evolved without this experience and without my two daughters in my life. The most important lesson I learned by having children was selflessness. Before they came along, everything I did was essentially about me and for me. After having them, nothing I did was for me. I learned to give, and

I learned to give without expectation. Giving without expectation is the single most important skill I know for making and keeping friends, fighting depression, and making the world a better place. When a person is thinking about other people instead of him- or herself, it is hard to be depressed. When a person's total work effort is focused on doing good for everyone and not just for oneself, it is hard not to find joy of some sort, and it's even harder to fail.

Military Duty and Joining the Technology Industry

Besides parenting, I somewhat enjoyed my stint in the U.S. Marine Corps. I say "somewhat" because I was only really functional and happy when I worked within my intelligence group at my job. Whenever I ventured away from these "smart" people, I managed to get into some sort of trouble. The military was a good fit for me because the rules were very clear. How I was supposed to act and what I was supposed to say were all scripted. I did well with that part of it. I also did well with my job as a linguist and analyst. I didn't do as well in the training exercises, which involved a lot of explosives, smoke, and chaos. And, like all strong-willed, logical people, I did have some trouble with authority if the person demanding my respect was deemed illogical or was not as smart as I was (hence the frequent trouble). I did enjoy the physical aspect of the job and did a lot of running, long road marches (endurance marches of 10+ miles with battle gear), and marching drills. The marines taught me a lot, but the single biggest lesson I learned from that experience was gratitude. I can think of no lesson greater than witnessing the damages of war to make a person appreciate the things she has in peacetime, including life itself.

I Became Social at a Technology Company

I have been in the high-tech industry for more than 20 years now. After my Dessert Storm duty was complete, I joined a small software company in Santa Monica, California, in 1991. The country was very supportive of its servicemen at the time, and this company hired me even with the minimal experience I had in software engineering. I remember how great it felt to work for that company. I smiled all the time from the relief of finding such a like group of people and from leaving the horrors of war behind me. As a result, the 5 years I worked for this company constituted the most social time of my life to date. I made friends there that I still see or write to today. Back in those days, it was not uncommon to work 70 or more hours a week, so my team and I became like family. We were inseparable, and work/play became one and the same. My two little girls actually had a room next to my lab, with beds, so they could sleep over while Mommy worked the night through. The work was perfect for me, and I could really be myself and immerse myself in it. Additionally, the atmosphere was relaxed, and I could wear the same casual outfit to work every day and not be the only one doing it. In fact, in that world, I was less eccentric than many.

I grew technically as I moved into software program architecture and even earned patents for some of my more leading-edge/unique technical work. However, the single most important lesson I learned in this industry was not even technical. It was formal program scheduling.

I had a most amazing mentor at this small company. He worked with me tirelessly to teach me how to track and manage complex programs. As it happened, I was very talented at this with my natural, laser-sharp attention to detail and huge capacity to remember those details. Nothing escaped my eye, and I was eventually able to do very large programs in my head. From this work came the most important life lesson of that time period. In this life, you can either be a victim or be empowered. It is a choice, and there is *always* a choice.

Computer Programming Helped with Life Planning

Yes, the programming was fun, but this scheduling work really carried over into my life as the years went by. With scheduling knowledge, I could take better control of my life through planning any task that was challenging for me (from an executive-level perspective). I could map out all the subtasks, figure out all the risks, and then make alternative or contingency plans for when those risks got in the way of the original plan. It helped me to see all the choices and to discern how those choices might affect the end goal.

All of a sudden, I was less anxious and more flexible, because I had a bigger vision than I had ever had before and understood the actions to take if my first plan failed or if things did not go the way I expected them to. I highly recommend that any autistic person with challenged executive functioning and flexibility learn *planning skills*. I teach these all-important skills to the kids I mentor today.

I Work Best with the Right People

Besides these primary jobs, I had many other jobs that failed in one way or another. My first job was at Kmart, working in the shoe department. It was horrid and caused me anxiety every time I had to go to work, but I toughed it out until I had paid off my car and had a few dollars to spare. Quitting that job was one of the best days of my life. I think I was going to be fired anyway. I was actually fired from a few jobs just for being weird and fired once for not sleeping with my boss. I also walked out on jobs where I just could not tolerate the environment or the people who were in charge. I once spent the entire day in California, applying to become a sheriff. After scoring the best out of several hundred applicants, I was singled out. The staff made a big deal out of my scores and all wanted to meet me and talk with me about my new career with them. During the final processing step, I was working with one of the sheriff staff members on some paperwork, and she treated me with disrespect. She was obviously physically out of shape, and her uniform was sloppy. I walked out without even looking back. I remember an officer in the U.S. Marine Corps who said to me, "You are a really good worker, so long as you are working for the right person." He sought the "right" placement for me to keep me out of trouble, and that worked well enough for me to get through my contract in the marines. Since then, I have always kept that statement in mind and have always realized that I need to be in the right place and with the right people to do my personal best.

I Worked Hard to Stay Off Welfare

There was a time in my life when I had very young children, after my husband abandoned us, when I contemplated applying for financial assistance of some sort. After spending a few hours in the local welfare office, I made the bet of a lifetime. I wagered that I could indeed make it without any help. The smell, the sights, and the sounds of that office kept me from ever wanting to go back again. The people and their energy made me sick to my stomach. The paperwork was confusing. I left, and I never went back.

I was poor during those first years. I was very poor. I had no TV or phone and ate many peanut butter sandwiches just to be able to buy milk for my kids. In fact, for decades after this time period, I would not touch peanut butter. It was a trying decision to walk out of that welfare office that day, and if I had really known the enormity of that wager, things may have gone differently. In the years that followed, I worked so hard and made so little that by the time childcare expenses were paid, I would have made more from the welfare payments. Still, I kept faith that this was only temporary. I believed that if I stayed the course, worked really hard, and never allowed the forward movement to stop, that one day things would pay off. I continued to build the "raft" in my mind to search the oceans for that seemingly elusive island. I threw myself into my work and my parenting. I became that raft, getting stronger and stronger with each year. And the bet I made that day at the welfare office eventually paid off.

RELATIONSHIPS IN MY YOUTH

I was exceedingly aloof in my youth. I adored my brother and played with my cousins on my own terms, but other kids were largely just "dead" to me. I do not remember playing with other kids during recess in elementary school, and I do not remember wanting to or caring, either. On occasion, I was forced to join in team sports, and I was always the slowest runner and was picked last for teams. If I ever had to work in a group, I could only do so if I was the leader or if I was in charge. Otherwise, it was a disaster and I threw a tantrum. I was never shy, but I worked and played better alone. So at recess, I was fine to just sit at the top of the playground and daydream or talk with the teachers as they came by and sat with me. I did always have one or two people in every class who would actually talk with me (the geeky or outcast kids) and who offered to hang out with me after school sometimes. I always had plenty of interaction with others.

No Interest in Fashion or Clothing

I remember that the social dynamics were far more complex in junior high. I was vaguely aware of things like school dances and other social functions, but I never attempted any of those. In junior high we elected a student body president for the first time, but again, I never engaged. It really never crossed my mind that any of these things might be fun or that I should be part of them. I didn't vote in student elections, because I did not know anyone. I remember the kids all starting to get into fashion and clothing, but I had no interest in that, either. One day, a well-meaning classmate (a very nice young man) actually had a frank talk with me about how beautiful I was and how much better I would integrate if I just wore feminine clothing and became more fashion conscious. I thought it was sweet of him and actually tried it for a day by wearing a different shirt. He was thrilled and complimented me highly. Alas, the shirt was scratchy, so I went back to my jeans and t-shirt for the rest of the year. I did go out for team sports—even football tryouts. I was ridiculed off the field by the coaches, as well as by the boys. It never occurred to me that trying out for the team would not be acceptable, as I regularly played tackle football with my brother and his friends. My brother was not in this school to protect me, so I was much more on my own.

Camping Was One of the Best Experiences of My Life

My parents had a permanent camping spot by the Susquehanna River during these "middle school" years, and we went nearly every weekend, year round. My father bought me a small boat that I painted bright yellow and named "Sunny." It was only about 6 feet long and was a single-man, flat-bottomed rowboat. Every single day I was near that river, I rose with the sun, caught bait, loaded up my boat, and went out alone to explore the river. I rowed upstream for miles and miles, toward intricate series of islands in the middle. There, I spent the days alone, fishing, daydreaming, exploring, and talking to nature. At night, I let the current carry me back to my family's site just as darkness closed in. Then I'd eat dinner and go find my brother and the other kids at the park. These were perhaps some of the best times of my life, though I mostly spent my time alone. I vaguely remember that one of the boys from the park had a crush on me and thus became my first official boyfriend. I had no clue what that meant, but we held hands, kissed sometimes, and told everyone we were an item.

In high school, I was back in the same school as my brother and his friends, so I felt instantly more at ease. He was two grades ahead of me, but we were in many of the same classes, so I saw him frequently. One of my neighbors was a friend at that time, and I went to her house on occasion, but I mostly enjoyed talking with her parents. Every now and then, I asked her to go camping with us by the river. Otherwise, I mostly talked to adults or to friends of my brother and my mother. I had plenty of people in my life to talk to, but none of them felt very "close." I felt alone on my raft in my mind, even though I was surrounded by people.

When I went to Germany for my 11th-grade year, a neighbor befriended me, but I wasn't really interested in reciprocating the friendship, and it died quickly. In fact, I didn't stay in contact with anyone upon my return to the U.S., not even my host family. I saw "friends" (relationships) in a very nontraditional way then, and it's still that way today, although my awareness of these beings as people with their own needs has increased significantly, to where I can actually keep friends now. I was not really able to reciprocate a friendship at all until my early 30s, though by then, many people sought me out as a friend or mentor.

When I returned from Germany to enter my senior year in high school, I had a strange and instant popularity. Everyone knew that I was the person who spent the year abroad. As a result, people greeted me in the hallway, invited me to parties, and talked to me. I never learned their names and was always perplexed as to why they greeted me so much or how they could even remember who I was. This is the year that people really started to be attracted to me. I actually went to a few parties and to some people's houses, but for the most part, I was not that interested. I did, however, enjoy conversations with their parents most of the time. I also never went to a school dance, prom, homecoming, or any formal social event of that nature, though I did go out on graduation night with a group of kids who liked me. I generally felt that sort of thing was way too much effort for me to even bother figuring out.

RELATIONSHIPS AS AN ADULT

I Felt More Connected to Animals, Nature, and Computers

Before I start talking about relationships as an adult, I should stop here to say that I have always felt more connected to animals, nature, and my obsessions (especially computers) than to people. I think this is true of many autistic people. Animals in particular gave me much joy and a sense of "connectedness" to this planet when I was a youth, as did the trees in the woods by my home. If I were brutally

120

honest, I would tell you that these things were my real childhood friends. And this theme continues throughout my life in some form. Though I am good at being a friend now, I enjoy *things* more than *people* on the whole. I remember the day my last long-term romantic relationship ended (I was nearly 40 at the time). After citing a lack of emotional reciprocity, he said to me, "I feel like you love your computer more than me." I stood there in total shock, not knowing what to say. I was not shocked that he would say such a thing; rather, that this fact would be a problem. I assumed that everyone felt as I did about their work or their obsessions. I realized when he left that I needed to never again enter another romantic relationship, and I subsequently learned that I am better off alone.

The Military Made Me More Aware of Other People

The military helped me to be more aware of other people. The tasks that we performed were very repetitive, but they were also designed to increase awareness of your squad and platoon mates. We were often paired or partnered up, and with the stakes being as high as "death," it was essential for me to learn to care about others a bit more. Also, as I achieved rank, I became responsible for these other people and could not just ignore them. I also learned to live with many people of various races and backgrounds in very close quarters. Because the rules were very clear, I could do this with relative ease. It was after boot camp and in my Russian-language training school in California that my first husband entered my life.

I Felt Like I Was "Supposed" to Be with Someone

I had no experience with men, really, at that time. I was only 19 and was pretty immature about everything socially. I was flattered that a man might actually pursue me, so we ended up actively dating and

121

exploring. Before long, I was pregnant. I went through counseling to have an abortion, but the pain of the counseling and the thought of undergoing surgery were less appealing to me than being pregnant. In short, I did not really think the whole thing through, so I got married the way you are "supposed" to, and my first daughter was born. I can honestly say that I never had any feelings toward my first husband. I was very confused during our relationship. He left me when I was in a 6-month school/deployment for the U.S. Marine Corps. I was actually glad that he did.

A few years later, I fell into another relationship. This time, it was with a person I met while on a mission in Yuma, Arizona (teaching pilots about radio protocols and intelligence). He and I had a long-distance relationship that ended almost immediately upon our moving in together. I discovered then that he was drug and alcohol dependent. Again, I did not really have feelings for this person, but I always felt like I was "supposed" to be with someone, and if "someone" made himself available in this way, I just obliged. I never pursued anyone romantically or even put thought into the decisions I made. I was really just along for the ride during this time in my life.

I Benefitted from My Last Relationship but Did Not Connect Emotionally

My final relationship happened in my late 30s and actually resembled a "real" relationship. This occurred mainly because of his efforts to teach me about relationships, more than my ability to actually step into one in an emotional way. I did everything I could for him and my children, but I did it more in actions than by way of emotional fulfillment. In the end, he simply did not feel that I was able to give him what he needed emotionally. And I knew I could not. Somehow, I managed to do okay by my children, but I could not translate this to another adult. It wasn't logical to me.

I actually benefited greatly in this relationship in that he spent hours and hours discussing social behavior with me to help me understand it. It really was not much different than the social skills therapy I'm aware of now. In fact, he tried to convince me several times to seek therapy for my seemingly uncaring attitude about other people. He knew that something wasn't quite right about my social abilities. Of course, I thought he was being silly, but still, I learned a lot about other people's feelings from his perspective, and he taught me many scripts to use. During our years together, I was the best I had ever been at dealing with people socially and put up a good front at social events. Unfortunately, it was also during my years with him that I suffered the most physically. I experienced constant panic attacks, necessitating subsequent emergency room visits. I developed a bleeding ulcer. I received a diagnosis of exhaustion and had chronic infections in my body. When this man finally left me to pursue his other options in life, I actually sighed a bit in relief and enjoyed better health, although I did really miss him and felt bad about hurting him.

My Partner Left, and We're Still Friends

When he left, he said it was a very tough decision to make because he also saw the good qualities of being with me (and there were many). In fact, overall, I'd say we actually had a pretty good go of it, despite the eventual breakup. We were close friends for years, before we were ever romantic. But once romantic, we were also very sexually compatible. Our years together were great years of exploration. We discovered the high-tech world together.

I eventually found my island on a 40-acre tract of land near Portland, Oregon. We bought the land together, and I was finally able to buy and raise horses and surround myself with my old friends—trees and nature. When my partner left, I stayed on and bought the farm. It is where I live today, quite peacefully and happily. I can be in the city in an hour, yet I'm far enough out that I can be very much alone. He has moved on and is with "like" people now, enjoying a more social life. We are still friendly today, and I believe that had we entered our friendship knowing about the autism diagnosis I now have, we might have stayed together. Or, we may never have entered into a romantic relationship in the first place. My current belief is that it is "right" that I remain alone and not enter another "mixed" (autistic/neurotypical) relationship, as there really are too many differences. I honestly do not get the whole romantic relationship concept.

Besides—I like being alone on my island.

DIAGNOSIS

Grieving over My Father's Death and Having to Get Help

"Have you ever been tested for Asperger's?" The doctor looked at me curiously. I was furious and looked intently at the wall. What did this have to do with grief therapy? I contemplated hitting him and/or walking out. I was receiving cognitive services for the first time in my life, because I had witnessed my father's death from a major stroke on my 47th birthday a few months earlier. I went through the "right" grieving processes, but I struggled to integrate back into useful work because of the fact that all I could see were details. Nothing "came together" for me—everything remained fragments and bits of data. Normally, I receive data in pieces and can very quickly assemble these pieces to create objects that I recognize. But with the loss of my father, my ability to piece things together went with it. When I explained my issues to my boss, she encouraged me to seek out grief therapy. I was very much against the idea, but I was afraid I would lose my job if I did not try it. I made it to therapy with much trepidation and angst. My whole body shook as I filled out the mandatory introductory paperwork. This "doctor" asked me about Asperger's after a mere 5 minutes of describing my "details" problem to him. And THIS was supposed to somehow help me?

Finally, I spoke to him as calmly as I could. "Doctor. Let me remind you that I am VERY successful and highly functioning—one might argue, even more than *you.*" He wasn't fazed by my smug attitude and replied in a calm but very matter-of-fact way, "I know, and I still think you have Asperger's." In that moment, I realized this was "real." I really was different, and this difference had a name. I could not believe it. My mother had been telling me for nearly two decades that I had Asperger's. All my friends told me I was unique, different, and "eccentric." Some of them even mentioned autism. But only then did it hit me as being the truth. All of a sudden, this condition was real, and this doctor was not backing down. When I left that session, I called my mother and told her the doctor wanted to test me for Asperger's. She laughed and said, "Tell him to save his pencil—I'll just tell him myself that you have it." I just assumed all these years that she and everyone else were teasing me!

Accepting the Asperger's Diagnosis Was Difficult

Now I had to replay my whole life, with this *thing* that was deemed a disorder by this doctor and his peers. Of course I knew I was different my whole life. My mother called me a Martian, but she never made a big deal out of it, and I quite frankly never cared. It was in about the 5th grade when I realized that I was actually able to direct adult conversations and think differently—and also more clearly—than most adults. At first, this realization made me feel very alone. If I understood things differently than most adults did, then they could not really help me. It disrupted the rules of child/adult relationships, and I struggled with that for some time. It was, in fact, the very reason for the "raft" image that was always present in my mind.

At the time of this discovery, I just assumed that I had been given a Martian superpower. I was very aware of my "powers" but was very careful with them during my childhood. Throughout my life, I would often help people with my unique perspective or viewpoint, and others, in turn, sought me out for this and were largely nice to me. I was also different in that I did not dress like the other kids and had no knowledge of pop culture. So in my mind, my differences were always a good thing. In fact, as I got older and my ability to help other people grew, I moved from referring to myself as a Martian to referring to myself as an angel. I just figured I was placed on this earth to help the earthlings by disrupting their "normality." In fact, I always said that "Normal is boring."

Diagnosis Made Me Feel Like a Social Outcast

With my recent diagnosis, it is hard not to feel like a social outcast or like I am doing things "wrong," despite how amazing my results have been in life. Of course, a lot of my struggles now make sense. My broken romantic relationships and constant confusion about my sexuality, my inability to deal with large crowds, my constant physical health issues…I grimace as I remember that I once foreclosed on a house because the mortgage company sold my mortgage to another company and I had to change the address in order to pay them.

I just wouldn't do that, and I walked away from the house rather than make a simple change. It was a hard lesson, and I did learn to not do that with mortgages, but just this past month I paid a late fee on a bill that came with a change, and I was reluctant to adjust to the change and pay it. It is overwhelming to think about the struggles I've faced because of this thing I have. This disorder impacts *everything*. Every morning for months after my diagnosis, I woke up with a pit in my stomach, and I hoped it was a dream…but it was real. I have a disorder, and a "big" one, at that.

A few weeks before writing this chapter, I was presenting a new assistive-technology patent idea to another senior manager at Intel. I told him about my diagnosis. This person had firsthand experience with autism spectrum disorders because he has relatives on the spectrum. At first he was shocked, and he asked me how I felt about this news. I did not have words for that question. I just shrugged my shoulders and looked at the wall. He then asked the million-dollar question, "I wonder just how much of you being here, now, is because you never received a diagnosis."

Reflections on My Diagnosis

I am only now getting comfortable associating myself with my diagnosis, a year later. In fact, it is possible I have actually reached the point of acceptance.

Not too long ago, a psychologist asked me for advice on how she can help youths with recent diagnoses accept their autism spectrum disorder. After several back-and-forth e-mails on the subject, it occurred to me that she was assuming these kids would be relieved or even happy to hear this news. I do hear that some people are relieved and even happy, as it explains much that they previously had no answers for. For me, however, this was not the case. With my diagnosis came a realization that the unexplained hardships, medical issues, and struggles were not something I could just "get over." My diagnosis felt to me like a mountain, and one that continues to loom large over my entire life. I now know I have a pervasive disorder that has no cure, no "fix," and no easy answers in terms of going forward. Mountains and walls have always been things that stopped "other" people. Now, I have had to stop and realize that continuing to try to summit this thing will only continue to hurt me.

The facts are that "acceptance" of a label can take the same course as acceptance of a death or other traumatic, life-changing event. At first, I denied it vehemently and refused to even discuss it. I then went through grief, followed by a very long anger phase, during which I found myself going back through my life and looking at everything that happened, only through this new lens.

Everyone asks me what it feels like to find out about autism spectrum disorder so late in life. I never have an answer and cannot really articulate this for anyone. The thing that helped me the most in finally coming to accept myself in this new light was not how I *felt,* but rather what I *did.* During the past year, I challenged my feelings by learning about autism and joining my peers in advocacy work. I attended adult autism meetings, became a mentor to autistic youth, and started a youth advocacy program for autism. I created autistic models on relationships and emotions and taught autism professionals in schools and clinics about my experiences as a person with autism.

As I get the chance to work with more professionals, parents, and caregivers, I find that the topic of labels seems to have two very specific "camps." I am currently working with a speech-language pathologist who is very clearly against the use of labels in her work. My social-skills coach (who has a doctor of psychology degree) also does not believe in diagnoses and labels. Another doctor I know well, on the other hand, specializes in assessing people and very much believes that people need to have this label as an entry point to treatment and better health. When I recently polled my adult autistic friends as a group, they concurred 100% that having the label empowers them, versus hurts them.

I see both sides.

Professionals who deem labels disempowering usually tell me of experiences they have with young people (since most of them work primarily with young people) who "abuse" the label and use it as an excuse to not do or try something they are being encouraged to do. They also cite the fact that the purpose of therapies is to address a "disability" or weakness or what a person cannot do. Some professionals do not want to further promote a sense of disempowerment by allowing the person being treated to come from the entry point of "disability" or the limitations of the label applied to them. They want a person to approach therapy by thinking about the positives, the strengths, and the possibilities. At a high level, I think this concept makes the most sense. I see a lot of both autistic and neurotypical adults who experience depression and a lack of empowerment, and they tend to make up reasons why good things cannot happen to them. I always encourage these people to approach the problem they're trying to solve from the angle of possibilities, instead. This empowers them to see the way ahead more clearly, and it isn't until they "see" what they can do that they can take the actions required to work toward their desired destinations.

Recently, I had dinner with a renowned autism specialist who was so impressed with my abilities to cater to her whims and needs on our outing that she assumed my autism was not significant enough to warrant a label. What she did not know about or understand was the sum total of time and stress I had put into making that outing pleasant for us both. I had actually driven into the area where we were to meet the night before, so I could acclimate to the environment of the town. Then, during the day, I visited the place where we were to eat and walked the path to the restaurant several times to acclimate to that, as well. The result was that I could be very "social" in her eyes and focus my attention on her, since my sensory-processing issues and my anxiety were fairly minimized by preparing myself in advance.

In addition, what she did not know is that without my diagnosis, I would have lost my job last year. Because of my diagnosis, this year I am going to receive the very best review of my career. I have avoided going to the hospital for the past year for panic attacks, ulcers, high blood pressure, and/or physical exhaustion…because of my diagnosis. (This is the first year *in my adult life* that I have managed this). I was able to ask for help with my finances and actually find someone who was willing to work with me—because of my diagnosis. I am able to go to the doctor now without being ridiculed, because of my diagnosis. I no longer have any arguments with my friends over things I do not understand, *because of my diagnosis*. I recently avoided "theft" charges, because of my diagnosis! I could go on and on. The point is that one does not receive a diagnosis of an autism spectrum disorder without having a "significant impairment of everyday functioning."

Having a diagnosis of autism as an entry point to "Karla" makes my relationships, career, and overall life awareness so much easier and clearer.

More important, a label of autism gives me a framework. It gives me permission to take more frequent rests and to lower the expectations I have imposed on myself my whole life. I am not lazy, nor do I seek the "easy" way out. Coming to terms with my Asperger's simply allows me to set realistic expectations for myself, in terms of what I can and can't do. Without the label, I'm left to wonder why it is that all the people around me seem to be able to do more than I can. They do not get as tired. They do not go to the hospital for exhaustion, high blood pressure, or panic attacks like I do. Without the label, I am made to feel like an idiot because I have no awareness of my limitations. Then I feel like a failure, because there is no excuse for why I can't keep up. The "excuse" is actually an important piece in terms of understanding my health and determining my quality of life. So far, 100% of the autistic adults I have spoken with agree on this point.

Do kids use this label as an excuse sometimes when they shouldn't? Do adults use it when they perhaps should not? I don't know, to tell you the truth. I like to believe that people largely want to do well, succeed, and be valued. I believe that if someone is using their label to get out of something, then they actually need to do that. Even if I don't quite understand or "feel" the reason why, I think caregivers of autistic individuals should always try to look at situations from this perspective before applying judgment, because our perspective as autistic people may be different and may be even more valid.

MANY MENTORS HELPED ME

I have been blessed with many, many mentors in my life. As a young child, I had a large family who accepted me for who I was. I had many adult friends who befriended me as a child and taught me to hunt, fix cars, and ride horses. Even though I was largely socially clueless, I was not made to feel badly for the way I was. As I grew older, I heard advice that to become great, you have to hang out with great people. So that is what I did as I explored the many paths I've wandered throughout my life. Though obviously introverted, I was never shy or socially phobic. No matter what I wanted to learn, I sought out great mentors. When I wanted to learn about something in my computer job, I found a software architect who agreed to mentor me. Then I made sure to make and spend time with him. I rode on the shoulders of giants in my guitar adventures, my high-tech explorations, and my recent fitness and bodybuilding endeavors. Everywhere I've gone, individual people have always turned up with an "energy" that I wanted to tap into and soak up. In my view, the skill of finding a mentor and participating in mentoring programs should be taught to every child.

I BECAME A MENTOR FOR OTHERS

As I became proficient in my area of study and as my own kids grew into teenagers. Over the years, I also became a mentor to others. Some of the kids I mentored I met through my children, but many others sought me out. To date, I have mentored nine kids into adulthood and currently have a 13-year-old autistic kid whom I see pretty regularly. These kids often call me "Mom" or "Aunt," because they think of me like family. One evening, I received a phone call from a woman I had mentored some years back, when she was a girl. She had disappeared from my radar but finally got back in touch. She spoke to me with much happiness in her voice as she told me excitedly how she was graduating from the University of California, Los Angeles (UCLA) the next morning. She told me that she had entered and finished college because of my role modeling. She thanked me profusely. Touched, I sent her a plane ticket to visit me in Oregon the next week. She came to my farm, and, without words, popped a tape into the VCR. As the images of young people smiling and dancing filled the screen, she told me how she was teaching dance to the impoverished young people in Los Angeles. She was not making a lot of money, but she had learned about giving, and now she was giving, too. The smiles of all those children touched me, and I also found myself smiling. I thought how proud I was that this young woman really "got" it.

I get the honor of watching the kids I mentor graduate from high school and college and eventually get married. Most of them come from a troubled home environment or just plain need another adult in their life who sees things a little "differently." Mentoring is one of the most important things we can do on this planet, and it is a great way to give back and even to connect to other human beings. One of my own mentors once said, "You need to maintain a perfect triangle of learning, teaching, and performing in any subject to master it." He was specifically speaking of the classical guitar, but I think this is sound advice that I try to practice throughout my life.

LIFE LESSONS

My life has had many pivotal moments. Having the responsibility of another little person's life resting entirely upon your shoulders bears with it emotions so strong that I have never found words for them. I know I would not be even half the person I am today without my two daughters. While I do not advocate that everyone have children, I am glad I had my chance, and I'm glad they are in my life today as friends and mentors. My firstborn is a neurotypical child, and she completed her degree in theater at Portland State University. She works full time as a theater arts teacher in a Dallas middle school. My second child is on the autism spectrum. She joined AmeriCorps upon graduating from high school, to earn money for her college education. She informed me that she watched me work my fingers to the bone her whole life to provide for her and that she was not going to allow me to fund her college education, too. After her work in AmeriCorps, she got a graduate degree in sociology from Indiana University–Perdue University Indianapolis while working full time to support herself. She is now in Los Angeles with her husband, pursuing her PhD in historical languages from UCLA.

My Dad Gave Me Life, Love, and Self-Esteem

I see my father's death with vivid clarity, even today. I remember standing there, in his room, helplessly watching him die. I heard his last words. I remember thinking how cruel life was for causing this major stroke to happen at the moment it did.

My father was an interesting character, by every account. He had strikingly blue eyes that smiled all the time, except when he was having one of his bizarre temper tantrums. He had these all his life, and no amount of reasoning stopped them. (He even got fired from a job in his early 60s because of his temper.) He died in part because of constant anxiety, high blood pressure, and his reluctance to listen to anyone or to make changes.

My dad was remarkably clueless socially and was always making statements in public that embarrassed my mother. He could not be bothered to put together an outfit, and my mother always complained how she had to dress him like a child. She did actually care for him like a child, and he was very childlike. Many a friend commented to me how bizarre he was. That said, he was also full of life, funny, and fun. People generally loved him. (There were hundreds of people at his memorial service.) More than anything else, I remember that he was proud of his children, especially this little "apple," who fell so very close to the tree.

He gave me life, love, and self-esteem. He accepted me for who I was and kept me connected to this earth and to the family. His parting "gift" to me was his death, which caused me to seek out the doctor who finally informed me why I had always been so different.

Do What You Love to Do, and Who You Are Going to Be Will Happen

I once had a teacher in a corporate business class in California who taught us the quote, "Plan-do instead of doo-doo," and I have lived very strongly by this suggestion ever since. He said that you either choose to be a victim, or you take responsibility for your life, and the line between the two is very thin. Planning is a tool to help you take responsibility. I try to take one full day a year to make personal plans. I actually set long-term goals for each decade of my life, ever since learning this lesson. In my 30s, my goal was to get as far as I could in my high-tech career. My 40s is a decade of self-awareness and self-improvement. In my 50s, I intend to leave my legacy. In my 60s, I will start a new career. I haven't figured out my 70s yet.

"All who wander are not lost." People say of me that dust does not settle near me. I am always moving. My whole life is about exploration. It is about stretching my comfort zone and finding the place where I fit in and belong (my island) and can contribute to this world. I tell my children and those I mentor to find their "peeps." Don't settle for the first opportunity that comes by if it isn't right for you. I try to live by a phrase that I teach my kids—"Do what you love to do, and who you are going to 'be' will happen." Try out many different things and explore different places and paths until you find your talents. Then, make use of those talents until you have bettered this planet.

The Tech World Changed My Life and Keeps Me Doing New Things

When I finally discovered the high-tech world, my whole life changed. I was finally able to turn my passion into doing good in the world in a significant way. I "found my peeps." My work includes hours and hours of business-type communication training that is remarkably like social skills training, except without all the "you're broken/disabled" stigma attached. This environment has helped me grow significantly over the past two decades, and I have given it my heart and soul. It has been a true win-win.

When I hit 40 years of age, I made myself take lessons in music. It was a promise I made to myself to exercise the artistic side of my brain. This adventure affected me profoundly. I saw colors more clearly and even saw new things in my surroundings. For instance, I saw a cherry tree in my yard that I had not noticed for the previous

10 years! People at work noticed it, too. They actually dubbed me the "softer, gentler Karla," so it was not just in my mind.

I am terrified of doing things that are strange, different, or unknown. But that fear largely does not stop me. I remember sitting in guitar lessons and shaking for the first several months. My teacher could not believe that any grown-up person could have so much fear about taking music lessons. I could not explain this fear, but I overcame it and eventually became an accomplished player. Anything that is new will stretch my comfort zone. I once complained to a mentor that something new I was trying felt weird, and he quipped with much joy, "Great! Weird is good, because it means you're growing."

It's Never Too Late for Dreams to Come True

Perhaps one of the more surprising lessons I've learned is that it's never too late for dreams to come true. I found this out when I became a professional football player at the age of 46. One day, I noticed an ad in the window of a local store in my town, for a football team starting up in the area. But this was no regular football team— it was a professional women's team! I called the number and spoke with the head coach. I knew I was too old to actually play, being a full-contact sport, but I wanted to contribute in some way, given my love of the game. I figured I could do some office work or help set up games, at least.

The coach informed me that another tryout was occurring that very day, and he asked me to come out. I laughed and told him I was 46 years old—I was too old to play. He asked me if I was an athlete, and I told him I was currently preparing for a bodybuilding competition, so I was both athletic and fit. He repeated that I should come try out with the rest of the players. While the idea sounded completely insane on one level, another part of me figured that just trying out might be fun. I remembered the day in junior high that I was so cruelly ridiculed off the field. I figured, "Why not?"

I only had a few hours to get my things and make it to the tryouts. That was probably a good thing, since I didn't have time to worry about what would happen. Still, my heart raced as I drove to the field. The tryout was challenging, but I managed to exceed all expectations in terms of what a 46-year-old athlete could do. The coaches were surprised, and I was too. In fact, I believe I was in the top 10% of all the women who tried out. So when the coach announced I had made the team, I was floored! At the age of 46, I had finally earned my chance to play full-contact football. That was an amazing day, and I kept repeating over and over again, "I can't believe it!"

It just goes to show that it's never too late for amazing things to happen. For me, I've found that I just have to be willing to step out of my comfort zone and push myself to try something new—even if, at first, it may feel a little "weird."

Giving Has Always Been Part of My Life

One of the most human experiences I ever had was being a part of war. I remember watching mothers and children cry as the transport bus pulled away, carrying a load of U.S. Marines to Iraq. The anxiety, fear, and terror were so thick that I found it hard to breathe during those times. I lost platoon mates and friends to the mindlessness of a dark and evil war, and I witnessed things I hope to never see again. When I returned to civilian life, I practiced a life filled with gratitude and have never looked back.

Giving has been a part of my life since my early years. I learned about this most emphatically during the breakup following my second relationship. This relationship was with a man who was alcohol and drug dependent, and I feared for my children's well-being. I left him when he was away on a business trip. When he came back and found out what I had done, he hired a lawyer and tried to sue me. Terrified, I found my own lawyer.

I interviewed an attorney near my job in Santa Monica, and he took the case. We made it just a few hours into the mess of litigation when I realized that I simply could not afford to do this. I had no way to pay for this very expensive service. The lawyer took my case pro bono and made sure I got out of the situation I was in without implication. He explained to me what "pro bono" was and told me that I could pay him back by remembering to always give back to the world in a way that was "win-win."

I was so touched and relieved that I immediately took him up on his suggestion. I learned quickly how powerful this thinking was in terms of leading the "good" life. I will never forget him, and I am forever grateful for this lesson.

I AM NEVER LONELY

I have lived the past decade of my life as a single person and have concluded that it is not only okay for me but in fact better to be alone. It always concerns me when I talk to parents of autistic kids who think that their child is suffering from loneliness on the basis of societal perspectives about relationships.

While I think there are some autistic kids who are possibly suffering, I am never lonely. I have many friends and many options for social activities. But these things still don't really interest me as much as my other interests. Even at my age, I am a raft and I am strong, and while I have found my island, I still explore and push my comfort zone. I am surrounded by people who love and support me, and yet, still I am alone, and that is okay.

CHAPTER 5

MOPPY HAMILTON

Mother of Two and Retail Employee

MOPPY HAMILTON

Age: 62

City: Omaha, NE

Occupation: Cashier at a major retail store

Marital status: Divorced, with two children who went to college

FROM TEMPLE:

Moppy is honest about the fact that she isn't completely happy working at a large retail store. She keeps her job because it allows her to live independently. She has two grown children, who were instrumental in getting her condition diagnosed. Learning about her Asperger's syndrome helped Moppy learn to accept herself. She has some additional impairments, such as a hearing impairment and problems with staying focused. She shares a close bond with her two daughters, who support her in many ways. When life is really hard, it is important to have a few things to turn to that make you happy. Moppy loves to play with her grandson and her daughter's dogs. Watching old reruns of some of her favorite TV shows brings Moppy enjoyment. Both of her children went to college, and she writes, "It makes me so happy that they both turned out to be so smart and successful!"

MOPPY'S INTRODUCTION

I have worked as a cashier at a major retail store since 1993. One of the things I like best about my job is that it's the perfect mix of having solitude while also being around people. I don't actually understand how to do my job most of the time. Sometimes, having Asperger's feels like being an illiterate person who is able to hide the fact that she can't read. I don't steal, I'm not disrespectful of my superiors or the customers, and I'm pretty easy to get along with. But, ultimately, I just don't get it. I believe that I've been able to keep my job because of my near-perfect attendance record and my willingness to conform to the company rules. I wish I could do my job my own way, but I have to follow set policies. I have to be counseled sometimes about new procedures because it takes me a long time to understand them, especially if I think I can do it a better way. It seems like diversity used to be more encouraged than it is now. My company has switched to more rigid standards that we must conform to.

Unfortunately, I have experienced bullying at my job. I know a lot of people think I'm weird or different, but that doesn't really bother me. When someone is intentionally mean to me or thinks I'm *trying* to act stupid, I get upset. I'm harmless and don't understand why some people would want to use up their own energy by making me feel bad.

Up until recently, I kept my disability very private at work. But I was having so much trouble conforming to a new procedure that I was really certain I was going to get fired. My daughters helped me go through the proper procedures to disclose my disability to my employer, and reasonable accommodations are now in place.

What makes me happy is spending time with my family— especially my grandson. I love to play with him and my daughter's dogs. My favorite thing to do is watch TV. I like reruns of shows from when I was a kid, like "Leave it to Beaver" and "Andy

Griffith." I like to listen to country music, and I try to take a walk almost every day.

EARLY YEARS

I have blocked out a lot of my childhood because I was so unhappy. I chose not to pay too much attention to the world around me, so I let my mind go blank. I was introverted and in my own world. I needed to protect "me" and didn't really care too much about what was going on with my family.

I'm the oldest of three kids, all 3 years apart. I always wanted a bigger family, probably since I was the only girl and because all my friends had bigger families.

I was never close to or impressed with my middle brother, who was very self-sufficient and confident early on. I was probably jealous because I could sense that my father favored him. He looked like my father, he was a boy, and he seemed to have the traits that my father considered good in a child, such as athleticism and popularity. Life seemed to come easy to my brother. We were violent with each other and fought all the time. There was always pushing and shoving.

My youngest brother and I bonded immediately. The two of us got along, and he looked up to me. We were both bullied, but for him it was less traumatic. We played with imaginary friends, "the Otises," whom I conjured up on the basis of Big Otis, a big gentle Scotsman on the box of Kellogg's OK's cereal. We shared a love of animals, a sense of humor like no other, and a love of Janis Joplin, which binds us to this day. The biggest thing is that even though we're not twins, we use a "special language" based on funny things we've heard and our own inventions. We share many words that aren't words. We start every conversation with an exaggerated New York accent, "Hello Dahlink!" We have so many inside jokes, like, "It ain't no soda in there," which is a type of slang that cracks us up. We totally *get* each other. In this way, he's my best bud. In fact, as a child I wanted him to be renamed Buddy, but my parents vetoed it. To laugh with my brother is one of the most positive things I carry around with me when I need cheering up.

I renamed myself many times as a child. Even my first name has been legally changed. I didn't like my name from the beginning, because I felt like it was a boy's name. I went by many nicknames. By about 3rd grade, I decided on one name and stuck with it until right after my divorce (I was 44 at the time). My coworkers teased me with an abbreviated form of that name. After correcting them all the time, I realized this new name was just right for my divorced status. It is my legal name to this day. In the autism community, I'm known as "Moppy," which is an inside joke with my two children.

My mom always said she was too young when she had me (she was 22) and that I was a handful. I danced to my own beat. My father often said he was embarrassed of me—I was never sophisticated and always a klutz. He was verbally abusive and mean, but not violent. He criticized me all the time about everything: having bad posture, being clumsy, and not being feminine enough. Probably our biggest disagreement was my love of rock 'n roll music as a teenager. He was a semiprofessional jazz musician and couldn't accept rock. He passed away from what was believed to be early-onset Alzheimer disease in his early 50s. Now I have a stepdad, whom I get along with.

My family is Jewish, and in my early childhood, I attended Sunday school at the synagogue. But ever since I was a toddler, I was jealous of my friends who celebrated Christmas, and Christmas got into my blood. So, we adopted some Christian traditions, like having a Christmas tree with presents. When I was about 14, my parents no longer felt it was necessary to follow Judaism, so we freely enjoyed the fun and excitement of the holidays. Holidays for us were about family, food, music, and decorations. We were taught to do good and that God watches over us, but we were never raised in a spiritual way or taught to worship God or Jesus or to believe in heaven or hell or any of that. Although that made me different, I *loved* it! We were still taught manners, respect, and all of that without religion. I always said we turned out okay, considering. We never got spanked like our friends did, but our punishments could be rough. We lost TV privileges, dessert, play privileges, and the like. (I rarely obeyed my parents.) I think I do believe in God, but I'm not dominated by it. I am against religion, because I don't think you need to live your life on the basis of pleasing God. I also don't like the image of someone superior to me being a male.

I feel like I can sense other people like me, and sometimes I judge them or feel awkward around them. This also confuses me, because I was raised to be very accepting of all kinds of people.

SCHOOL YEARS AND BULLYING

School was hell for me, from preschool onward. Even though I had friends, I was bullied from the start. I was called "skinny" and "ugly," so I was conscious about my looks early on. I got okay grades until I shut down and lost interest. As my mom puts it, I simply stopped progressing.

I was very healthy and never could get away with faking illness, so I had to go to school every day. I went to four grade schools, but that's because we moved. In 6th grade, I started a new school and was targeted by our male teacher, whom I believed really hated me, and the other kids picked up on it. I did admire a boy with a sense of humor, and I like to think I used him as a role model to jumpstart my own sense of humor.

Junior high was bad too, but I did have friends and hung out with a group of "couples." One rather immature boy kind of became my boyfriend. We all had lots of fun together.

I transferred to a new junior/senior high for zoning reasons. It was new and "experimental." This new school accepted kids with behavioral problems, with no questions asked. For me, attending this school was a big mistake. This was where I got bullied—violently—every day, even though my closest girlfriends did not. I was called names and told I was skinny and ugly (which I think I probably was). I was uncoordinated and couldn't keep up with structured sports in school. In a "WASP-y" (White Anglo-Saxon Protestant) neighborhood of blondes, I stood out because I'm a brunette with a darker complexion. In high school, there was a group of girls that were friendly with one of my friends, but they singled me out because I obviously didn't know how to defend myself. It all started when I told my girlfriend in a note that I considered those girls to be the "cream of the crap." My friend betrayed me by showing them the note. They started shoving me around in the hallway, and none of my friends defended me, I guess because they were afraid. The "cream of the crap" girls chased me into the bathroom on the second floor of the school, took off my clothes, and threw them out the window. I waited there naked until a student I didn't know came into the bathroom, and I asked her to get help. Someone got my clothes, and the counselor came in to get me. She took me to her office and called my mom. Unfortunately, this counselor determined that I was the source of the trouble. I never returned to that school. I transferred out and subsequently repeated the 11th grade elsewhere.

The next year was better. I reunited with my boyfriend and the crowd from junior high I had always been drawn to. We played "Twister," which in those days was looked down upon by our parents. We rode around together, and sometimes we made out. We gave each other nicknames. I was always jealous of and admired the "bad and tough," in my mom's words—the "white trash" kids. I suppose it was because they didn't get pushed around.

I Did Not Care about School

Obviously, the most difficult thing about staying in school was trying to avoid the bullies and the fighting. I didn't give a hoot about grades or classes, and I was never forced to excel by my parents, so all that's kind of a blur. I think my favorite class was geography. I never took the honors classes and got average grades. I don't know if I was dumb or uninterested, or both. Nothing was easy, because I had attention-deficit disorder (ADD) but never received a diagnosis and was never placed in special education. During these years of turmoil, one would think I would have been suicidal, self-destructive, and depressed, or felt that I didn't have a future to look forward to. However, I was never even remotely into harming myself. I don't know why!

My business teacher in the first high school I attended served as a mentor to me. I always got along with her. One time when I was being harassed by the bullies, I asked if I could hide in her classroom. She let me hide in there, allowing me to skip my own classes to avoid the bullies. Also, I consider my ex-husband's grandma a mentor, as well as my own grandpa. They accepted me and never tried to change me.

I took some general-education classes in junior college and thought they were too hard. I found myself more interested in the graffiti on the desks in the library. I copied it all down and put it into a blank journal I call my "Nothing Book." I did finish a full school year, but between financial issues and my lack of interest in school, I didn't return. I decided, *I'm done! NO MORE SCHOOL!*

EMPLOYMENT

My first job was in my grandparents' grocery store at the age of 14. I worked on weekends for $20. I took it very seriously and got free food, which was a plus.

I hated work. I was always in trouble and got fired a lot. My parents encouraged me to work, though. I even bought a car (a 1968 Rambler American that I named "Melvin"). I mostly worked in retail, but I never was a rule person or a team player, and I lost and disliked most jobs.

My best job was working in a casino in Reno, Nevada. I had nice bosses and liberal rules. My worst job is probably the one I have now. As I get older and I meet people with disabilities who in my opinion *could* and *should* work and would be better at it than me, I get really depressed. I can't get a doctor to medically excuse me from working, and, moneywise, I have to. I know it's bad for my health, because I'm so stressed out and my feelings of how much I hate my job could give me a stroke. But I don't want a new job. I want NO job. I've often worked two or three jobs at a time. I've always been stressed about being forced to coexist with people I don't choose to be with—people who are different from me. I don't like how we are all supposed to please each other. I know I do things my way, and, finally, with the help of my daughters, we told my supervisors I have Asperger's and I must be permitted to perform my job in a way that fits me without hurting the company. I feel like I can't tell everyone I'm different, and I get no respect. They just don't care.

As for volunteer work, I never had the appropriate empathy to do any of that. I always felt I was the charity case.

RELATIONSHIPS

I had friends from my neighborhood all my life, so that was nice. I didn't have many in school. In fact, my first memory of negativity directed at me was when a girl I didn't like invited me to her birthday party in the 4th grade, and a crippled boy pushed me into the cake. I believe it was prearranged and done on purpose. I had to call my mom to come get me.

My first dating experience was in junior high. I was scared of sex, and I was always afraid of being raped. When I was about 18, my girlfriends and I started going up to the army base for dances and social activities with the servicemen. I went "parking" with a guy who told me that he wanted to have sex, and if we didn't, it would cause him pain. I knew there was an all-night drug store, so I said I would go buy a condom. He said, "No, it doesn't work like that. We have to do it now." We were in my car, but he said if I didn't do it, he would drive off and leave me in this secluded place. And I believed him, so I did it. I wasn't happy with the situation, but I couldn't make myself hate him, either. We stopped dating after that, and soon after, at another army dance I met the man I would marry.

As I got older, I knew I was straight, but I never really loved men. When I was 14, I had an opportunity to go away to camp. A female camper tried to kiss all of us girls and made physical advances. It felt disgusting to me. At this same age, the Beatles became big. Although I was young, I imagined myself being with Paul McCartney, as much as my 14-year-old mind would allow. It was a great feeling. I love the idea of sex, and I love looking at men who turn me on and fantasizing about them.

We Both Wanted Kids

I never wanted a frilly wedding—I don't like sophistication. My ex-husband convinced me to get married. It was his idea. We realized we would make more money from the military if we got married. And I realized we had been loyal to each other for a year, which was rare in those days. We both wanted kids, but he didn't want to start a family without being married. I was perfectly happy to spend the rest of my life with him, but as his girlfriend only. He wasn't Jewish, which didn't bother me. I admit that I never liked being married. Two daughters and 22 years later, we divorced, having lost the desire to be together. There was just too much fighting. There was no violence, no adultery, and no drug abuse. We just weren't compatible.

I don't believe in marriage or commitments and never will. I believe it's okay to have kids and not be married or in a relationship. It's fine if the partners are together, but it's not necessary. Since I'm not religious, I don't associate marriage with religion. To me, you should/can have sex without love, because it's pleasurable. You should take precautions, of course. I have no moral guidelines on this topic: Teen sex and even any sex is okay if it's pleasurable. Why deny yourself? While it's possible to love someone, I refuse to love a man. It's also possible to love more than one person, so the whole thing confuses me. I love fantasizing—I just don't want a commitment. That leads to too much violence, cheating, and negativity.

Men don't find me attractive. I resent that men talk to my girlfriends, all of whom have boyfriends. Men ignore me most of the time. If a man does happen to notice me, I don't respond appropriately. I overestimate his attention.

Once, I had a long-time country-dance partner who was happily married. His wife did not mind him spending time with me. We were very close pals. He gave me things and paid when we went out dancing. He died, and I miss him. We both had inferiority complexes, and we both made each other feel good. At the dance bar, another man said the regulars considered us a couple.

I think that if you have to work on a relationship, it's not worth it. When I see weddings in the newspaper, it makes me so sad. They might divorce! I have no desire to make the sacrifices required to live with another person. I refuse!

Having Kids

I wanted kids. When I had mine, I was young and inexperienced, like my mom. My ex-husband was involved but was overly critical of how I mothered them. I never had any interest in learning to cook or sew. We were poor. But, we weren't violent.

Affection doesn't come naturally to me, unless it pertains to an animal. I don't like being touched, but I don't mind being hugged. I just won't instinctively initiate a hug. I did enjoy snuggling with my children when they were babies. I liked being a mom. It was a new kind of love. My children made me happy in a way a partner or pet couldn't. Being a mom made me feel like I had more purpose in life.

My oldest daughter was always self-sufficient. She was a happy, contented kid, and we got along great. She didn't have any behavioral problems that weren't solved easily. Now that she is a mother, I am so proud. She "gets" motherhood in a way that I never did, and she and her husband share the parenting responsibilities.

My Youngest Daughter and I Are from Different Planets

I always felt that my youngest daughter and I were from different planets. She was more intense, more anxious, and more needy than my first child. When she reached the age of about 9, our bond started to unravel. I don't know if it was because of my Asperger's (which we didn't know about at the time), but my daughter constantly craved a "normal" mom. She compared me to her friends' moms and criticized my untraditional parenting style. When my husband and I got a divorce, she lived with her father, and we became estranged for several years. She always felt I wasn't in tune with her struggles. We've bonded now and are stronger than ever. This child, in conjunction with her sister, is the reason I am involved in this book.

Role Reversal: My Children Act as Mother

We all seem to be content with the role reversal that has taken place in our family: In some ways, my children act as the mother, and I play the part of the child.

My oldest daughter, nicknamed "Leroy," is an elementary-school teacher. She is an outgoing, fun-loving person. She is the perfect description of a social butterfly. Everywhere we go, she knows someone! It takes us three times as long as it should to leave a restaurant or a store because Leroy is usually chatting with someone or making new friends. She has been married to her "prince charming" since 1999, and they have one son—my only grandchild. Her husband and I get along pretty well. Sometimes he gets frustrated because I ask too many questions or I interrupt when my grandson is talking. Leroy is a really great mom. She is attentive and affectionate. I think motherhood comes very naturally to her. I love to hang out at her house, because not only do I get to spend time with my grandson, but I also get to cuddle with her pets, which I adore. She helps me with things like Facebook and e-mailing.

My youngest daughter, whom I call "Fred," has worked in nonprofit organizations for a long time. She has always been involved in the arts, as a dancer and performer. She volunteers with many different arts and special-needs groups around our city. Fred is the one who really encouraged me to seek out a diagnosis of Asperger's, and she is very involved in helping me have a higher quality of life. She has become an autism advocate and speaks at autism conferences about our story. She is currently the vice president of the Autism Society of Nebraska. Even though our relationship was difficult for many years, now we get along better than ever.

Both of my children went to college and completed graduate school. I never thought I could raise "normal" children. It makes me so happy that they've both turned out to be so smart and successful!

ON AUTISM

In 1st grade, I overheard my current teacher and my soon-to-be 2nd-grade teacher discussing me and how I was a "troubled" student.

I distinctly recall hearing one of them saying, "Well, she's not *retarded.*" Here was further evidence that I was misunderstood. Even these days, I still struggle to survive in a "normal" person's world. I recently had a disagreement with a coworker, who said to me, "You're not as dumb as you act." What does that even mean?

I've always felt like I just don't get it—and by "it" I mean "life." All my life, I knew I was different. Most of the time I just don't know how to act. I feel life-challenged. I hate chaos, noise, crowds, and people. I constantly drop, break, and lose things and I can't figure out how to open or close containers. I am an absolute and total klutz. I can't figure out how to make my bed or keep my shoes tied. I hate baggy clothes and sleeves, especially things that hinder my comfort at work. I feel cursed. I have bad luck all the time. I get mad enough to have a stroke upon hearing certain words, phrases, and commercials. I consider unnecessary, "extra" words "ear pollution," and I get so frustrated when extra words are used.

I am addicted to TV. I call it my boyfriend/husband/drug/liquor. I NEED it! I think about it all the time. Other obsessions and fixations I have are country music, anything redneck, and tractors. I love tractors!

I live in low-income housing and get food stamps and go to food pantries. My disability (I'm also hearing impaired) isn't noticeable, so people don't accept it and sometimes don't believe I have it. I'm very impatient and can't organize tasks. I so wish I were normal.

Because of my ADD, I'm very impulsive and can't stay focused on a task. If I want to do something, I jump up and do it. Multitasking is my enemy!

Also, paying a compliment to someone makes me feel as vulnerable as lying naked in the middle of the street.

INSPIRATION

The people who have inspired me have always been "real," and not famous. People who seem to have good luck all the time inspire me. I am very much impressed by the funny things that people say, whether they are famous or not. I try to remember these gems and make them my own. Humor is so important to me. If someone thinks I'm funny, I find it consummately flattering.

OUTLOOK

I think September 11th and a lot of other tragedies changed us all. But being a mom and a grandma changed me for the better. I'm more accepting of diversity, especially now that I know I have a disability myself. I know I'll never embrace the technological changes. I'll never understand computers, DVD players, iPods, or smart phones, so I don't buy them. I know my limitations. And I thank God I have daughters who do use these things for me. I guess knowing I have a condition that has a name and knowing that my family members have made their peace with it has changed me the most.

CHAPTER 6

STEVE SELPAL

Freelance Artist Who Found Success through Art

STEVE SELPAL

Age: 60

Resides in: Palm Bay, FL

Occupation: Self-employed artist for Steve Selpal Art Production, Inc, a graphics and art consulting business

Marital status: Single

FROM TEMPLE:

Steve has done freelance art for many years and fully supports himself with earnings from his art. One client wrote, "Steve's artistic talents are a true asset to our small company. His ability to put down on paper ideas that I have in my head is uncanny." Steve does a variety of art, ranging from corporate design and advertising to fine art. His fine art is sold in both galleries and direct sales. Steve states, "My condition of autism gives me stubbornness and a willpower to survive." As the son of poor immigrant parents, he used this powerful motivation from his experiences as a youth to succeed.

STEVE'S INTRODUCTION

Everyone is different. Art as a career choice is certainly not for everyone, including those who have natural artistic ability. For anyone who has a diagnosis of Asperger's syndrome, I strongly recommend undergoing counseling with psychologists and psychiatrists, plus aptitude testing and pursuing an education. Autistic people are focused individuals, and I see that as our strongest attribute, because we can impact society in a very positive way. Our difference from the norm is a good thing, not a bad thing. The awareness of and legislation for autism is an ongoing movement, similar to civil rights and women's rights movements throughout the world. This movement will eventually help autistic individuals and their parents overcome their differences and show their similarities. It will also help bridge the differences between neurologically typical people and autistic people. In our global culture, our definition of what it is to be human will surely change for the better.

EARLY YEARS

My two sisters are younger than me and are both neurotypical. I was born in London, Ontario, and my sister Helen is 3 years my junior. Betty May is 7 years younger. I was born in a Catholic hospital, because my father's parents were Catholic. They wished me to be dedicated to the Catholic faith and to become a Catholic priest when I grew up. My siblings and I had lifelong religious conflicts imposed upon us from birth. The religious differences in our family play an important role in understanding our peculiar dysfunctional dynamic.

I loved my baby sister Helen with fascination, but I was affected more than a normal child would be from the attentions placed upon my new sibling. These feelings of abandonment are normal for all who have experienced the arrival of a new sibling. What was going on in the background, from my birth until the appearance of my new sister, was a very strange religious battle waged between my Calvinistic mother and my father's parents, who were Roman Catholic. No one on either side of my family had any schooling or literacy. They always reacted to changes by the status quo of what other people told them. My father's father, Stephen Selpal, owned and ran his own barbershop at the picturesque street corner of Richmond and John streets. Some of his customers were the local catholic priests, who were Irish, Scottish, and British. This neighborhood of old London, Ontario, was home to both Saint Joseph Hospital and Saint Paul's Cathedral. Knowing my grandfather as I did, I knew from his repeated remarks that he had promised me to become a catholic priest.

My Dad Had Asperger's

My *nagytata*, or grandfather, showed his love for me in strange ways. I remember some events very clearly from my early childhood. My first words were in magyar (Hungarian). My mother, who was raised in the John Calvin Reformation Presbyterian Church, was totally against raising me to be a Catholic. The loud arguments and anguish of my mother left an indelible and tragic imprint on all of us. My father, Stephen Jr, played a very small role in all of this. Most of my life, he was nonexistent because, by his own admission, he was totally dominated by his own father. Posthumously, I realize that he was actually a gentle and kind man with Asperger's syndrome, who had no willpower of his own. His dominant and dictatorial father and his strong-willed wife laid waste to all of his own opinions.

Stephen Sr made his own homemade wine in his basement at 11 John Street, beneath the barbershop and his residence. My parents and I lived on the second floor of this building, which was formerly a Bank of Montreal. He initiated a strange fondness for me. For teething pain, he gave me his wine in a shot glass. I remember swooning and feeling sensations of pleasure as he lay next to me, fondling me. Any child only understands creature comfort, coddling, and love. I only knew that I loved my *nagytata,* and for each new word in Hungarian that I learned, I was awarded with his affections.

Around 3 years of age, after my sister Helen was born, Stephen Sr's wife, Jenny, my *nagymama,* or grandmother, told me that my parents loved the new baby and not me, but that they (my grandparents) truly loved me. Jenny always called me *kis majom,* which means "little monkey." My parents made me wear a red leather "monkey harness," which was apparently a common way to control hyperactive children. I remember hearing the moniker *kis majom* from many other adults, as well. I felt withdrawn and wanted to die. I had my own mind, my own imaginary friends, and my own music in my head, and I didn't want anyone else.

Difficulty with Speech

My outside world swirled around me, and I experienced anxiety and panic every day. There were good things sometimes, too, especially in the calm of winter. I could understand most of what the adults around me said, but no one ever listened to me, and I didn't realize that I really couldn't talk very well. I thought I could talk, but the replies that came back never made any sense. I got dizzy from confusion and exhaustion and had to lie down. Trying to talk always exhausted me.

Later, after my sister learned English faster than I did when she was around 3 years old, I felt a deep hatred toward her because I became aware of a secret bond between Helen and my mother. I felt this to be wholly unfair. The groundwork and impulses for love or hate between Helen and me were already established, and I had no bearings or control over them.

I was a just a "monkey." Curious George was one of my role models, but I didn't know exactly why. I loved the Red Rose Tea commercials on TV, with the chimpanzees acting the way humans did. In those commercials, the chimps danced the jitterbug while a jazz orchestra of chimps "played" musical instruments. I dreamed of chimpanzees an awful lot in those days. I often thought I was a chimpanzee more than a human, and I felt gleeful about it.

My sister was also a pawn in this family drama. For a time, there were occasions when my Uncle Alex, my mother's brother, visited with his new wife, Marie. Everyone talked about Helen and myself as though we had no brains. They also talked about us as though we weren't even there. Marie was pregnant and told me she had a football under her shirt. I believed it. They talked about how I attacked Helen all the time.

Grade 4 was a major transition for me, not the least of which because of my new teacher, Miss Landon. In my school system, kindergarten through grade 3 was the first "step," although I don't know exactly what they called it. Miss Landon was a real looker. She reminded me of a picture of Audrey Hepburn that I saw printed on candy wrappers. I just knew that Miss Landon was my own angel. Her legs were extremely long, statuesque, and white as snow, like marble, just like the Greek goddesses in my encyclopedias. I was 9 years old when she came into my life.

The County Fair Was a Landmark in My Life

At the beginning of every school year, just to make life even more confusing, we went to the Western Fair. In London, which was the county seat of Middlesex County, this was a grand event that lasted 8 days. I remember that particular year's Western Fair very well, as a landmark year in my life.

Grandpa didn't want to take anyone else to the fair except me. I felt all grown up. As we were leaving for the fair, Helen started bawling loudly and hideously because she was being left out. *Nagytata* said, "*Bőgő masina!*" This magyar expression was meant to be derogatory. It actually means "bass machine," like a double bass in a string orchestra. He and I left for the fair.

It was still daylight, and Grandpa put me on an elephant that had three ornamented saddles, just like horse saddles. The poor elephant walked around in circles and pooped a lot. Then we saw amazing shiny cars and green farm tractors, as well as all kinds of farm animals—sheep, pigs, cattle, and horses. Many of the animal stalls had colorful award ribbons and chevrons. Everything was grand, and many of the animals liked me. I tried to rub their faces with my hand. They were just like me—they were more like me than other humans, I thought. The smell of poop was everywhere. Animal poop was nice and sweet smelling, because of the aroma of the sweet golden hay in it.

Then we went to the same tent that we visited the year before, with the burlesque shows. Wow, I had forgotten all about it. Last year, it had been too overwhelming, and I remember hiding and pulling my jacket over my head. It was a cacophony and too painful for me to bear. This year, it was the greatest show on earth! After meeting Miss Landon, my new teacher, this spectacle made perfect sense. The ladies on the stage were like angels, with shimmering beauty and intoxicating perfume. Their breasts were like airplane propellers spinning round and round with shiny metallic gold, blue, red, and green streamers. I loved Grandpa for bringing me here. The music was loud and jazzy sounding. Razz-a-ma-tazz, razz-a-ma-tazz! While my *nagytata* bought beer, I ran up to the front of the stage and stared. My grandpa gave me beer to quench my thirst, and it was way better than the red wine he always gave me. The beer was golden, and I gulped it down. Water or milk or apple juice never tasted this good. I remember how everything was golden in there and brilliantly bright. The shiny red lips and smiles of those ladies were intoxicating, as well as their shiny white bellies and bulging thighs. One of them looked like Miss Landon. One of them was very dark skinned and smiled the brightest. She reminded me of an Aladdin cartoon I had seen on television. I loved her the most because she looked me in the eyes, and I felt like I merged with her, as her eyes melted into mine. She was my destiny, I thought. I replayed that moment in my mind for years to come. Soon the pretty ladies with blond hair noticed me, too. I was thrilled beyond what any language could describe. I felt that I was at home and that I belonged there. I wanted to experience this forever. Then the music stopped. The lights went dim. We left, along with everyone else, and I thought, why couldn't we smile like this forever? *Nagytata* took me home. I couldn't talk, but I knew that I had seen heaven.

Realizing I Was Different

At the age of 11, I realized that there was something terribly disturbing about me, in juxtaposition with most people—even *all* people. Actually, at the age of 11, I believe I was "older" and "wiser" then I was for most of my adult life. At that tender age, I realized from my readings that art throughout the ages assisted people in deciphering their own cultural meanings for life, the very justifications for life itself, and the perimeter of each significant culture on earth. At 11, I could see it all, and I could see the path before me. I had already had my very personal existence shattered at that age and had my own immature physical body violated. So what? I always had my incredible pluck and crazy raucous sense of humor. No matter what happened to me, I could always perceive a keen sense of the ridiculous and laugh about it. Most people in my life liked me for my spontaneous sense of humor and laughter. I could always laugh at myself at the age of 11 and any age after that. That was a very special year in terms of my mental awakening, although I hadn't yet gained all the skills required to defend myself. In public school in Ontario, I knew I had an aura or stench all over me that caused most kids, especially the girls, to change their desks and ask the teachers to be able to move away from me. I already knew that I was not like my classmates, siblings, or kids down the street.

My parents, especially my mother, thought I was a perfect child. I didn't cry very much, and I wasn't much of a problem until I turned 3. After that is when I remember wearing a monkey harness to help control me. Any doctors had to deal with the fact that we were Hungarian, and my parents had both language and literacy problems. I was told that I would line up toys in a row instead of playing with them normally. I do remember very clearly, just like a motion picture, staring at my alphabet blocks and their variety of colors. I remember wearing shirts with horizontal stripes, and I can still see the color combinations.

My Mother Was Shy and Awkward

My grandfather invested in a motel on the east side of London that comprised 12 units in a row in one long, skinny building that ran parallel to Dundas Street. It had a 200-foot square space in the middle, with a very large old farmhouse sitting on it. He bought this property in the summer of 1953, when I was not quite 3 and my mother was pregnant with Helen. My grandfather had envisioned using my mother as a slave to run and clean all those units. This was horrible and frightening to my pregnant mother, particularly because she was exceptionally shy and awkward when dealing with anyone in public. Being "too ethnic" and European did not help. I remember spending very long hours by myself at the motel, but I had some happy times. I loved staring at leaves and colorful items, like the rosette stained-glass window on the stairs landing. Everything looked different through the colored filters of the stained glass.

SCHOOL YEARS

I was not understood to be mentally different by my family, because my poor hapless parents had no idea. They were very simple, shy, and awkward immigrant Hungarians. I ate regularly, and I was potty trained by 3 or 4 years old. Having anyone touch me or assist me on the wooden potty chair made me hostile, and I screamed. I don't think I underwent evaluation by a doctor until I was in kindergarten. If I wandered off for a few hours, nobody noticed, because eventually I came home to eat. My report cards described me as a daydreamer. I fluctuated between being overly anxious and hyperactive on the one hand and in a "sleepy stupor" on the other. None of this was evaluated any further. I was bad at arithmetic, but I taught myself to read extremely well—and quickly. The phenomenon of hyperlexia (early reading accompanied by difficulties with language and social skills) is probably very appropriate in my case. I adored encyclopedias and solitude. Reading and staring at my encyclopedias was like a narcotic. Nobody understood my meltdowns or my appetite for solitude with my books. My immigrant parents had no idea how their firstborn should or should not behave. I can never direct any fault at them for not seeing or understanding my mental differences.

My Immigrant Parents Had a Hard Life

My parents each have grade-6 educations. My mother's schooling began in a log-construction one-room schoolhouse in Saskatchewan, where her family had emigrated from Hungary. The Canadian province of Saskatchewan in 1926 had the technology of Kansas in 1880 or even earlier. My mother has a very severe outlook on life. Her family arrived in Saskatchewan when she was 4 years old. The whole modus behind their immigration was a complete travesty. In Europe, the newspapers advertised "free land in the new world." In war-torn central Europe, this was a beacon of promise. When they arrived, their promised allotment of land had no lumber or electricity, but they had a small lake on their boundary, with fresh water and ducks. My mother's beginnings were harsh, and her public schooling was harsh, as well. As of this writing, she is still alive and here with me in Palm Bay, Florida. Her family arrived in Saskatchewan when she was 4 years old. The whole modus behind their immigration was a complete travesty. In Europe, the newspapers advertised "free land in the new world." In war-torn central Europe, this was a beacon of promise. When they arrived, their promised allotment of land had no lumber or electricity, but they had a small lake on their boundary, with fresh water and ducks. My mother's beginnings were harsh, and her public schooling was harsh, as well.

My dad's family came from Arad, in Romania. He emigrated in 1929. He didn't fit in at school very well, as they put him in the 3rd grade or so to learn English. His schooling was broken up periodically from the violence and changes due to the Great War and subsequent violence after the war. He was shy and awkward then, and this was a persistent trait throughout his life. He had abdicated direct responsibility of the kids to my mother, and for years, he remained something of an enigma to me. I dreamed about what I wanted to do with him, like go to the north pole or visit ancient ruins, like what I read about in the encyclopedias.

When my father was born in 1914, the region was a vast county of the Austro-Hungarian Empire. Hungarians at that time dominated the population, where nowadays there are far fewer Hungarians in lieu of Romanians and others. This heartbreak over the breakup of Hungary was a deep scar on the national psyche. From the earliest age, any skills that I learned or little jobs that I did around the motel were addressed in terms of bolstering my sense of Hungarian pride. They would say, "Don't be lazy and sloppy like the English! Do this sweeping like a Hungarian, not a slouchy cigarette-smoking Englishman." Their maniacal fanaticism for hard work was imprinted on me.

My parents never really taught me enough English to get by, so kindergarten was hell. I was overwhelmed. I was born late in the year, so I was still 4 when I started. It was like a confusing, never-ending LSD trip, so unreal, with the stress of a new language I was forced to learn. I remember being laughed at constantly by the other kids. "Oh, to learn English faster so I don't keep getting scolded by the teachers." "Oh, to learn English faster to comprehend what these hellions are saying." I remember their faces hovering and swimming over me. I fainted frequently. Kindergarten was traumatic for me and affected me very deeply. I would do anything to avoid the repercussions of my teachers. I'd get lost in reverie when I was in school, thinking about being at home with my books and my imaginary toys and friends. I heard radio stations in my head. These "radio stations" played music, announcements, and even advertisements. This was truly auditory hallucination. Until I turned 11, I thought that everybody had a radio in their head. I couldn't communicate my grandfather's trespasses. My kindergarten year, school was such a shock to me that in early February, I became so ill I couldn't breathe. I had a fever and was kept out of school until springtime.

Doing Things Wrong Was a Frightful Embarrassment

At home, I was taught that doing things wrong was a frightful embarrassment. "Nem sül ki a szemed?" This means, "Aren't your eyes burning out of their sockets?" This idiom also means, "Aren't you embarrassed by what you've done?" This meant admonishment and verbal punishment. I was always getting yelled at. My ears got red hot, too. However, the suggestion about my eyes burning manifested in such excruciating eye pain that I often fell where I stood and cried out from the agony of my eyes burning out of their sockets. This strange and painful physical reaction persisted into my teen years. My sisters never reacted traumatically this way, but I always did. Besides my mother, some of the other Hungarian adults used this same phrase, with the same disastrous results of my falling down and holding my eyes and rocking back and forth. Anything I did that required discipline resulted in a knee-jerk reaction to being scolded. I cringed when adults raised their voices at me. By trial and error, I realized that I had better be careful, or the next time, my eyesight might never return. I had a fear of becoming blind. I thought that this was okay, and I actually thought that everybody, like my new English friends in kindergarten, plus my 2-year-old sister, Helen, had this same reaction to scolding and spankings.

My teddy bear would come alive and console me and hug me. Other toys, too, came alive to introduce me to their friends. To me, they actually existed. Each night, I went to sleep with these imaginary friends, and every day there was some kind of hell and yelling. These friends always reminded me that I was all right, and my radio in my head lulled me to sleep with imaginary music.

When my sister Betty May was born in May 1957, I was already aware of what babies were. I was in the 1st grade. By that time, I was somewhat functional with English, so I could teach Betty May English words.

"Le vágom a kakas!" This idiom means, "I'll cut off your cock!" I heard it so many times from my mother, and it utterly frightened me. Sometimes I was frozen with fear. Other times I ran away down the street. I had seen how my grandmother tied up roosters upside down by their feet on the clothesline and cut off their heads. This was an ordinary occurrence on the farm, but I didn't like watching it. However, whenever my mother yelled, "Le vágom a kakas!" I knew I had better run away. I could feel a distinct pain in my groin region.

Bonding with Animals

As a kid, I was often dumped at my grandparents' farm. On the farm, I could always gaze into the eyes of a chicken or a pig or a cow or a horse and see how they felt. They were just like me. I could always hear their inner voices, and they told me things. If they told me they didn't like their water, I went to find out why. Often their water troughs were muddied by too much activity and dirt. I got them a bucket of water and tried to help. I loved the animals very much, and I dreamed about them, too. Because of them, I liked the farm.

Whenever I met the gaze of other people, I heard a whooshing sound and felt a distinct sucking sensation. I could feel my mind and my thoughts being sucked into their greedy human souls. Of course there were exceptions, usually when I looked into girls' eyes. The farm animals never caused this to happen.

Carol Ann Henderson was the love of my life at the age of 8. I will never know why, but we could stare into each other's eyes and it was okay. In the spring of 1959, we held hands and walked behind the motel to the parking lot of a factory that made fluorescent tubes.

We didn't talk very much, but I looked into her eyes, and it was calm and comforting, like looking into an animal's eyes. That spring, I walked with Carol Ann to her home. Her mother was very nice, just like Carol Ann was. Her mom asked me where I lived, and I couldn't tell her, but I pointed with my finger. Her mom drove me home, and as she drove, she announced the names of the streets where we turned. Then I realized I had better read the street signs and learn the names of the streets. In September of that year, I asked my grade-3 teacher where Carol Ann Henderson was. My teacher, Mrs Fox, told me she had moved away. Oh how I anticipated seeing her again. I dreamed about Carol Ann for many years. She wasn't snippy and insulting like everyone else. When I dreamed about her and our walks together without talking, I always felt good. I dreamed about her eyes and her kind face for the next 10 years.

Dissaproval of My Interest in Art

After the age of 9, I was influenced the most by my uncles and my extracurricular fixations—Boy Scouts and my fencing master. These were important for a few years, but ultimately every one of them severed ties with me. My long hair and my new fixation with art was too much for them to bear. They all spit me out. Their shutting me out almost drove me to insanity.

From 1960 to April 1965, I worked my way up from Cub Scouts to an advanced status as a senior scout and patrol leader. Then our old scoutmaster, Mr Belden, retired, and a new man with a Dutch-sounding name took his place. This newcomer openly ridiculed my longish hair, and after 3 weeks of his abuse, I quit. He scolded me, "Why don't you speak properly?" Mr Belden and I had shared signatures on the troop's bank account, and I had the meticulous job of figuring out which items were required purchases. Our events were mostly camping trips. Some of our camping trips involved hazardous winter camping under harsh and cold conditions, which required very exact inventory requirements. My troop did well with those camping trips, and we also went on many excursions during the milder spring season and autumnal conditions. For well over a year, being a treasurer and planner, I had the respect of the whole 43rd A Scout troop. But the new scoutmaster didn't understand my mannerisms or the way I talked. He hated the way I looked and probably thought I was effeminate. I had spent years gaining trust among the Scouts, and I loved the concept of scouting for boys. I had taken our guidebook, *Scouting for Boys,* very seriously. The knowledge about survival and practicing outdoor skills outlined in that book was very important to me. For years, I pondered why I had to quit the Boy Scouts, which had educated me so thoroughly in survival skills and personal responsibility. But, I felt I had to move on.

My fencing master, Lorant Kafka, gave me a stern warning about going against my parents' wishes in terms of studying art in September 1967. Before that moment, he had always accepted me. But now that I'd told him about my curriculum changes, he was against me. My anguish was severe. In his stern Austrian mind, my longish hair and my talk about my new art program were unacceptable and triggered his hatred and disappointment. I had thought that the disciplines of fencing and pursuing art were compatible and respectable. Was I wrong! I had practiced fencing with Kafka since the age of 9. I had helped him to speak English properly through all those years, so that Canadian newcomers to the sport could understand his heavy German accent. My father had paid for the Maple Glen Cup, the trophy of our fencing club. Also, my dad paid our friend Tam Ozaki, a skilled carpenter, to build freestanding wooden dummies to hold a foil for drill exercises. My mother had sewed and stuffed many heart-shaped targets to be hung on the walls of the gymnasium. Many years later, when I was studying the art history of war-torn Europe, I had an epiphany. I realized that Kafka must have remembered the fate of many of the avant-garde dissident artists of France, Austria, and Germany, before and during World War II. He was just trying to warn me that I was entering a very precarious profession. Lorant knew me very well, and he was actually very protective of me. He knew that the greater part of society would be against me if I took up art. My severe Austrian fencing master inadvertently stiffened my spine and defense mechanisms, in spite of his woeful warnings.

My Uncles and Good Art Teachers Inspired Me

Among my relatives, I had four uncles who inspired me the most. I stayed with them during summertime visits. Just like my influential schoolteachers and professors, their dialogues helped instill in me good lessons I've carried with me all my life. However, they were unsteady, and I could not trust them after I entered my 10th-grade year, when I majored in art. Especially after February 1968, they all openly shunned me and were outspoken in their fears for my future. Worse than that, they professed all of this to my poor parents. Since I stayed with these uncles during school vacations, I didn't have much choice but to learn the lessons they presented, and they contributed greatly to my strength and my determination.

My mother's sister Emma married my uncle John Thomas. Emma and my mother were opposites in every way. Aunt Emma was modern and helped Uncle John run their corporation. John Thomas was educated, with a degree in chemistry. He was fascinated with electricity and Amateur Radio Relay League radio (or ARRL, otherwise known as "ham" radio). To be good at ham radio, you had to have a very well-formed knowledge of electricity, and the ARRL was a help resource. In 1953, he began experimenting with television antennas that he formulated and built in a rented garage. Within 2 years, he had a factory building with a laboratory and 60 employees. Each year, his TV antenna business doubled, and so did his roster of employees. In the summers of 1962 and 1963, I spent 3 weeks studying electricity, radio theory, and Morse code. I built an oscillator with a headset to practice Morse code. John was very firm and serious all the time. He scared the hell out of me. He explained that there was a strong likelihood that President Kennedy's United States and Premier Khrushchev's Soviet Union would have a nuclear war. In the school year after my first sojourn with John, London installed a warning system of sirens. Throughout the autumn, winter, and spring of that year, the sirens underwent drill exercises. This is what it would sound like if there were a nuclear war. At Prince Charles Public School, they showed films of what a nuclear strike would be like. Maybe you have seen some of those black and white films. John impacted me more than any of the other uncles.

Trusted Art Teachers

My succession of teachers was the only true, steady, and impartial form of daily contact that I could trust. These were mostly art teachers. During my formative years in high school and college, I attracted attention from certain teachers, and I didn't know why. Later, in my adult years, I had only brief contacts with any of these teachers. Throughout my working career, every day, some circumstance reminds me of a memory about a teacher and what he or she said. I have always been able to look back and trust the wisdom of my teachers.

I found that tobacco helped me a great deal. Nicotine helped me focus. Many years later, I realized why. As a teen, I didn't have Adderall or Ritalin. Tobacco was a crude substitute to help with my ADD. Today, however, tobacco is taboo. It is politically incorrect to even talk about it in terms of its effects. Outside of the motel business, all my summer jobs were at tobacco farms. My mother's relatives owned tobacco farms, and because of them I always had the money to buy my art supplies and proper winter coats and boots.

The social countercultural changes inspired by the peace and antiwar movement, The Beatles, and the rapid changes from 1963 to 1969 inspired me the most throughout my life. Unlike Forrest Gump, the hapless protagonist in the fictional movie, I was very much aware of all the social changes happening around me. I felt like an African American in my heart. I cried bitterly when Martin Luther King's assassination was announced. However, all of my mentors from my early adolescence were extremely conservative, and eventually they all shunned me for my feelings and the way I identified with the underdogs of society. My own long hair and conviction to studying art caused many adults to reject me. I acquired a stiff upper lip, shrugged it off, and laughed.

Friends Were Art Majors

I was one of the first long-haired young men in London, Ontario. That affiliation with the counterculture was not unique to me. Many people the world over felt the same changes of heart and observed and assimilated the very same new, sparkly feelings that I had. In my case, the physical changes that occurred from puberty to early adulthood were mixed up with a much greater phenomenon going on throughout the whole world. As an early teen, I told my teachers that I was a citizen of the world. However, my peers in East London saw that I was very odd. They called me a "freak." Before long, I realized that anyone who thought the same way I did was called that. It's not really possible to understand the term "freak" and the connection to the countercultural changes of the early 1960s if you didn't live it. In those days, many people thought that the pop-culture influences of The Beatles and other such groups were spreading homosexuality and lax discipline. As a long-haired kid, I managed to find friends in an ever-widening circle, and many of those also attended Beal and majored in art, as I did.

My high-school years at H. B. Beal were indeed wonderful years. The 10th-, 11th-, and 12th-grade years were followed by a special art-certificate year, when I majored in sculpture.

EMPLOYMENT

Art has been my life. Form follows function—that's one of my many rules, which are so brilliantly easy to follow that they're automatic. Art is not meant to be "pretty." It must spur questions in the minds of viewers, or else it is impotent. I have never had a New York art gallery show. Yet, I don't consider myself a failure. I think that I have done quite well. I specialize in commercial and fine art, but neither supersedes the other. Because art is a major function of my life, I must earn money doing it. The ideas that I put into my art, whether it's a project for hire or for an art gallery, have to satisfy both aesthetics and my meager life requirements. Both my art and my life are humorous.

My life developed much more slowly than most people, and I've been called a late bloomer many times. While this is very true, now I accept myself for who I am as an individual with Asperger's syndrome. Recently, I have come up with new goals for my life. I have done only two public-speaking presentations regarding autism, plus one television interview, but I can strongly identify with the prospect of doing many more. I hope I can do this to instill confidence in people affected by autism. I want people to know that they can get an education and focus on a career of their choice through persistence, as I have done.

Outlook and Discovering the Importance of Art

The following series of events has had a powerful impact on my outlook and my destiny. In 1964, my 7th-grade teacher, Bob Wood, and the principal, Mr Deeley, had a conference with me and told me that in the 10th grade I would be majoring in art at the H. B. Beal School of Art. Entering Beal in September 1966 changed my life forever, because it taught me the importance of becoming an artist. The experience made me realize the roles of artists versus nonartists. The critique of my senior show requirement at the Kent State School of Art in 1979 offered me a penetrating analysis of both my art efforts and who I am. The comments by my panel of faculty members had the proper mix of positive and negative points, which helped form my character, regarding how and why I do art. When Hickok, Inc, hired me in 1985, in Cleveland, Ohio, my confidence was reinforced because I had a professional role as a creative staff member in a viable corporation.

An LSD experience I had in February 1968 changed my speech capabilities, allowing me to no longer stammer when engaging in sustained eye contact with other people. This was the single most important, life-changing event for me. Prior to this, I was very introverted and always forgot what I was saying. After this experience, I had the ability to speak, and I felt that I was being heard. My first psychiatric hospitalization in 1970 made me realize why I had failed to socialize properly. This was a deep analysis that was ultimately very constructive. It marked the beginning of a series of psychiatric evaluations that I underwent over the years.

Developing My Freelance Art Business

In April 2001, I sold my house and downsized my existence to include what is truly important to me. During this time I learned how to be cautious with others, in terms of protecting my business. In 2003, I realized I could serve my customers via long-distance communications. I had moved to Florida, and my main customers were in Ohio. My skill of expository writing had improved dramatically, and this skill is my greatest asset to both myself and my customers. My enthusiasm for helping others with my artistic talent is not diminished in any way by doing freelance work for businesses. I see all of it as problem solving. I focus my energy and visualization to make all of my clients successful. I can do detailed work that many designers refuse to do. Immediately after my layoff from Hickok, Inc, I planned the best path for my business. In October 1997, Steve Selpal Art Production, Inc (SSAPI), became an S-Corp. I like to do everything the proper legal way. My sole proprietorship, Stevo's Digital Donut Shop (SDDS), creates art for music acts. SDDS began in 1990, while I was still at Hickok. Ever since I played bass as a teenager, I always loved music. I was a member of a business organization called Cleveland Music Group (CMG), which offered camaraderie. Modern music genres require unique insights, with special logos and images. The fine-art production I do for galleries falls under SSAPI.

Surviving a Down Economy

In 2000, the "Internet crash" caused many Internet businesses, plus brick-and-stone affiliates, to liquidate. Soon, most of my clients were gone. The event of September 11 made things worse. There were many newly graduated graphic designers and many printing and advertising specialists unemployed. There was a succession of customers who could not fully pay for my services. I sold my house and downsized to a rental space. September 11 awakened my sense of patriotism, and I wanted to help. From 2001 to 2003, I served as a loss-prevention officer. Even though I was over the age of 50, I was vetted and even had the qualifications for firearms. My skills were evaluated, and it was decided I could guard stores in uniform. I made arrests, and my sketching and writing abilities helped. In 2003, I moved to Florida and kept my mother from entering a nursing home for 8 years. My sister and mother forbade me to do fine art. My mother entered a nursing home in September 2011, and I'm finally doing fine art again.

My main customer at present is a hobby rocket company in Ohio. A thousand miles does not deter us from doing business. The owner of this business gave me permission to add this quote: "Steve's branding expertise has given personality to all our rocket kits, and his expository writing skills enable us to communicate seamlessly."

In May 2006, a psychologist working in vocational rehabilitation for the Board of Education of Florida diagnosed my condition as autism and Asperger's syndrome. This was crucially important, because all my life I carried the labels of mental illness, which must specify a date of onset.

Upon receiving my diagnosis, I finally understood what I think I had always known—that I was born this way.

CHAPTER 7

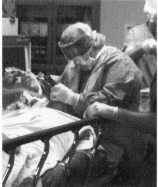

ANITA LESKO

Nurse Anesthetist and Aviation Writer

ANITA A. LESKO, BSN, RN, MS, CRNA

Age: 52

Resides in: Pensacola, FL

Occupation: Certified registered nurse anesthetist and military aviation photojournalist

Marital status: Single

FROM TEMPLE:

Anita handles the anesthesia for complicated brain surgeries. She is very good at what she does because she is highly technically proficient and highly motivated. Life has been challenging at times. Work colleagues have done awful things to her, such as spreading hurtful lies. Anita dreamed of riding in a fighter jet, so she started writing articles and taking pictures for aviation magazines. She found a way to make her dreams come true, which culminated in a ride in an F-15 jet. She realizes she may be missing out in some ways when it comes to personal relationships. However, she also knows she's accomplished exciting things that many others may never get to experience. Anita works with an Asperger's support group and voices concerns that too many younger individuals on the spectrum are not willing to work hard to make the most of their abilities.

ANITA'S INTRODUCTION

I have been employed full time as a certified registered nurse anesthetist for 24 years. I graduated from Columbia University in

New York City in 1988 with a master of science in nurse anesthesia. I have been at my current job for 12 years. I administer anesthesia for all types of surgery, but my specialty is anesthesia for neurosurgery. I especially love doing the anesthesia for brain tumor surgeries and aneurysm clippings. There is a lot of brain physiology going on that I can control by the drugs I give and by the anesthetic techniques used during the surgery. There is a tremendous amount of detail to tend to for my patients, from putting them to sleep and keeping them asleep to waking them up. It all has to be planned very carefully, especially bringing them out of anesthesia at the end of the surgery with a smooth awakening. I thrive on all the details! I also administer spinals, epidurals, and arterial line placements.

The only challenges I have faced at my job have been bullying. It only occurred with several individuals, but one in particular bullied me for 10 years. The following was something that haunted me for many years after the event. I own horses, and one day I needed to purchase hay for them. However, I was going to be at work for 14 hours that day and therefore unable to get to the feed store. My mom offered to drive me to work and then take my truck over to pick up the hay for me. There was only one problem: When I got out of the truck at work, I didn't realize this bully was watching me. About a week later, several coworkers asked me if it was true that I'd lost my license for driving drunk. I don't drink, and I'm very much against drunk driving. To say I was shocked is an understatement.

"Where on earth did you get that from?" I asked these people. It was unanimous: the bully. I went to my boss about it, to which he replied, "Well, she's like that, and everyone knows it." I didn't find that response very helpful. Four years later, that drunk-driving rumor was still going around about me. I corrected people when they asked me, but how many didn't ask me and believed it? That was an extremely stressful experience. I cried over it for sure, but in the end I just picked myself up and kept forging ahead.

EARLY YEARS AND BEING CALLED NAMES

I have a half-brother, Warren (not his real name), who is 9 years older than myself. We were not raised together. I was raised with my mother and my nonbiological father in northern New Jersey. My half-brother was raised by my mother's parents and her sister in Wilkes-Barre, PA. During our younger years, we were often together because my parents and I went to Wilkes-Barre to visit him almost every weekend. I was never able to get close to Warren. He always seemed to have lots of friends his own age, and I was like an outcast no matter what.

One thing that did seem to really bother Warren was the fact that I didn't have any friends. Even during our childhood days, he and his friends teased me because I didn't have anyone to play with, and they asked me what was wrong with me. Then there was the night that changed both our lives forever. One evening, when I was about 18 and Warren was 27, he and his wife Tammy were at our house having dinner, along with two of the neighbors' daughters, Leah and Jenny. Warren started in on me about not having any friends, not having a boyfriend, not going to the prom, and not driving. Tammy, Leah, and Jenny all joined forces with him, calling me names and saying all kinds of horrible things about how abnormal I was. My mom broke up the argument and sent the neighbor girls home. After that everyone went to bed.

My brother, however, was fixated. The next morning, he started up all over again. My mother finally solved the problem by ordering

Warren and his wife out of the house. She told them never to come back. They packed their bags and stormed out. That was the last we saw of them for the next 10 years.

Just before my grandmother died, she begged my mom to repair relations with Warren. Reluctantly, Mom and I did start talking to him again, but it was very strained. We spoke now and then over the years, and it always felt like a struggle. It would have been easier to talk to a complete stranger.

Warren and his new wife have been to my home in Pensacola several times, with their two young children. About a year ago when they were visiting, my mom brought up the fact that I have Asperger's syndrome. This made Warren very angry, and he walked outside to avoid talking about it. He knows very well what it is, because he has a PhD in psychology and is a dean and professor at a large university. He couldn't pretend he didn't know what Asperger's syndrome was. I had the pathetic hope that once he knew this, he would finally understand why I am the way I am. However, it actually seemed to make matters worse. I'm still estranged from my brother.

I Was Always Left Out

My mother discovered my differences the day she first took me to a playground when I was 4 years old. Prior to this particular day, there never seemed to be anything unusual about me. I only had adults to interact with, and nothing appeared different. Then, on that bright and sunny day, Mom realized that something was very different about me indeed. I remember it very clearly. She took me to a park near our house, and I saw a number of children playing on a merry-go-round. It looked very inviting to me. I excitedly ran down the little hill toward the other children and arrived at the merry-go-round, ready to participate in the fun. However, all the children—and I mean each and every one of them—took one look at me, turned around, and walked away. I didn't understand what had happened, but I did know that I now had that merry-go-round all to myself. At no time did I have any urge to follow those children or wonder why they left. I just wanted to spin on that ride as long as I could. I loved spinning. I don't know how long I stayed on that merry-go-round. I just kept making it go and go and go.

What I didn't realize was that my mother was sitting in the car, watching it all. She saw the children look at me as if I were from another planet. As she watched, I decided to try out some of the other activities. It didn't matter where I went, however—the children all walked away from me.

The following week, my mom put me in a different outfit and took me to a different park…and got the same results. By this time, she realized there was something amiss. She began wondering what she was doing wrong to make me this way. As it turned out, she was left wondering this for the next 50 years, until I discovered I have Asperger's syndrome.

I Was Taught to Be Kind to Others

My mother always taught me to be kind to others, to never make fun of anyone, and to work hard, no matter what I choose to do. She raised me catholic and had me attend Sunday school until I received my first holy communion. After getting through communion, complete with the miserable, torture-chamber frilly white dress with the stiff, scratchy ruffled lace and the tight shoes, I voiced my distaste for organized religion. After that, we stopped going to church but formed a deep spiritual relationship with God in its stead. To this day, I am often outside on my farm, looking up at the beautiful blue sky with wispy clouds, watching a hawk soar effortlessly on the currents above me, and feeling One with God and the universe.

I can still remember Mom telling me to be kind to others and to never make fun of anyone. She instilled in me that it is very hurtful to someone if another person makes fun of him or her in any way. I remember the first time I saw a crippled person in a wheelchair, at the grocery store. I tugged on my mom's sleeve and asked her why that person was like that. She very quietly explained to me that something bad happened to that person and that they could not walk anymore. I felt very sad. That moral character has remained with me my entire life. It also applies to everyone who's different, in whatever way that may be. I also think that as my life went on and the bullying and harassment became a daily event, I realized just how emotionally painful it is and I never wanted to inflict that on anyone else. I was also taught to treat everyone as an equal. To this day, and I'll use work as an example, I treat everyone the same, whether they are the housekeeping people or a neurosurgeon. I treat everyone with the same respect.

I Was Taught Many Basic Skills

Regarding my responsibilities as a child, personal hygiene was very much instilled in me early on, as well as completion of homework each night and kitchen duties. Mom cooked everything from scratch and felt it important to have me right beside her, learning the ropes. I think I learned enough skills to have my own cooking show. Being of Eastern European descent, a lot of dishes were made with fresh vegetables. Dough was often used, so I learned how to make all kinds of things, including artisan breads—those crusty, old-world kinds of breads. As an adult, I am a gourmet chef and cook up elaborate dinners to rival professional chefs.

SCHOOL YEARS AND BEING HAPPIER AROUND ADULTS

I dreaded the prospect of starting kindergarten, knowing there would be lots of kids and noise. As a young child, I thrived on peace and quiet and was happy to be around adults. I was most upset knowing that I had to go to kindergarten myself, without my mother. That first day was like a nightmare, and it pretty much didn't change for the next 13 years, until I graduated from high school. School was, simply put, a torture chamber. The external stimuli were overwhelming. It was too noisy, with children playing, teachers talking, and bells ringing. The school bell that rang every hour was enough to send me into a tailspin. I started to cringe minutes before it rang, and when it did ring, it sent a shudder throughout my entire body. My school had strange smells. I got bullied and was forced to do things against my will. I hated being away from the security of home.

I recently found my kindergarten report card. The teacher wrote that I appeared anxious all the time and never seemed to calm down. My mother was frequently called in to the school to discuss my noncompliance with the rules. The teacher said I wasn't like the other children, I didn't listen to her, nor did I fit in with everyone else. I just seemed to do what I wanted, and I was in my own little world. Sadly, bullying became a normal way of life for me.

One thing that stands out from elementary school was Valentine's Day in the 3rd grade. The teachers knew my mother was a skilled artist, and for holidays they always asked her to make something special for the classroom. This time, it was a request for a big Valentine's Day box to hold all the valentines. Mom went all out, decorating a huge box the size of a TV. She spent days on it, even trimming it with beautiful lace. She brought it to my classroom and set it up on the front table. Everyone was excited, including the teacher, who praised my mom for all her hard work. This was 2 weeks before Valentine's Day. On the day itself, the plan was for the students to put their cards in the box, have a big party, and then distribute the cards.

There was only one very big problem.

As I sat in class each day, admiring my mom's handiwork, the realization set in that there were not going to be any cards in that box for me. Not even one. It was going to be very embarrassing to be the only kid in the class without even one card. I came up with the perfect solution to this problem. My mom had bought me a box of valentines to be given to each kid in the class. My secret plan was to write them all out to myself, using different handwriting for each one. No one would ever suspect! After I filled out all the cards, I snuck them into that box over several days, using great caution so no one saw me put them in there. Once the cards were successfully housed in the box, I felt quite smug, knowing I would receive 35 cards on Valentine's Day.

Finally, the big day arrived. The teacher had beautifully decorated the classroom. Two students were assigned to hand out the cards. As they were delivered, I sat and watched the pile of cards grow on my desk. I felt so proud to be like everyone else, getting lots of cards. When it was all done, the card-giving turned out just as I'd expected. Other than the valentines I sent to myself, there were no other cards. I was thankful I had dreamed up my scheme, because I would have wanted to crawl under a rock and hide rather than sit there with an empty desktop. As everyone opened their cards, I looked around the room and thought how lonely I felt at that moment. The consequences of being different and not fitting in were starting to sink in. The realization was overwhelming.

I thought I was going to fool even my mom with my large collection of valentines. When I got home, I took them all out to show her. She never let on that she figured out exactly what I had done. Nor did I know that she cried herself to sleep that night.

Teachers Did Not Know What to Do with Me

All throughout elementary school, the teachers and administration didn't know what to do with me. They admitted to my mom that they knew I was smart but indicated that I could not, or would not, be part of the class and participate like everyone else. My total lack of coordination tormented me. I couldn't learn to tie shoelaces, so Mom had to find shoes that just slipped on. I couldn't catch a ball—not even a huge medicine ball. Not even in high school. I can remember one of the "in-crowd" girls in high school throwing that medicine ball at me with all her might. It hit me in the face and knocked me down onto my back. The laughter that ensued still echoes in my mind. In kindergarten, when we had exercise time, the teachers took us outside to run around a big field. I could hardly walk without tripping, so I dreaded running. I couldn't keep up with the other kids with my awkward running and constant tripping. It just served as another avenue for mockery. I couldn't get the hang of most games, like jumping rope or hopscotch—anything that involved coordination.

Handwriting was another issue that plagued me. I could print very fast, without giving it a second thought. Handwriting, however, necessitated concentration for every letter I wrote, which greatly slowed my ability to take notes in class or write essays for tests that had time limits. I was a mystery to everyone.

I was in the 5th grade when I started taking riding lessons. I never liked to play with dolls—I preferred plastic horses. I had earned money doing odd jobs and used it for this venue. A very peculiar thing happened when I went for my first horse-riding lesson. The uncoordinated kid suddenly became coordinated. I think it was because I *wanted* to be coordinated.

Somehow, I made it out of elementary school. I absolutely dreaded junior-high school. As I feared, the bullying got worse. The sensory overload was incredible. Being different seemed to get more pronounced as I went along. The bullying ranged from being called all sorts of names to getting pushed and shoved and having things thrown at me. Once some kids even threatened to throw me over a bridge into a river.

Sensory Overload in High School

High school was just a continuation of the nightmare. It seemed to last a hundred years. In high school, having to migrate each hour from class to class among an ocean of people was a dreaded event. To me, the noise level was deafening and seemed to make everything around me "echo." I worried that if I tripped and fell, the tidal wave of students would run me over and trample me to death. There were endless aromas of perfumes and colognes that added to my sensory overload. Another thing I dreaded was lunchtime, from standing in the lunch line to the task of finding somewhere to sit that minimized my exposure to the bullies. That walk from the cashier to an empty seat or table seemed totally overwhelming. I'm sure there were only a few hundred students in that cafeteria, yet it seemed like millions, with the drone of chatter, utensils, students yelling out names at me as I walked past them, food being thrown at me, and so on. By the end of the day, I was exhausted. I hated every minute of it.

I was very thankful when it was finally over. I almost didn't graduate, however, because my physical-education teacher gave me a failing mark and wrote that I was so uncoordinated he felt I needed remedial training. My mom paid a visit to the principal. She took with her two huge, 30-inch photographs of me jumping horses over 6-foot fences. She let the teacher talk, and then the principal, about how uncoordinated I was. Then she showed them the two photographs. They didn't say a word. The principal changed my grade to a C and sent Mom on her way. I was thrilled on graduation day to finally be free.

Organic Chemistry Class Was Easy and Fun

Interestingly, organic chemistry was my best subject in school. This is where I discovered I'm a visual thinker. I had to take a full year of organic chemistry after general chemistry. General chemistry was all based on mathematics, which was a struggle for me. I absolutely dreaded organic chemistry, as I heard so many people talk about flunking out of it. I got pretty scared as the fall semester approached. If I couldn't pass it, I wouldn't be able to get into Columbia University for the nurse anesthesia program.

On the first day of organic chemistry, I sat in the front row, in front of Dr John Isador. To the students, he was known simply as "Izzy." Little did I know I was about to make an unusual discovery about myself. That first day, Izzy told us what he expected of everyone and then pretty much said, "Go buy the textbook, have a nice day, and I'll see you tomorrow." I went to the bookstore and bought the off-putting book, which was literally 4 inches thick. I was too unnerved to even open it. But that night I had no choice—I opened it up and read the first chapter.

The next day in class, Izzy drew chemical structures on the blackboard and explained the basics. He said our knowledge needed to grow from the basics, like building blocks. The more he talked and drew, the more fascinated I became. Understanding organic chemistry involves being able to imagine the chemical structure in your mind and going from there. I was able to see these chemical structures in my mind, as if on a huge movie screen. I could mentally manipulate them into whatever shape was necessary. Organic chemistry rapidly grew to be my favorite course of all time. I got 100's on every test and had a blast learning it all. I simply could not understand why others found this subject so difficult. Of course, now I realize why it was so easy for me. Aspie brains are great at visual thinking. Izzy was a terrific teacher too, and I still remember him well.

EMPLOYMENT

My First Job Was Cleaning Horse Stalls

I was 12 years old when I began to work. My first job was mucking out horse stalls. My parents couldn't afford riding lessons or a horse, and I desperately wanted to learn to ride, so I became a working student at a big riding center near my home. The more stalls I mucked out, the more lessons and riding time I got, so that motivated me to keep on shoveling!

I also spent hours painting endless miles of fences, picking rocks out of the big paddock where the privately owned horses got turned out, stacking hay bales—you name it. As I got older, like around 16 or so, I was put in charge of the school horses—about 25 of them. I cleaned their stalls, fed them, brushed them, and got them tacked up (saddled) for the endless lessons that went on daily. I also cleaned all the tack (riding gear) daily. No matter how many times I walked into that tack room and saw all those saddles and bridles hanging up, I never tired of cleaning them and keeping everything neat. In fact, I never tired of anything—not even mucking out yet another stall.

Being a working student at this stable was the best job I ever had. I worked there until I was 18. That job helped build my strong character. I developed a strong work ethic, and I realized I have tremendous perseverance. I learned that the harder I worked, the luckier I got. I say that because people would see me ride a horse over an open-jumper course and say how lucky I was to be able to ride like that. Then I'd tell them how I got there—that I did extremely hard work, nonstop, to achieve my goal. I just kept on going until I got where I wanted to be. Even I could not explain my drive to do it. Of course, I didn't know it was my Asperger's laserlike focus at work!

I never needed encouragement from my parents. My motivation was getting riding lessons and riding time. The more I worked, the more riding I did, and the better I got at it. My big dream was to compete in open jumping, and by the time I turned 17, I reached my dream and competed for several years in the jumpers. I had worked my way up to being a top-level rider and was then getting privately owned horses to compete. By that time, I was riding multiple jumpers each day. It was a dream come true. I savored each and every moment when I was on the back of those powerful jumpers. Taking flight over a 6-foot-high obstacle, soaring over the top of it and landing, already looking at the next fence, is a feeling like no other.

Discovering Nursing

In my early 20s, I worked as a volunteer at a local hospital. They placed me on an orthopedic floor, where patients recovered from things like hip replacements or pelvic fractures. Most of the patients were elderly and had no visitors. The nurses, most of whom were around my age, did not appreciate my presence at the nurses' station. The patients, however, did appreciate my company. Each Saturday morning I'd offer any help I could to the nurses, then start visiting the patients. Some were there for months, so I got to know them well. It was during this time that I decided to go into nursing. I could see the difference I made in those patients' lives, and it made me feel really good about myself.

The worst job I ever had was cleaning houses in college. I worked between classes, when I had a layover of several hours until the next class. I never minded the hard physical work—I was used to that from the horse days. It was the attitudes of the people I worked for that I strongly disliked. They constantly said demeaning and demoralizing things to me about being a cleaning person. They knew I was a college student, but that didn't seem to register with them. They always had to say something to make me feel like less than I was, that I was worthless and only capable of cleaning houses. I noticed that if I was exceptionally tired, their words almost started to have an effect on me—that for a moment I believed it. Once rested, I realized exactly how dangerous it is to say things like that to someone, because maybe another person would take that negative thought and really start believing it. This can be so detrimental to a person's self-esteem. From that experience, I learned the power that negative words can have on a person, and thus the opposite—that the power of kind words and positive thinking can be equally as powerful, if not more so.

Being a Successful Nurse Anesthetist

I have been working full time as a certified registered nurse anesthetist for the past 24 years, since graduating from Columbia University. For the past 12 years, I've worked for an anesthesiology group that provides anesthesia services for the largest hospital in the area. I specialize in anesthesia for neurosurgery, including brain tumors, aneurysm clippings, and spinal fusions. I have also specialized in anesthesia for trauma, transplants, and burns. All of these specialties require very intense concentration and skill, and I thrive on these types of cases.

RELATIONSHIPS

I began to realize I was different in elementary school, probably during 1st grade. I started noticing that all the other children in school didn't want to be anywhere near me. Initially I attempted to go over by them, but after numerous rebuffs, I eventually gave up. This seems funny to me because of my exceptionally strong perseverance for everything else—but not when it comes to trying to pursue friendships among my peers. I really just wasn't too interested in working at it. I had plenty of thoughts and ideas floating around in my head to occupy my time, so I didn't need friends to fill my life with. I was very content to be alone.

As a young child, my mom had a friend with three children my age, and when she came to visit, I played alongside those three children—but not really *with* them. For example, if we all had coloring books and crayons, they interacted with each other to decide what colors to use, and I sat over at the other end of the table by myself, coloring in silence. That was my version of "playing" with other children. I never had any friends from school—not a one. I simply could not interact with peers my own age. Except for ones who were crazy about horses, like I was.

My Friends Shared My Interest in Horses

As a teenager, the only friends I had were two kids who were also working students at the stable. They were my own age, but the difference between them and the kids from school was that they were hooked on horses like me and were also working students, so we all had that bond. Thinking back, I'm extremely grateful for both of those friends, because their friendship enabled me to have a moderately normal teen stage. We often worked side by side at the stable, then walked miles to a burger place, ate together, walked back, and rode together. Then we worked some more. Everything was horses, horses, and more horses. As hard as they worked, I worked even harder, because my invisible driving force was making me do it! Recently, I looked up my old two friends on Facebook, and I found one of them. I wrote to her and was glad to hear back. I then wrote and asked her what she remembered most about me. She said she was always very jealous of me because I rode better than everyone else. She elaborated that I seemed to have a magical way with every horse I rode, and it always bugged her. I was a bit let down. That wasn't what I wanted to hear. I was hoping she'd have said she remembered how hard I worked. Plus it irritated me that she could have been jealous of me in light of the fact that she knew just how hard I did work to get there.

I Made Friends at an Asperger's Support Group

As an adult, I didn't have any friends until I started an Asperger's support group last November. It was there that I met a brother and sister, aged 51 and 50, both with Asperger's syndrome. We connected instantly, and we all speak the same Asperger "language." Prior to that, I didn't have even one friend. There are people at my job that I enjoy talking with while I'm there, but that's the extent of it. I never could figure out how to make friends or keep them if something did get going. By the same token, I love being by myself. Between working full time, taking care of more than 50 animals, caring for my elderly parents (who are both handicapped), and writing books, there isn't really much time left to hang out with friends. Let me put it this way: I don't sit around wishing I had friends.

I've Become the Person I Was Meant to Be

I haven't been on a date in 14 years. I realize this is shocking to most people, but it just happened this way because of all the things I've been doing with my time. I didn't make a conscious decision not to date—it just happened. Earlier in my life, I had three long-term relationships. The first was when I was 18. The guy was 30. That lasted about 3 years. Then I got engaged to another guy for 4 years, then several years later was engaged again for 4 years to someone else.

At this point in my life, I feel really ready to meet someone to have a serious relationship with. I feel very settled in my life. I have a sense of self-confidence that I've more than earned, I can communicate extremely well, and I've become the person I was meant to be. Obviously, I'll always have Asperger's syndrome, but I've grown as a person so much that I feel it's only an asset to me now and not a hindrance.

Looking for a Relationship with Good Communication

I would very much like to meet an accomplished and exciting person, and one who believes that communication is a very important aspect of a successful relationship. Someone who could understand that, yes, I do have Asperger's, and I do have some quirks about me, but my other qualities override those quirks. I feel that an Aspie and a neurotypical person can have a successful relationship, if it is approached like two different cultures merging together. If a Jewish man and a catholic woman are together, they each need to learn about the other's religion and celebrate them both. I've known two such couples, and they both celebrate Christmas and Hanukkah, Rosh Hashanah, Yom Kippur, and Easter. (You get the picture.) There has to be a willingness of each partner to accept the other person as they mesh together. It can be done.

I'll also talk about intimacy, something that most probably won't be willing to discuss. In general, I don't like to be touched by people—like at work, someone will give me a hug and I don't particularly like it. I stiffen up, and I assume they can sense my distaste for it. However, I very much enjoy being touched by a romantic interest. The unusual thing is that I can go many years without having sex, yet when I'm interested in a person and have deep feelings for him, I want to participate in this activity as much as possible. I'm extremely romantic, and I absolutely love to create a romantic setting in front of my fireplace to spend an evening right there. I'm a very sensuous person regarding sex, and I leave all my Aspie traits at the door when it comes to passion.

INSPIRATION

My Mother Inspired Me

Without a doubt, my mother has been my biggest inspiration. Following is the dedication I wrote in my book, *Asperger's Syndrome: When Life Hands You Lemons, Make Lemonade:*

> I dedicate this book to my mother, Rita, who enabled me to become the person I am today, and for everything I've accomplished throughout my life. She has always believed in me and encouraged me to work hard and follow my dreams, no matter how far-fetched they seemed to be. I've always dreamed big, and she's right there to cheer me on. Because we didn't know I had Asperger's syndrome when I was a child, indeed there were endless struggles with my "Asperger ways," but somehow, she instinctively knew exactly what to do with me to keep me calm and focused. I can well remember endless times of getting upset or stressed out over something, but she always remains calm and works to bring me back to my natural state of peace and calmness. She has devoted her whole life to me, and because of that I

have accomplished things that others only dream of, because I focused on the gifts that I was given when I was born with Asperger's.

My Mother Used My Passion for Horses to Motivate Study

One particular area that my mother always focused on was my education. She began to stress the importance of a good education very early in my life, always emphasizing that I needed to get a good education to enable me to be able to take care of myself someday. At one point, while I worked on my master's degree at Columbia, I was under a lot of stress due to social issues. The work itself wasn't stressful—it was the problems I had with my classmates and two of my professors that bothered me. I started to feel overwhelmed. One evening I returned to my apartment to find a brand-new beautiful halter for a horse waiting for me. Earlier in the day, my mom made a trip downtown to Miller's Saddlery and purchased the halter. She knew my big dream was to own my own horse, and I needed to get my degree to accomplish that goal. That halter signified the horse I would own one day, and it even had a brass nameplate on the side, awaiting an inscription with the name of my first horse. After wiping the tears away, I got my laserlike focus back on track, pushed all the extraneous stuff out of my head, and got to work on what was important, like learning how to administer anesthesia.

OUTLOOK ON LIFE

There are two very significant events that have really changed me. First, my local newspaper published an article about me last October. The article explained that I have Asperger's syndrome and that I was starting a support group for the Pensacola and surrounding areas. They also published the date and time of the first meeting. More than 50 people turned out, with 25 "regulars" who attend my meeting monthly. It was during these meetings that I started making discoveries that have truly lifted a weight off my shoulders. Other discoveries have greatly troubled me.

One of my big issues was driving, or rather a lack of it. I thought I was the only person in the entire world who was afraid to drive back when I was 17 and had to learn to drive in high school. It was simply overwhelming to me, not only the sensory overload but the realization that if I did one wrong thing out on the road, it could cost me my life or that of someone else. It wasn't until 10 years ago that I started driving regularly. Until then, my mother drove me everywhere. Occasionally I drove with her in the passenger's seat, but that really made me nervous, because I feared I'd get us in an accident and something would happen to her. I felt better driving by myself. At the meetings, however, other people started bringing up their fears of driving. I was very relieved to finally find out I was not the only person on earth with this problem!

Shocked to Discover Young Aspies Were Not Employed

The discoveries that troubled me included the many people, from young kids to adults, who learned they have Asperger's and literally shut down on life—particularly the young people. It was like a death sentence to them. Their life was over from the day they received their diagnosis. I was in utter shock at this. When my condition was diagnosed, I felt *relieved* to finally understand why I had the problems I did. Now, I was hearing things like, *"I'm glad I didn't find out I have Asperger's more than 3 years ago, because my life would have been over long ago."* This totally flipped me out. Here they sat—a handful of healthy people who had given up on living. I questioned a 22-year-old woman about whether she works. Looking up from her needlepoint, she stated indignantly, "I'm not ready for that." I was floored. Sometimes when my alarm goes off at 3 AM for work, I don't feel ready, either! Being in the medical profession, I've seen a lot of really bad things happen to people, as well as people who are born with severe physical handicaps. Yet, they choose to make the best of what they have. This "victim" mentality was extremely foreign to me.

I was also troubled by how many parents take their child with Asperger's from therapist to therapist to therapist, never allowing the child to just be a kid instead of a diagnosis. Additionally, I believe these children will truly begin to think there must be something wrong with them. This, in turn, becomes a self-fulfilling prophecy. These people need to think of the future and what they CAN do for themselves. I was also shocked to find out how many people are collecting disability payments because they "can't" work. *Can't work* because they have Asperger's syndrome? I was at a total loss. For the ones that don't come from a multimillionaire family, which is most of them, don't they realize that when their parents are gone, they're going to end up in some kind of institution or home? They need to start working—at whatever job that might be—and do something other than sit at home feeling sorry for themselves. They need to get over the fact that they have Asperger's. It's not a disease—it's just a way of life. We need to get these people up and functioning.

The single most life-changing event for me was writing my book, *Asperger's Syndrome: When Life Hands You Lemons, Make Lemonade*. This was the very first time I actually stopped to think about my life and what I have accomplished. Until this point, I've always just worked diligently toward my next goal, never looking right or left and never looking back. As I began to write, all the events of my life started flooding into my mind like the bursting of the Hoover Dam. At times, I could hardly type fast enough to keep up with my thoughts. It was a daunting task, because along with all the memories came the emotions, as well. There were endless times I started typing only to have to stop because I couldn't see any longer for all the tears. I learned to stop, sit back, and cry it out. Then I started typing again. It was very cathartic, to say the least. But most importantly, it showed me, in black and white, all the things I have accomplished in my lifetime, and I accomplished them *not knowing* that I had Asperger's syndrome. Oh, it wasn't easy by any means—but I never gave up. Perseverance became my middle name.

I Do Lots of Interesting Things

In addition to earning my master of science degree in nurse anesthesia and working full time, I became an internationally published military aviation photojournalist and flew in fighter jets and helicopters. I was an accomplished equestrienne. I did ice dancing for about 7 years. I started an Asperger's support group and began speaking publicly about Asperger's and my life with it at universities, schools, and hospitals. I wrote my book.

The most exciting thing I've ever done is fly in an F-15 fighter jet and a military helicopter! It all began when I saw the movie "Top Gun" in 1997, and my special-interest laserlike focus took over. By the end of the movie, I made up my mind that I wanted to fly in a fighter jet. I started picking up every military aviation magazine available and began writing articles for several of them. I taught myself how to use a very expensive camera, with a foot-long lens, and eventually started getting top-quality photos of jets flying at speeds of more than 400 miles per hour. Before long, my military aviation articles and photos were being published worldwide. I got to spend time with the Blue Angels of the U.S. Navy and a Fighter Wing of an air force base. It was at that point I got my F-15 flight. I can still remember to this day the thrill of being in the backseat of that multimillion-dollar combat aircraft, getting ready for takeoff. As the pilot eased the throttle forward, the jet turned onto the runway. The massive jet began to feel like a racehorse in the starting gate. We were cleared for takeoff, and off we went! I could feel the roar of the engines with full afterburner. I watched the treetops turn into a blur, then we went straight up to 15,000 feet. The G-forces were unreal. I felt like I was in heaven. All my hard work had finally paid off.

Working Hard to Succeed

I've done a lot of exciting things in my lifetime. No matter what I did, if one door closed, I kept looking for another one to get my foot in. Obviously, having Asperger's and not knowing it made for an endless array of obstacles that got in my way. Sometimes I felt like the ball in a pinball machine—no matter which way I went, something was blocking me. But it didn't matter. I knew that eventually I'd find a way to get where I wanted to be. I was willing to work hard.

When I completed my book and saw with clarity all the things I've accomplished in life, despite having Asperger's syndrome, it enabled me to be the hope and inspiration for others with Asperger's. I believe that they, too, can achieve their dreams by thinking positively and believing in themselves. Like I say in my book, "When life hands you lemons, make lemonade!"

CHAPTER 8

WENDY LAWSON

Psychologist

WENDY LAWSON, PhD

Age: 59

Resides in: Warrnambool, Australia

Occupation: Psychologist

Marital status: In a committed relationship, with two children

FROM TEMPLE:

Wendy went back to school at the age of 38 to get the credentials needed to be a psychologist. Her family life as a child was structured, and conversation at mealtimes was encouraged. She was a resourceful child, and at age 9, she walked people's dogs and mowed lawns. In addition to autism, Wendy had a series of physical problems that complicated her life considerably. However, she raised four children, and today she works as a psychologist, helping others with autism.

WENDY'S INTRODUCTION

I currently live in Australia and am well known in the southern and northern hemispheres as a trainer, conference speaker, and campaigner for the rights of people on the autism spectrum. After years of misdiagnosis, I finally received a diagnosis of autism in 1994. Having returned to school, then to university to study psychology, I did eventually become a psychologist. I needed to become a professional so that other professionals would listen to me. I am also an artist, author, and poet, and I've operated my own business for nearly 20 years. I am a lecturer at a number of universities, as well as a tutor in the University of Birmingham's distance-education autism master's program. In addition to my professional and research knowledge, my life experiences and personal insights provide professionals and parents with an invaluable gift when I share my autistic understanding with others. I married and had four children, and two of my sons are on the autism spectrum.

Being on the autism spectrum, I am passionate about the rights of those who so often cannot speak for themselves. In my work, I aim to promote justice and equality for all. During my growing years, I was not always treated as an equal by my peers. I like to say I grew up with a *diff*-ability (a difference of ability). Although my autism wasn't diagnosed until I was an adult, I lived with all the issues that came with it.

I am proud of my autism. In 2008, I was awarded fourth place as "Victorian Australian of the Year"—an amazing feat. It was humbling and exciting all at the same time. It was certainly an honor that I took very seriously and one I continue to hold respectfully and responsibly—and one I feel really good about.

For me, life as a young student was fraught with difficulty. Learning the typical things that children are supposed to catch onto quickly just didn't happen easily for me. Challenges included things like sharing, taking turns, looking at people who spoke to me, and coping well with sudden noises, changes, and expectations.

Receiving diagnoses of high-functioning autism, attention-deficit/hyperactivity disorder, and dyslexia (learning difficulty) as an adult has helped to explain why I couldn't keep up with other children at school. Also, in some ways it has served to explain the specific skills and abilities I have (eg, poetry and writing). However, my success and achievements, amongst years of distress, abuse, and emotional and physical pain, are not just the result of interventions by others or professional support. They are born from an ethic founded upon hard work, commitment, good self-worth, and a healthy belief system.

Much of my belief system is the result of family upbringing, inspirational friendships, encouragement by dedicated teachers and great mentors, and my own decisions, personality, and perseverance. Sadly, there was a time when my family and many professionals thought I'd end up living in an institution permanently and would never lead a successful life.

EARLY YEARS

When I was born, my brother Tony was already 9 years old. My mother had miscarried two other babies. Mum went into labor with me after going for a Sunday ride with my father in his 1950 Morris Minor Estate car. My birth was very quick. I was born a month early, but I didn't require any special support.

Wendy

Baby little, bald and wrinkly, welcome to this world.
Your arrival, abrupt, survival,
All arms and legs unfurled.

Being 'cross eyed,' watery, with sight so blurred,
And distant noises all unheard,
You'll find your way around.

But for a while we'll not notice your smile,
Nor hear your voice of silent choice.

Till one day, quite far away,
Things click and find their place.
With fury friends and modern trends,
You'll make small steps and we'll accept
You're different, but not less.

My brother named me Wendy, apparently after a young girlfriend of his (Wendy White) who lived on our street. They often played together.

Apart from having "sticky eyes" that were turned oddly, causing me to develop a squint, initially I seemed to be developing typically. By the time I was 3 years old, however, Mother had given birth to my sisters, Alison and Ann (a year apart). Their arrival caused much distraction and occupied my parents for some time.

Both my sisters were premature—Ann by 2 months and Alison by 1 month. Ann also had a twin, but he was stillborn. Ann needed lots of help because she was so tiny at birth. In fact, she was not expected to live, but she did.

Maybe because Mother was so busy, or perhaps because it was easier, I was often left to my own devices. I didn't talk until well after my 4th birthday and was in diapers much longer than my sisters. This didn't seem to bother anyone, though, and I was expected to partake in family life just like everyone else. I received no special attention and was treated just the same as the other family members.

For my 5th birthday, I remember being given a kitten by my maternal grandmother—a grandmother who accepted and loved me, just the way I was. I always found it much easier to connect to and spend time with animals, insects, and birds, rather than people. My grandmother understood this. My sisters knew the kitten (whom I named Sandy) was mine. If they wanted to play with him or hold him, they always asked me first, and, in exchange, I was offered time with a favorite book (which I couldn't read but simply enjoyed having) or puzzle.

At times, my sisters and I squabbled over trivial things, and my father made it very clear that we were to behave and make up with each other. I remember taking rides upon Father's back during the summer months at the seaside and in the ocean. My sisters and I often played leapfrog and got along well with one another.

Much of the time, I actually didn't notice my brother and sisters. They were like the furniture—always there. If they were not where they should be, however, I found this very troubling. To gain my cooperation, Mother employed the support of a young friend— Margaret—who lived next door. This young friend (aged 12 years) later joined the family and lived with us as an "adopted" sister. She took me out and let me run, climb, and explore the outside world. With her encouragement, I learned about everyday things that my Mum just wasn't able to show me. Margaret was my first hero.

I Worked Out Social Relationships with Puppets

My brother went to a special school because he had trouble reading and writing. My sisters and I went to a typical school but, owing to the difficulties I had with learning, I was kept in a class for slow learners. In spite of this, though, I taught my sisters to ride bicycles, play chess and checkers, and put on puppet shows for the rest of the family and our neighbors. I always found it much easier to talk through the hand puppets I made and to work out social interactions from our pretend "theater puppet stories" rather than doing it face to face with other people.

By the time I was 3½ years old, my parents definitely knew I was different from my siblings. At age 2, I already had a diagnosis of intellectual disability, even though this was considered to be very mild. Only my left eye had full sight. I wasn't good at joining in family social times and didn't really understand the games my siblings played. This wasn't seen as a problem, though, because the family simply found ways to engage with me.

In later years, puppetry and homemade theater with a cardboard box and some old curtains always excited me and my sisters. We acted out the stories we read in books with our homemade hand puppets. I was used to seeing "Punch and Judy," a puppet show performed on the beach near my home, and it always intrigued me. Eventually, my family realized that puppets were a great way to interact with me, and they proved a useful way of helping me understand the social domain—a kind of early social-story model.

My parents structured our daily lives, and I was expected to do chores, just like my sisters and brother. Mother wasn't as firm with me as Father was and, unfortunately, I didn't always do as she told me to. I didn't like to be touched and, on reflection, I think Mother found this difficult, although she was never big on affection or cuddling.

I loved to stroke soft material and, sometimes, other people were wearing it at the time! No matter how often I was told not to do this, I still found it difficult to resist. Eventually, I was given soft pieces of material to carry in my pocket and was told I was allowed to stroke only this material. Having this substitute cured me of stroking soft material that others wore.

Family Mealtimes and Conversation Were Encouraged

I do remember family mealtimes. As I got older, meals were always conducted around a large family table. Most of the time, I had a book in my hand—I could read basic material by age 9 and was proficient by age 13. However, I was not allowed to read at mealtimes, which I found distressing—but it became a rule we all observed. Conversation, on the other hand, was encouraged. There was always lots of discussion, debate, and laughter. Mostly, I observed rather than joined in, but I learned lots from these times, and I'm sure these experiences have given me confidence in my current work, since I talk in public settings so much of the time.

My family was not religious, but I was sent to Sunday school with my siblings. Church life, with its ritual and structure, became a great love of mine. Eventually, I joined the church and became a Sunday-school teacher and, for a short period of time, an assistant pastor.

As a teenager and young adult, I loved to spend time with the local vagrants that slept behind my father's restaurant. I enjoyed being with the local gypsies ("travelers"), too, and often sat around their campfire, eating eggs and bacon cooked on the fire in well-worn fry pans. As a child, I rode bareback on a pony that belonged to a young "traveler" companion and spent hours listening to the stories told by the older men and women.

My sisters and I shared a room, and on Saturday mornings, we snuck out of our bedroom window to go to the local picture house. There, we watched children's cinema. Although my parents were not keen on this idea, they turned a blind eye when we snuck out. However, I was always in trouble when I got home! Books, movies, musicals, and theater are still very much a love of mine today, and I sit in awe and wonder each time I see a show, no matter how many times I've seen it before.

SCHOOL YEARS

My early school years were very hard. I felt confused and alone. I was constantly teased and mocked by other children. I just didn't know what was going on. I did my best to please the teachers and loved to listen to the voice of one teacher in particular. That one teacher's acceptance, patience, and support gave me a reason to keep going to school.

I found school rules difficult to understand, so I was often in trouble. I hated school dinners in the primary school because they usually had "hard" foods like "peas," and I couldn't eat them. Today, of course, I recognize that I have a number of sensory issues and have worked out how to get around these. For example, I combine foods with uncomfortable textures in a blender (or mash them) so they are easier for me to eat.

I Felt Safe in the Library

Other issues at school were mostly to do with my processing difficulties, meaning I needed more time than other children to take in information and make sense of it. Metaphors were always hard for me to grasp, being so common in language and me being so literal. The only way I managed to survive in school was by spending as much time as possible in the library, among the books, where it felt safe.

I loved books and the world they allowed me access to. It was a world of color, magic, science fiction, animals, and places of kindness, where the goodies always won. It was a world I was determined to be part of, rather than the world around me, which made little sense and often seemed so cruel.

High school was even tougher than primary school. I failed most subjects, except history, English, and art. I was hopeless at math, science, geography, and any other subject that consisted of formulas, recipes, and/or symbols. This left me feeling like an idiot, and it was very hard for my teachers to understand the huge gaps and holes in my learning.

I think my easiest subject at school was English. Once I mastered reading (and it took me some time), I loved to read. Mostly, I read the classics *(Jane Eyre, Biggles,* and *The Famous Five,* by Enid Blyton) and adventure, biography, and animal books. I didn't always appreciate that some things were fiction and not meant to be taken literally, but the heroes in the stories inspired and encouraged me.

I Was Thought to Be Lazy and Uncooperative

My skills were so uneven that it was assumed I was lazy and uncooperative. This was far from the truth, however, and it wasn't until I received my diagnoses of autism and dyslexia as an adult that I made sense of my difficulties at school. Had it not been for my love of reading, research, and knowledge (usually about specific topics), I would have remained convinced that I could never achieve anything, and I likely would have given up years ago. As it was, I attempted suicide and was misdiagnosed with mental illness at the age of 17. But, there were people who saw the real me, believed in me, and were determined that I get a fair go at life.

Starting at age 10, I was in and out of the hospital for several years. First it was because of a bone disease in my left tibia that left me in leg braces and in need of much physical rehabilitation. Later, I was placed in a mental institution. Several people, including one very special nurse, a psychiatrist, and a social worker, invested heaps of time and energy into singing with, reading to, and walking with me during my late teens and early adult years. Many of these individuals are my heroes, and I owe them a great debt.

There was a whole year where I stopped talking because, as a 13-year-old, talking seemed to get me into so much trouble! One nurse, in particular, shared her sandwiches with me and sang to me while she played her guitar. Eventually I joined in and sang her songs. Over time, I returned to using speech. This nurse remains a great friend, even to this day.

I did not attend any special schools or clinics during my school years, even though I stayed mostly in the lower-level class for us kids who found learning difficult. It was only in the mental hospital when my condition was incorrectly diagnosed as schizophrenia that I was made to go to group sessions, music, and discussion groups. These sessions were very uncomfortable, and I often hid to avoid them.

Being Different Is Hard

Realizing that I was different from other young people my age took me some time. In fact, I thought *they* were the strange ones! And I waited for ages for them to become more normal, like me. I was 17 when the "penny dropped" (a metaphor meaning, "when I finally understood or got the message"). This was when I realized it was *me* that was the different one. It was me who was the minority, and they were the majority.

This realization caused me great stress and anxiety. Knowing you are different and that there isn't anything you can do about it causes hopelessness and even depression. This is what happened to me. Thank God for those individuals along my path who cared enough to sacrifice their time and hang with me during those years.

Initially, I left school at the age of 15. After 8 weeks of summer holidays, I was then able to go to college for 2 years to complete a cadet nursing course. After completing this course, I went on to study for my state nurse registration, but, owing to my processing difficulties and sensory issues (I am troubled by fluorescent lighting, loud noises, sudden sounds, and certain fragrances), I wasn't successful with this training. I did well academically (against all expectations), but not practically.

It wasn't until much later in life, when my youngest son was 8 years old, that I went back to my local high school (with students 17-18 years of age) to complete my high-school certificate and gain entry into university. University life suited me, and I loved having the opportunity to study. I didn't do too well socially, but this wasn't the emphasis at university! I attained one degree after another and, at the age of 57, I received my PhD in psychology. This was the most incredible day of my life—one I will never forget and one that most people believed would never be possible for me.

Although the social elements and processing of general information had been the most difficult things for me at school, these were not so tough at university. I think this was the case because I could study more independently, work more at my own pace, and record lectures and listen to them over and over again. Also, at university, I had a note taker. It was not possible for me to take notes and listen to the lecturer at the same time. I have a very singular focus and am only able to concentrate upon one thing at a time, unless there happen to be related aspects within or connected to that same interest, like branches of the same tree.

EMPLOYMENT AND ENJOYING WORK

Work was something I really enjoyed doing. Whether it was walking a neighbor's dog as a child of 9, doing "bob-a-job" week (knocking on neighbors' doors and offering to wash their car, cut their grass, weed their garden, or wash their windows), or earning money for charity or for Christmas presents, I just enjoyed being busy and being helpful.

When I was growing up, all the members of my family were expected to work and, as children, we were encouraged give a concerted effort in whatever we did. If we didn't feel like doing something, it was explained to us that it wasn't about feelings but more about necessity. If Father didn't work, he wouldn't be paid, and we wouldn't have food for Mother to cook, which meant we couldn't eat. I am someone who loves her food (okay, only specific foods), so I was motivated to work hard at anything I did. We were also encouraged in the things we loved the most, and our interests were fostered and rewarded.

Unfortunately, however, any work I was offered needed to be structured, written down, and timed. I began and finished each job exactly as I was told to. This in turn led to occasional problems when other people ran a few minutes early or late! As I got older, I managed to keep some part-time work cleaning neighbors' homes, walking their dogs, and babysitting local children.

I Found Jobs in Areas That Interested Me

As a teenager, I kept busy with things that interested me. At 15, my first job was working at a wildlife safari, animal, and adventure park. As someone who cared for the animals, I got to walk the brown bear, feed the tapirs and anteaters, clean out their pens, and keep up the pet corner. At the time, I had 2 months to kill before going away to nursing cadet school.

One memory from my time at the safari park is going to the big house at Longleat (in Somerset, England) to collect my pay. There was a large black cat tethered outside the front door, gnawing on a marrowbone. The cat seemed so silky and inviting. I walked up to it and stroked its fur, burying my head into its soft neck. The cat purred loudly, and we spent several moments together before we were discovered. The manager who noticed me was shocked and called from a distance for me to move away from the animal slowly. Of course I did as I was told. I was informed that this cat was in fact a puma, and not a very tame one at that. It was not to be touched by anyone other than its owner and trainer. I had thought it was simply a large kitty cat—a very large kitty cat indeed! Whatever I was told about this animal, I just loved it, as I have and do many others. Animals have such unconditional love and are so accepting. I reckon they know when they are safe and respond in kind. Of course, I would never disrespect an animal or invade its space in an uninvited way.

Later, after cadet school, I attempted to train as a nurse and loved the hospital life. I think this was reminiscent of the years I spent in and out of hospital. The institutional life suited me. It was structured, routine, and familiar. But, unfortunately, my sensory issues and processing difficulties meant that my practical abilities were constantly sabotaged, and I eventually had a mental breakdown. I had so much knowledge on an intellectual level, but, practically, the demands of having to think and act at the same time left me wanting.

In spite of this, however, I wholeheartedly loved nursing. I loved the institution, the medical paraphernalia, the gleaning of medical knowledge, and the routines outlined by my nursing duties. When I had to stop nursing, I tried working as a dinner lady at a private boys' school. That lasted a single day! The noise, people, demands, social expectations, and general chit-chat were intolerable. I'd say that was the worst job I ever had.

I Was Not Successful in the Traditional Workforce

I wasn't very successful in the traditional workforce. When it came to working for other people, I experienced difficulties with processing spoken information and social expectations. So, for a long time, I retreated into the security of home life with my animals. But, I certainly worked hard at caring for and looking after them. I fed them, cleaned out their cages, exercised them, and loved them.

After marrying, I served as a Sunday-school teacher, bible- and prayer-group leader, and unofficial counselor to our church community. When I was first married, before my children were born, I loved working in kennels with the dogs that came for holidays while their owners were away. This was a job that only lasted a few weeks, because it was hard to get to work on time owing to poor public transportation. Of course, once my babies were born, I focused on them, and it became a full-time job. When my children were much older and I returned to school, I also took up some volunteer work, caring for women with human immunodeficiency virus, or HIV. Most of these women were very poor and were living in a hostel that offered pastoral and nursing care.

I would say that working with animals was my favorite job, and nursing was second. Much later in life, I found a career in teaching and writing. In many ways, my current job brings all my knowledge and skills into one place. I am blessed indeed!

RELATIONSHIPS

I got married at the ripe old age of 20. *Why* did I marry? Because my youth pastor said it was a good idea. But, even though I stayed married for 19 years, it turned out to be a bad idea. Not because I was hopeless at relationships but because the relationship was abusive and very difficult to maintain. Still, I became a mother and had four children with my husband. In due course, many years later, I connected deeply with a woman who joined my family, not knowing that she, too, was on the autism spectrum. She is my Beatrice, my companion and lifetime partner.

I Have Two Sons with Autism

Two of my sons are on the autistic spectrum. My oldest son, now 37, is a musician who works in a band by night and builds roads by day. He has a partner and several furry "children" (cats and dogs). My youngest son, now 29, has Asperger's syndrome (high-functioning autism). He worked for several years as a cook at a very busy inner-city deli and shares a home with two other chefs.

My middle son, Mattie, was killed at the age of 19. He would be 31 years old if he were alive today. Although he was a troubled young man with a learning disability, Mattie had kept a job for 2 years and had a girlfriend at the time of his death. My second eldest child, Katy, now aged 35, is a teacher. She has been with her partner for 11 years, and they have two gorgeous little girls.

As a young mother, church folk helped teach me to cook and keep house, and they supported me in parenting my children. When my kids were small, it was not uncommon to find the bathtub full of not only my kids, but some local church kids, too! Their families often brought over dinner and games for us all to play. This spoke to their love and commitment to our well-being. Those times were great learning experiences for me and helped establish my appreciation for family life.

Wise Words from a Church Friend

Even though my first marriage ended in divorce, I incorporated the lessons I learned into my future relationships. Accepting divorce wasn't easy, but I was helped into understanding and acceptance of this by the wise words of a church friend. She said, "Wendy, marriage is until 'death do us part.' Your relationship is dead, and you are carrying a corpse around with you. It stinks! It's time to give that body a respectable funeral. This is called *divorce*." Her words strengthened me and allowed me to take a road less traveled, one that opened doors to a future I might not otherwise have known.

Friendship was always a difficult thing for me in general. I found it hard to "make friends" and maintain friendships. Most of my friends were either older or younger than me. Some were travelers whom I saw only seasonally, when they were in the area picking fruit or shearing sheep. Others were misfits, like myself.

I was sexually abused as a child, so I found it difficult to know what I should or shouldn't do in so many situations with others. If an adult required something of me, I was obedient, because I had been taught to do what grownups told me to. It was years later, when conversing with a great and wise friend, that I was able to separate those years of abuse and come to understand what true love is really all about.

Processing Fast Conversation Was Hard

As a teenager I tried to fit in better by going to youth camps and such, but I couldn't keep up with the social networking expectations. Processing fast conversation was too hard, and other young people made fun of me. At one particular youth group, I was sexually assaulted by a group of typical (nonautistic) teens. They seemed to think it was fun to pin me up against a wall and take turns sexually abusing me, while the others looked on and laughed. Today I realize that if you are different and confident, you can earn respect. But if you are different and insecure, you become bait for the waiting pack animals that some people seem to be.

My furry friends, however, I indulged and loved immensely. My attachments to my own pets and any others I came across often caused problems because I chose to eat and sleep with them whenever possible. Dr Doolittle was one of my favorite characters, and I never doubted that he could talk to the animals or that they understood him.

Most of My Friends Love Animals, Music, and Movies

As an adult, I now have some wonderful and amazing friends whom I have come to know and trust over many years. Like me, most of my friends love animals, knowledge, music, theater, movies, and reading and are probably a little eccentric.

When I look back over my earlier years, I realize I did *try* dating. Mostly it was because a couple of young men approached me and asked me out. In my naivety I agreed, thinking we would go for a ride into the countryside. This was my take on "going out." Once these young men wanted to kiss or touch me, our relationship didn't last long. My husband was different because our "dating" consisted of going to bible meetings, prayer group, and church in general. Otherwise we mostly walked the dogs and rode or fixed his motorbike. In fact, it was our mutual love of animals, church, and engines that brought us together.

Forming relationships with the opposite sex comes naturally to me, as long as they are not romantic relationships. I feel very much at home in the world of men's clothing (often made so much better than clothing for women), men's frankness and logical thinking (less social small talk), and many of the interests that men share (science fiction, technology, engines, and facts). I am not attracted romantically to the opposite sex and have not been successful in any romantic encounter with a man. The fact that I married someone of the opposite sex and that we had four children was more by another's design rather than by own truly informed choice.

A NUMBER OF MENTORS

From quite a young age, I had a number of mentors and people who took an interest in me. My parents found me a difficult child to handle, so when I was 11, my family "gave" me to a paternal aunt to raise me through my teen years. As a result, my aunt had a very meaningful role in my life. A primary school teacher who allowed me extra time in class is another example. And then there was my very special nurse, who gave up her own personal time to talk or sing to me.

INSPIRATION FROM GOOD DEEDS DONE BY OTHERS

I have been inspired by different people and animals at various times in my life. As a youngster, it was the courage and determination of my animal heroes that inspired me the most—heroes such as "Skippy" the bush kangaroo, "Champion" the wonder horse, "Flipper" the dolphin, and "Lassie" the intelligent collie.

As an adult, I have continued to be inspired by the thankless deeds of so many. Principally, there is "The Christ," who gave his life for others. He is my ultimate role model. Then there are my everyday heroes, such as Gillian, the lass who wheeled me home from school on my bike when my legs were too painful for me to walk (my teacher thought I was just being difficult). Or Suzette, who spent her lunch breaks with me and almost lost her job for becoming "too familiar with the patients." And, of course, there is my current partner, who left all she knew to come and share my life in a foreign country, with its foreign ways and a society that generally disapproves of our relationship. Her courage and commitment have stayed me through many a crisis.

Recently I read the life story of Douglas Mawson, the famed Antarctic explorer and geologist. I realized that he lived his life by example. Even as a leader, he never asked his men to do anything he himself would not do first. Such courage and conviction can only build the same in us, if we allow it.

Who I am today is the result of an accumulation of experiences, choices, and interventions by others that have shaped and further developed my character, personality, and ability. It's because others have believed in me, expected the best of me, and walked with me that my life has meaning. As I accept who I am, including my limitations and shortcomings, I continue to grow and prosper emotionally. Physical and material gain are not as important as the sheer fulfillment I get from being loved and being able to give love back. The joy and enrichment I draw from my life might not always have been visible to others in typical terms, but they exist in abundance when one knows where to look.

Love is not only a beautiful feeling—feelings change like the wind. At times, it's an act of our will.

CHAPTER 9

NEIL McRAE

Veterinary Surgeon in Scotland

NEIL McRAE, BVMS

Age: 51

Resides in: Isle of Skye, Scotland

Occupation: Veterinary surgeon

Marital status: Divorced

FROM TEMPLE:

School was easy for Neil, until he attended veterinary school. Social life at the university level was difficult, and he was desperate for friendship. Neil writes, "I thought I was the only person in the whole world like me. No one mentored me, and I did not have a shoulder to cry on." For a time, Neil thought he was in the wrong profession, but he gradually found a deep satisfaction from his work with animals. Although relationships can still seem troubling, Neil continues to hope that he will grow socially and find meaningful connections with others along the way.

NEIL'S INTRODUCTION

My current profession is as a general veterinary surgeon in a mixed rural practice in Shetland, an archipelago of inhabited islands far to the north of mainland Scotland. Most of my work is with dogs and cats, both preventative health care and treatment of all kinds of ailments. But I also enjoy a fair amount of large-animal work, with cattle, sheep, and horses.

Until recently, my likes have perforce been solitary activities—reading, long-distance hiking, and studying—as I was unable to break through the autistic barrier between myself and the outside world. Recently, however, I have at last been able to enjoy the pleasure of interacting with *small* groups of people. I love the Scottish Gaelic language, which I have learned as a second language. When I was young, I loved and learned to play the Highland bagpipe, and I still play.

My main dislike is the small, but significant, proportion of neurotypical people who react with condescension and disdain to people with autism spectrum disorders and attempt to undermine us. This is the most common type of bullying I have encountered in my life; there is at least one such person in every workplace above a certain size. I don't remember much physical bullying at school, although there was a certain amount of unthinking mockery. My most painful memories of bullying are from my university years, in the form of frank contempt expressed by a few fellow students for someone who was socially lacking.

Later, during my working life, there were sustained hate campaigns by a few troublemaking colleagues who homed in on me, perhaps sensing difference and equating that with weakness. Looking back, it is clear to me now that those were deeply unhappy individuals with no insights into their own dysfunctional psychology.

The main challenge I have overcome is finding a way, albeit late in life, to break down the autistic barrier between myself and other people. I cannot express how significant a step forward this has been for me. Neither can I explain succinctly how I did it. It is difficult to find words for something so subtle and nuanced, which has required me to honestly examine the ways I think at a very fundamental level.

I am single, with a failed marriage behind me, and I have no children, although I would love to have them. I have been in employment continuously since 1984 in a variety of veterinary posts.

EARLY YEARS

A Top Student with No Friends

I was brought up in a very average, "lower middle-class" Scottish household. While I have no frame of reference, it was, I think, a warm and supportive environment; looking back, I remember feeling safe and secure.

I can't say I had a close bond with either my little sister or my little brother; neither were there any severe clashes between us. Rather, I just accepted their presence. I knew they would always be there, just as I knew Mum and Dad would always be there to care for us. I believe I thought this way because I had no conception of time passing.

My parents were worried about me; I knew this because my mother would sometimes sneak "worried" looks at me (I am quite good at reading other people's nonverbal language). Also, I occasionally overheard my parents talking about me and their worries about me. It was my near-complete lack of friends, a lack that became more and more obvious as I progressed into my teens, that worried them the most. Indeed, it worried me enormously too, but I realize now that I put enormous effort into appearing placid and unconcerned on the outside. I did this instinctively—I can only assume it was a defense mechanism.

As for my parents thinking I was different from other children, it was not really an option to be seen as different from others. There was no concept of pervasive developmental disorders then—none at all. If your life seemed deficient in some way, you had to "give yourself a shake," as Mum would say, and get on with it.

However, my parents were not *too* worried about me because I consistently came out on top of every class in primary and high school. This was a source of some pride to my mother (a former schoolteacher), in particular.

I was brought up in a not-too-strict Church of Scotland (ie, Presbyterian protestant) background. This was around the time when churchgoing was ceasing to be a universal practice in Scotland on Sundays; nevertheless, my parents attended church most Sundays and expected us to attend Sunday school.

An Egalitarian Outlook on Life

As children, we were all inculcated with a profound respect for our elders and also for other people's property. Theft and vandalism were seen as the lowest, most despicable of crimes. (This was in a time before random violence and assault became depressingly common in the United Kingdom.) In hindsight, one of the very good things about Scottish small-town society in those years was that it was profoundly egalitarian; British class divisions were not evident to us growing up. The idea that we should defer to people who saw themselves as our "betters" was liable to provoke incredulity and laughter. At the same time, less-well-off members of society were not seen as our inferiors. I still have a deeply egalitarian outlook on life, which I believe dates back to my childhood.

SCHOOL YEARS

I attended primary school for 7 years, from ages 5 to 11, then 6 years at secondary school. I went straight to university and completed (with difficulty) a degree in veterinary medicine. I never attended any special schools or experienced any intervention for my problems, which in hindsight must have been more and more apparent as I progressed farther into my teens.

Academically, I never had any problems. My biggest difficulties began when I was around 13, in high school. My problem was social interaction (although I didn't have a word for it then). I wanted friends desperately. I was vaguely aware that there was a sort of parallel universe where people had lots of friends. For example, most (not all) of my other classmates had many friends, as did the boys in the adventure books I read when I was young.

Difficulties Making Eye Contact and Small Talk

A very strange thing happened to me whenever I tried to speak to people informally (like exchanging break-time banter between classes). I couldn't think of anything to say—not a word. Not even pleasantries. Another thing was that eye contact made me extremely uncomfortable; I couldn't meet the gaze of other people for more than a second. I had to look away, although I couldn't help being aware that this frequently annoyed others. I had no idea, none whatever, why this was happening, but I assumed that I simply wasn't trying hard enough or that I was a weak person. I assumed I was just unlike all the other people who, I thought, had experienced the same problems and triumphantly overcome them.

I repeatedly resolved, with what I thought was a steely determination, to try harder the next day. And so, I forced myself to plunge into the fear—because it was very anxiety provoking—and into social situations to try to exchange "banter." But, strange and deeply unpleasant things happened. My voice became shrill with an odd prosody, and I sensed that my nonverbal language (which I tried to improvise on a microsecond-to-microsecond basis, an impossible task) became inappropriate to a scary degree. This led to more negative outcomes.

The Soothing Effect of Zeroing in on Details

The distress caused by repeated social failures cannot easily be put into words. In later years, I discovered the soothing effects of zeroing in on some item of innocuous detail—a wallpaper pattern, for example, or the weave of a carpet—and simply staring at it, entranced. My parents naturally discouraged this behavior when I was young, so I pretended to be sitting quietly, watching the television, while I was actually "hyper-processing"—dysfunctionally going over and over the negative social events of my day, trying to reinvent myself as a "shiny new person" by sheer power of thought alone.

My school marks remained excellent with little effort, so my parents were still reasonably happy with me (they had no idea of the turmoil I was successfully covering up) and just thought of me as "the shy one" and "the quiet one." Even my peers accepted me as some kind of eccentric genius, although they didn't seem to want to hang around with me.

Veterinary College Was Hard, and I Had No Support

My problems intensified massively when I went to veterinary college at the University of Edinburgh. The sudden removal of my (however tenuous) family and peer-support network was deeply traumatic; also, I was totally unprepared for study at the university level, never really having learned how to do self-motivated study. At school, I was used to coasting through most classes with ease. Now, however, I was faced with a situation where I was usually at the bottom of every class. Of course, there were no support networks in place for students with autistic spectrum conditions in those days (the 1970s).

My sense of crisis was exacerbated by the secret knowledge that I had no vocation for veterinary medicine; I had, indeed, chosen that course simply because I had done well at science, and really high grades were required for acceptance. This was a ridiculous reason for choosing a career, but one, I think, that is typically Aspie. Once I realized I had made a hideous mistake, I knew of no other course than to grimly carry on, pretending on the outside that all was well. Nobody had ever given me any career advice or told me that professions like medicine or veterinary medicine were "vocations;" I didn't even know what the word *vocation* meant. Neither had I been truly aware of the vast panorama of rewarding career choices opening up for me as a bright pupil or even that I *was* choosing a lifetime career path. I couldn't think ahead in those terms.

Failing to Engage with Other Students

Then there was the social interaction problem; I was aware that university was supposed to be the highlight of one's life, and I was desperate for friendship and human contact. But, I simply could not engage at all with my fellow students. I could tell from their body language that they were uneasy around me. They rebuffed me, sometimes gently but sometimes not. This lasted throughout my whole 6 years at university—a situation that makes me almost unbearably sad now, looking back and understanding the reasons for it. (In the United Kingdom, a veterinary degree requires 6 years of college. In the U.S., 8 years is required.) At the time, I had absolutely no idea why this was happening; I again concluded that I must be a bad or weak person, and I constantly resolved to try harder the next day—to start *living*—tomorrow. This failure to engage was always uppermost in my thoughts, when I should have been devoting mental energy to studying. But, as always, I hid my enormous distress beneath a placid and reserved exterior.

I thought I was the only person like me in the whole world. No one mentored me, and I did not have a "shoulder to cry on."

EMPLOYMENT

Working as a Teenager

My first experience of work was as a teenager, doing odd jobs for my father's printing business at night and during the holidays. I think my father instinctively knew I had no notion of following him into the family business (and was perhaps secretly grateful). But he liked to give me odd jobs to do—minor, repetitive tasks at which, it was found, I excelled.

My first employment was a holiday job, filling shelves in a supermarket when I was 16. It didn't last long, however, as I was called to the manager's office and told without warning that I wasn't suited to the work and would never master it. I was shocked by this, as the job had been so simplistic that it took almost no brainwork at all; perhaps the problem had really been that I failed to get on with any of the other staff. While I never really fell out with them, I remember struggling to understand why the other staff members were so socially polished (it seemed to me) and interacted with each other so well, although they all had very low educational attainments compared to me. I equated social success with intellectual effort.

I have never done any volunteer work, although I think I am an altruistic person. I was attracted to certain types of voluntary work, for instance voluntary service overseas (a British program for graduates). But the knowledge that I would find it impossible to interact with the other people involved put me off.

I Felt Veterinary Medicine Was the Wrong Profession

Despite feeling that I was in the wrong profession, I stuck it out and earned my degree, with some difficulty. I drifted into a succession of jobs in the companion-animal sphere, usually in large cities, without any sense of direction or a career plan. I never really fit in, but I always did well enough to hold down a job and get by. Sometimes I tried to persuade myself that I was happy by thinking hard about it and picturing myself as successful and admired. Other times I had moments of clarity, where reality broke in and I saw myself wasting my life in a profession I didn't really want to be in and one that did not want me.

Developing a Deep Satisfaction from My Profession

Then, slowly, a rather wonderful thing happened. I started to gain a deep satisfaction from my work and realized that I was, in fact, at least reasonably good at it. I came to feel a deep affinity with my patients, especially dogs and cattle, and I developed an ability to interact reasonably well with their owners. The professional-client relationship during a consultation is not informal (which would be terrifying to me) but is semiformal, so it can be managed. Also, I absolutely adore dogs and own one myself, so empathizing with clients who have dogs is not a problem; I only need to think about how I would feel if my own dog were sick or injured to put myself in the client's shoes.

I moved to the Isle of Skye to pursue my studies of Scottish Gaelic (one of my autistic special interests, I now realize), and this necessitated me finding work as a locum (freelancer) all over the north of Scotland, as there is no regular employment for me in Skye. This has facilitated a rediscovery of my love for farm practice in rural areas.

I Bought a House and Paid It Off

The best job I ever had is probably the one I am in currently, in a general veterinary practice in the Shetland Isles, replacing a veterinarian who is on maternity leave. Though it is extremely busy and involves a lot of hard work, the atmosphere is relaxed and supportive. Every day presents new challenges. Working in veterinary medicine is a constant learning process, which is one of the most fascinating and rewarding features of the work. I have built up a good relationship with the clients and, funnily enough, I have ended up working for and beside two of my fellow students from years ago. Although I liked them at university but could never get to know them, I have grown much closer to them now. I think they would like me to stay permanently, but I know that my heart is in the Isle of Skye and with the Gaelic language (there is no Gaelic spoken in Shetland). I have built a house in Skye and, by working full time away from home, I will soon have it paid it off. Then I will be able to downsize and spend a lot more time there.

In my experience, every workplace includes at least one "underminer," someone who is instinctively antipathetic to autistic people (although ignorant about autism and, indeed, their own psychology) and reacts negatively, ranging from mild disdain to vicious personal attacks. However, this sort of person has so far been in mercifully short supply in Shetland.

I feel that as my self-knowledge and understanding of my condition has increased slowly over the years, starting in my 40s when I read Tony Attwood's book, my insight into and appreciation of my veterinary work has grown proportionately. I feel privileged to be a member of the profession, but I am mindful that I am a locum without any permanence of employment. I will have to move on eventually.

RELATIONSHIPS: THE INVISIBLE BARRIER

As a very young child, I had friends. But, as described earlier, they all faded away in secondary school, which was a terrifying phenomenon I simply couldn't comprehend. I went through 6 years of university without making a single friend, although I was desperate for them (especially girlfriends). Once qualified as a veterinary surgeon, I managed to hold down jobs, but I still failed to make any friends, although I tried and tried. Luckily, my parents were always there for me, although I think they found my lack of friends a little mystifying. I in turn found it impossible to communicate with them honestly about my problems—problems that I could hardly put into words even to myself.

Just like when I was a teenager, I forced myself into social situations, making a huge effort to control every aspect of the interaction by way of enormous intellectual effort. When that failed, as it inevitably did, I sat alone afterward, obsessively processing and reprocessing every aspect of the negative social interaction that had occurred to try to make sense of it. I think, looking back, I was making an instinctive attempt to reconstruct—in my head— the outside world, everything that was *not me,* into one of order as opposed to (as it seemed to me) meaningless chaos. All my instincts tell me to do this almost constantly—even now. I think this is perhaps typical of an autistic person's relationship with the world. When we are sitting, apparently quietly, we are desperately trying to reconstruct the world in an all-encompassing way that makes sense. That's my theory, anyway.

Occasionally, friends from childhood looked me up and tried to reestablish a relationship, something I would have liked, too. However, each and every time, I came up against the invisible barrier and felt instantly awkward and embarrassingly tongue-tied in their company. I could sense that they in turn felt uncomfortable and moved away from me.

I Wanted Relationships with Women

I never had a relationship with a woman until I was 30, and that was only possible because of a year of cognitive behavioral therapy led by supportive psychiatric nurses. I achieved some kind of "breakthrough," and suddenly I felt a lot better about myself, without any real diagnosis or insight as to the real cause of my problems (my symptoms were misdiagnosed as "social phobia").

In Denial about the True State of My Relationships

The euphoria I felt then is difficult to put into words, when I felt I was "cured" and could relate to people—to some extent, anyway. I quickly got a girlfriend and, when that relationship didn't work out, I got another straightaway. This was the first time in my life I had been able to do this. In fact, the relationship with my second girlfriend was so strong for a while that we married after 4 years. However, neither of us knew that I was autistic, and without the benefit of a diagnosis and the self-knowledge that comes with it, I slipped back into Aspie ways of thinking. For instance, the relationship was turning bad before we married, and I could sense that. But, because I had been so happy, I thought if I just "thought" hard enough, I could "think" my way back into a happy relationship, like it had been before. I was in denial about the true state of the relationship. I believe this is typical Aspie behavior.

Our marriage inevitably broke up, and quite quickly. Luckily, there were no children. Although I would love to be psychologically healthy and have a wife and children—it's all I can think about some days—if there had been children from my marriage, they would have grown up in a broken home. Additionally, I would not, in hindsight, have been able to relate to them, as I reverted to my Aspie ways for years before understanding and awareness finally dawned in my late 40s.

True Understanding Led to a Degree of Acceptance

I have been celibate and single for more than 7 years now—and not by choice. But, increased understanding of my true condition has led to a degree of acceptance of the huge difficulties involved in my ability to form relationships. Lately, I have been increasingly hopeful that it might happen again, but it hasn't yet and, as I get older, it may be increasingly less and less likely, although I think I am young looking at 51. However, ordinary friendships, which were unattainable for me for so long, are now within my grasp. I know how to breach "the wall" I always felt between myself and other people. This, for me, is a massive step forward.

ON AUTISM

The people who have inspired me the most have been artists and writers, particularly the ones who have tried to encompass a whole world in their art—for instance the writers F. Scott Fitzgerald and Cormac McCarthy, or the composer Gustav Mahler. I now think I was instinctively drawn to them because I, as an autistic person, was struggling to balance and understand every aspect of the world's chaotic sensory input, effectively creating an entire world in my head.

Moments of Insight

All my life, I have had intermittent moments of insight, which showed me with terrifying clarity the yawning gulf between the quality of my life and the lives of others. For instance, I remember realizing that other people don't need to obsess and agonize for ages beforehand and afterward when they want to interact socially. Generally, before I became self-aware in terms of my autism, I rationalized away these troubling feelings and suppressed them, reasoning with myself that I was really no different from other people and that, if I was patient, my turn to have friends was just around the corner.

Other people had experienced the same problems I had, I rationalized, but by means of some strength of character they possessed but I did not, they managed to overcome them. If they could, so could I. This was, of course, a miserable self-delusion, which ensured that I remained socially isolated. No matter how long I waited, there would be no friendships around the corner until I recognized and came to terms with the central fact of my autistic nature. My moments of insight were in fact the only times I saw things as they really were. Without a framework of knowledge about autistic spectrum conditions, however, I could not build on them.

Still Socially Isolated

Both times I have made a determined attempt to confront my problems of social isolation, back when I was 29 (which led to misdiagnosis) and then again in the past few years (which led to a correct self-diagnosis and finally independent clinical diagnosis), my resolve has come from an honest admission to myself that things could not go on as they were. It culminated in a visit to people I thought of as "friends" one New Year's Day. I arrived uninvited, but they welcomed me warmly enough. However, "the wall" appeared again, and I could not reply to their attempts at conversation. As I sat there dumbly, I finally thought, "That's it, I am a broken human being. I cannot cope with this, and I need help." From that moment on, I sought and obtained as much help as I could, from books and, after a long wait because they were hard to find, from qualified professionals.

It was difficult to find help. Clinically qualified personnel, from general medical practitioners to psychiatrists, proved altogether unhelpful. Somewhat reluctantly, I accepted the services of a speech and communication therapist who, although not medically qualified, turned out to have considerable experience with and insight into autism spectrum disorders. This therapist was enormously helpful. As I tried to explain how I experience the world, she listened without being dismissive. This was perhaps the single biggest turning point for me. She gently prodded me in the right direction as I worked out my problems for myself. Slowly—ever so slowly—I came to feel that maybe I *was* a part of the world around me after all and not so removed from it as I have always supposed. This is so difficult to put into words! There are still times when interfacing with neurotypical people is problematic for me. The old discomfort returns, along with the jangling nerves, the mutual incomprehension, and the sheer mental effort of trying to reinvent oneself, second by second, as a *human presence* that others can be comfortable with, rather than an "absence" that makes others uncomfortable.

But, things are getting better. I cannot help but wish I could have found such help 30 years ago.

CHAPTER 10

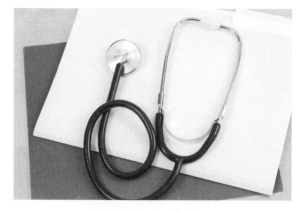

KIM DAVIES

Successful Physician

KIM DAVIES

Age: 57

Resides in: New England

Occupation: Physician

Marital status: Single

FROM TEMPLE:

Kim's life story has many similarities to mine. When Kim was a child, she loved to do all the same kinds of things I liked to do. She rode horses and enjoyed building things with Erector Sets. As a teenager, she took up many activities that taught responsibility. Every day, she had to feed her horse and clean its stall. She did volunteer jobs, helped with her brother's paper route, and worked as a bike mechanic. Her family taught her the importance of helping others and working. Today, she has a successful medical practice. Practicing meditation and becoming involved in alternative medicine has helped her greatly. Also, Kim Davies is not her real name. For professional reasons, she chooses to remain anonymous at this time.

KIM'S INTRODUCTION

I did not receive a formal diagnosis of Asperger's syndrome until earlier this year, and I am 57 years old. Three years ago, I participated in several transcranial magnetic stimulation, or TMS, brain studies, and those studies showed that my brain function is characteristic of a person with Asperger's syndrome.

I am a practicing physician, and I also have a degree in Chinese medicine. Outside of my work, I teach meditation and have completed a 3-year teacher training program for meditation.

I have had the advantage of being born into a good family and having the support of my family members, as well as many excellent teachers. Their support has helped me tremendously. I also have a mild degree of disability, which has made it easier for me to fit in than if I had a more severe disability.

My disability mostly involves taking things literally, an inability to understand jokes or sarcasm, difficulty with reading subtle expressions and tones of voice, some challenges with executive functioning, and mild sensory issues. I also have a lot of difficulty with time management. Most of my interpersonal challenges have revolved around interactions with classmates in school and ongoing struggles with my employees.

LEARNING MORALS AND RESPONSIBILITY IN MY EARLY YEARS

I am the oldest of five children and have four younger brothers. I spent a fair amount of time playing by myself when I was young. Building things with my brothers' Erector Set, constructing projects out of wood, making model cars and planes, and spending time outdoors were some of my favorite activities. I especially enjoyed being in the woods.

I also spent a fair amount of time playing with my brothers. They used to tell me I was bossy. I remember thinking that they should do exactly as I told them and play according to my rules. It wasn't until they got bigger than me that they started to rebel against my rules.

My mother treated all of her children as unique, capable individuals and made us feel as though we could all achieve what we wanted by working hard. My mother thought I was intelligent but knew I had difficulties with time management. She had to have many conferences with my grade-school teachers because I was not usually able to complete my assignments. I tended to do things slowly and tried to make every project perfect. I also spent a lot of time daydreaming.

My mother tried to teach us good morals, both by example and through education. She was very interested in helping people and volunteered for many different types of organizations. She taught Sunday school for a number of years and took us to church. When I was in junior high, I used to accompany her when she taught. I enjoyed being around the little children.

My parents stressed the importance of being responsible. We had to do our homework or practice our musical instruments before we could go out and play. We were involved in an organization called Pony Club, which taught horseback riding to young people. We learned a lot about responsibility through Pony Club, as we were expected to take proper care of our horses and tack. In fact, the responsibility of taking care of our horses came before taking care of ourselves. We had to get up early in the morning and clean the stalls before going to school. When we got home from horse shows, we had to brush the horses and feed them before we could shower and have dinner.

SCHOOL YEARS

When I was very young, my brothers were my primary playmates when I wasn't playing by myself. As I got a little older, I played with some of our neighborhood friends, as well. When I was in about the 2nd grade, I became best friends with one of the neighborhood girls. She was 2 years younger. We remained best friends for several years, until I started junior high. At that time, she told me she did not want to be best friends with me anymore. This was extremely hurtful, and I didn't know why she didn't want to be close anymore. I felt lonely at this time, as I did not really feel much connection with any other children. It was also confusing to lose a friend in this way, as I tend to be very loyal.

I Was Not Accepted by Other Children

Through grade school and into junior high, I had increasing problems with being accepted by the other children. I was bullied a lot, starting in about the 2nd grade. I remember trying to stay out of the way of the other kids and not really understanding what the problem was. There was only one other child that would play with me when I was at school. She was considered a misfit because her mother continued to walk her to school every day through the 6th grade.

One of my primary ways of dealing with the difficulties in school was to try to remain invisible. I made an effort to stay toward the back of the room and not say anything unless I had to. My other refuge was reading books. I always carried a book to read at school. When things became difficult, I buried myself in my book instead of attempting to talk to my classmates.

I used to have a hard time sticking up for myself. However, I remember one occasion when we were walking to school and an older boy began picking on one of my brothers. I hit him over the head with one of my schoolbooks and ran him off. Afterward, I felt bad that I might have hurt him. However, I was glad I could protect my brother.

For me, the most difficult part about school was being rejected by the other kids. This was particularly bad in junior-high school, where I was bullied frequently. The other difficulty was in trying to get all my work done. I have a tendency to focus with intense concentration when I'm working on something, but it takes me a long time to complete tasks. I tend to get lost in the details and want to keep improving a project until I think it's perfect.

I Was Interested in Science and Trigonometry

Throughout school, I was always most interested in the sciences, although they were not always the easiest. When I took trigonometry in high school, I used to spend many hours doing my trigonometry homework. I thoroughly loved it.

I don't remember when I first felt "different" from other people. I knew something wasn't quite right, starting when I was in grade school, but I couldn't figure out what the problem was.

I remember thinking that I was better than the other kids. I wasn't interested in gossiping or talking about who was doing what. Discussions about the latest fashions and "popular topics" like actors and actresses didn't interest me. I felt that a lot of the talk at school was stupid and silly.

The first time I had an inkling that something I said was a problem occurred at summer camp in about the 8th grade. Some girls were trying to put up a sail on a sailboat, and they were having difficulty. I went over to help them. I don't know exactly what I said, but I remember they got angry with me. I found it very strange that they should be angry, when I was only trying to help. Reflecting on it now, I probably didn't bother to introduce myself to them or start the conversation with any socially acceptable introductions. I most likely just said something like, "I can do that for you."

I Loved Building Things

The summer before 10th grade, my parents moved us to the country because the kids at school were giving me such a hard time. We had a small farm with several horses, and I enjoyed spending time working in the barnyard and taking care of the horses. At one point, we put up fences for a riding ring. My brother was not nailing the boards so they aligned with one another properly. I took all the boards down and put them back up so they were straight. I was angry with him for being so sloppy in the way he built a fence. I designed a gate for the pasture when the old one broke down, and I built it out of the fencing materials. It was easy for me to see how it needed to be constructed and stabilized so it worked properly.

After graduating from high school, I attended a small liberal arts college. My mother chose the school for me, knowing I would not do well in a big school. The school had a high percentage of professors to students, so each student could get a lot of individual attention.

I initially started taking premedical courses, with biology as a major. However, after I took a course in geology from a particularly wonderful professor, I switched my major to environmental science.

I have always had a tendency to want to work hard for someone who understands and appreciates me. He was that type of professor.

After college, I wasn't sure what I wanted to do. I really wanted to stay close to home and continue to be able to ride my horse. I thought about going back to school for an additional degree in geology or environmental science, but I couldn't decide. I ended up working for a temporary agency for about a year, doing menial office work. I didn't like it at all. It was not challenging and did not require any creativity or talent on my part. After a year, an employment agency finally got me a job operating a computer, with the ability to move into programming. After a year, I found myself in the programming department, doing business programming. Programming was interesting and fun, and I got along well with the other programmers.

The Deeper Meaning of Life

During this time, I wanted to find out what the deeper meaning of life was. I thought about the example my mother set regarding being of service, and I decided to do something more to help people. After spending some time talking to a physician and reading about medicine, I decided to go back to school. I graduated from medical school when I was 29 and attended a surgical residency program. I really enjoyed surgery, and I did well in the program, as I am meticulous and care about doing a good job. However, one significant difficulty I experienced during my residency program was when my residency director had some ideas that he thought were really brilliant. I thought they were dumb. I was simply unable to tell him that I thought he had great ideas, when I didn't agree with them. That made him upset.

After being in practice for a few years, I became increasingly interested in alternative healthcare and began informally studying different types of healing. I decided to return to school and earned an additional degree in Chinese medicine, which included herbal medicine and acupuncture. I really enjoyed learning the whole Chinese medical system and how it all works, even though it's quite different than allopathic medicine.

EMPLOYMENT

During my teen years, one of my brothers was very interested in cars. He decided to earn money by cleaning and waxing cars for family members and friends, and I helped him on occasion. I also assisted one of my other brothers with his paper route, especially if he slept too late and didn't have enough time to do it before school. I got my first real job in high school. I bagged purchases at a local five-and-dime store. I did not enjoy this kind of work.

One of the most fun jobs I ever had was working in a bicycle shop after my first year of medical school. I felt like I could apply for this job because I was interested in bicycles and had worked on my own bicycle for many years. When I was in the 8th grade, I decided I wanted a bicycle. I saved my allowance and bought myself a wonderful gold five-speed Schwinn bike. I also bought a book that explained how to maintain it. I loved tuning it up and making sure the wheels were true and the brakes didn't squeak.

I Loved Fixing Bikes in a Bike Shop

When I got out of college, I bought a blue 10-speed Fuji bike, which I loved riding around the backcountry roads where I lived. I took it with me to Philadelphia when I went to medical school. My bicycle was my primary means of transportation, as I didn't own a car. After the first year of school, I wanted a summer job and found an ad in the paper for a bicycle mechanic. I rode my bike to the shop on a Saturday to apply. It was a rainy day, and I had to ride several miles to get there. The owner of the shop checked my bike, saw how I had it tuned up, and decided to hire me. I don't know if it was because my bike was tuned well or because I was willing to ride through the city on a rainy day to get to the interview!

That shop had a very good mechanic, and he taught me a lot more than I had learned on my own. I really enjoyed working with him. I had great fun working on the bikes and getting them tuned up and running smoothly. It was also fun to be able to try out the really fine Italian bikes with Campagnolo components. Today, when I see a nice bike, I still like to check out what type of frame and components the bike has.

I Led a Girl Scout Troop

I have always done volunteer work, thanks to my mother's example. When I was in college, I volunteered at the Outing Club. I helped organize outdoor trips and maintain equipment. I also volunteered at Project Head Start. After I graduated from college, I led a Girl Scout troop with one of my friends. When the son of one of our family friends had difficulty reading, I spent a summer working with him, helping him learn how to read. I also helped tutor my brother when he studied for his Pony Club exams.

After completing my residency and working for several years, I served as an assistant residency director. I spent a fair amount of time teaching residents, both didactically and during surgery. That was truly one of the most rewarding times of my career, as I really enjoy teaching.

My Solo Medical Practice and Three Employees

Today, I work as a physician in my own practice. I bought this particular practice from another physician 10 years ago. I currently do not have any partners, but I have three assistants. My job includes everything from treating patients to managing the practice and my employees. I previously worked in group practices, where I was an employee.

On a day-to-day basis, I spend most of my time treating patients. This includes interviewing them, assigning a diagnosis, discussing treatment options, and administering treatment. Treatments may include surgery, and I am on staff at the local hospital where I do my surgeries. As part of the medical staff, I attend meetings with the other physicians and do consultations at the hospital. I oversee the work of my employees and give them directions as to what tasks are most important to do at any particular time. Management of my practice itself includes making decisions about marketing, negotiating my lease, managing the retirement plan, meeting with my accountant, and overseeing expenditures. I also do a fair amount of work on my computers to make sure they're working properly. If one of the computers breaks down during the workday, I usually try to fix it myself. If I'm not able to do so, I will call my IT people.

I currently use acupuncture and Chinese medicine as an adjunct and not as my main practice. Acupuncture can be very helpful in keeping my employees healthy, and I use it when my patients do not respond well to allopathic care. I also use acupuncture to treat my friends and family.

I am currently on the board of my local meditation center, and I volunteer at the center. I teach meditation in several venues, including our local Asperger's association. For a 2-year period, I taught meditation at a prison on a weekly basis. This was a very meaningful experience for me. I enjoyed listening to what each prisoner was interested in and his or her particular spiritual background. Once I got to know the inmates, I tried to find reading materials and techniques that would be meaningful to them.

RELATIONSHIPS

Before I started elementary school, my mother tells me I did not care to play with other children. If she asked me whether I wanted to have another young girl come over to play, I told her "no."

Aside from the one best friend I had, starting in about 2nd grade, I didn't feel close to any children other than my brothers. My best friend lived two doors down in our neighborhood. We enjoyed going down to our local creek and walking through the woods or pretending to ride horses. I really enjoyed being around her because she was always kind and never teased me.

I joined the Girl Scouts in grade school and belonged to a Girl Scout troop through my senior year in high school. In junior high, sometimes I did things with the acquaintances I had in my Girl Scout troop. I didn't have any friends in high school that I felt very close to, but I did get along with the other kids in my neighborhood. Sometimes I did things with them. Mostly I preferred to spend time by myself, working with our horses or hiking in the woods.

Doing Outdoor Activities with Friends

As an adult, I have many more friends than ever before, although I still have only a few very close friends. We usually spend time outdoors together, going hiking, kayaking, biking, or skiing. I may also get together to have dinner with some of my closer friends on the weekends.

I have studied communication techniques over the years, such as Marshall Rosenberg's nonviolent communication technique. I've also been meditating for 24 years now. These things have helped me understand people better and have allowed me to make and maintain some very good friendships. Since it still takes me a lot of time to do things, including my work, I generally don't have a lot of time during the workweek to get together with friends. However, I enjoy seeing them on the weekends.

Intimate Relationships

I have had perhaps less experience than many people with intimate relationships, but I did date a little bit through college and afterward. I had a boyfriend for a while in college but was never very comfortable with the whole dating scene. When I was in medical school, I had a best friend who enjoyed a lot of the same activities I did. She was a lesbian, and talking with her made me question why it was I felt different from other people. After looking into my thoughts and feelings about relationships, I realized I was attracted to women and had been in the past. However, I had not been open to it, owing to the religious beliefs I inherited from my mother. After several years of introspection, I decided that I'm bisexual.

About 10 years ago, I was in a 3-year relationship with a woman. Overall, I enjoyed sharing a home and having someone to talk with and be close to. When I was in that relationship, however, I definitely had Asperger's-related difficulties that affected my ability to communicate with her and understand her. My tendency to prioritize my meditation practice above everything else caused problems in our relationship. I wanted to spend vacation time on meditation retreats, which she was not really interested in. My time-management issues also caused stress. Since we separated, we have been able to maintain our friendship and still care about each other. Once I found out about my Asperger's syndrome, it put a lot of things into perspective. I am choosing celibacy at this time, as I put a lot of time and energy into my medical practice.

Getting Along with Coworkers Became Easier as I Got Older

In terms of relationships in general, things seemed to go much more smoothly for me as I got older. However, I continued to have significant problems with my employees. This occurred whether I was working for other doctors or for myself. They told me I was critical, mean, picky, or angry. I just couldn't see that I was acting in a way that was inappropriate. I am very detail oriented and want things done a certain way. However, I couldn't see that I was being mean or excessively picky. And I certainly didn't see how I came across as being angry.

I remember one occasion where an assistant said to me, "Talk to me normally." I asked her what she meant, but she wouldn't tell me. At that time, I questioned what was going on that was making it so difficult for my employees. One of my friends gave me another clue when she asked me why it was that I didn't ask other people for help. I realized that I just don't generally think about asking for help.

I Read Books on Asperger's

In 2008, I read John Robison's book, *Look Me in the Eye.* I had decided to read it to learn more about my nephew, who is on the autism spectrum. As I was reading, a lot of the things that John talked about felt very familiar to me.

I decided to try to find out more about Asperger's syndrome. I went online and took the Autism Spectrum Quotient questionnaire, published by Simon Baron-Cohen and colleagues, as well as any other tests I could find. It turned out that my scores were borderline on every test I took. I started to think that I might possibly have Asperger's. A lot of the information I read sounded familiar, but some of the cases involved such significant disabilities that I couldn't relate to them. I ended up going to the Asperger's Association of New England and had an interview with one of the social workers, who was very kind and helpful. She told me that I probably did have Asperger's.

I wanted to find out more. I met with a researcher at Beth Israel Deaconess Hospital, Dr Alvaro Pascual-Leone. He allowed me to participate in some of the TMS brain studies they were doing. During the studies, they stimulate certain areas of the brain that affect communication. I had some amazing revelations during these studies.

I realized that when I was reading sentences, I was deriving a literal meeting from them but was missing the emotional content. I also realized that if I read a word one way in a sentence, I tended to read it the same way in following sentences. This caused me to misread sentences sometimes.

I Did Not Understand Facial Expressions or Tone of Voice

When I participated in later studies, the researchers showed videos of people involved in social interactions. These interactions involved the people saying words that were not literally what they meant. When I first saw the videos, they were confusing, and I had a hard time answering questions about the individuals' intentions. However, after I underwent TMS, I was able to actually understand their intent, which made the videos both interesting and understandable. I realized that I was not able to fully understand the tone of voice, facial expression, or body language before undergoing TMS. This made me realize how much I miss during interactions with people, since I am unable to fully process facial expressions and tones of voice.

Recently, I have gleaned more insight into the issues I've had with my employees. After I underwent a neuropsychological evaluation earlier this year, I started taking medication for anxiety. I realized that I had often been stressed at work, but I was not really aware of how much anxiety I was feeling. I am generally good at focusing on one thing at a time; however, in my career, there are frequently many things happening at once and many decisions that need to be made in a short period of time. This was causing me anxiety, as I was required to keep shifting my attention to something new before I had completed the previous task. These feelings were coming out in my interactions with my employees, causing them to feel like I was angry with them or was unhappy with their work.

PROFESSIONAL AND SPIRITUAL MENTORS

I have had several mentors through the years. A long-time mentor of mine is Ron, another physician who was active in the local Zen center when I first started learning about meditation. He tried to provide a good example in many ways. He helped me professionally by inviting me to assist him in surgical cases. He has also been someone I can call and talk to whenever I have a question about my life or a particular problem I'm dealing with.

One of the most important pieces of advice that he gave me was about relating to my patients. He said the most important thing was for me to be present with them and listen to them fully. In many ways, this was a very foreign concept to me. My way of thinking was that I was there to try to fix their problem. The idea that the most important thing is to be present and listen is something that I still work on. However, the older I get, the more I understand that what he said is absolutely true.

Another mentor is Linda, one of my spiritual teachers, who has used meditation to transform her life. She had a very difficult life growing up in South Africa and had a lot of anger and emotional challenges. After many years of meditation, she has become very kind and openhearted. She sponsored me for the teacher training program and worked with me during the training. After working with her closely, it became clear to me that in most cases, I was trying to answer students' questions with an answer that was *technically* correct. At some point, I finally understood that their questions had to be answered from a completely different point of view—namely, an open and compassionate one. When someone asks me a question, my mind still goes to the technically correct answer first. However, I now put that aside for a moment and try to open my heart to the student and ascertain what it is he or she really needs. Sometimes it has nothing to do with the "correct" answer.

INSPIRATION

I have been very inspired by the example of several religious and spiritual figures, including a woman named Amritananda. She is a spiritual teacher from India who operates a very large humanitarian organization. She travels around the world to raise money for those in need and greets people with a loving embrace. She is a wonderful example of someone who completely accepts everyone exactly as they are. She has boundless compassion for the difficulties of all human beings. Being around people like her has encouraged me to practice opening my heart to myself and others.

My spiritual and meditation practices have had the biggest impact on my self-image and have helped me the most in my life. I believe that meditation has enabled me to understand myself and other people better, even though my brain does not process information in a neurotypical way. There seems to be another way of being in the world, which is more open and intuitive, where the mind is not as sharply focused on one aspect of reality. In this open space, relationships with other people flow more easily.

Learning about Asperger's syndrome over the past few years has also had a huge impact. I have read many books and attended conferences and support groups. I am grateful for the work of many writers, particularly Michelle Garcia Winner's work on social thinking. I've found that as I better understand myself and the way I interact with others, I am able to compensate accordingly. This in turn has significantly improved my relationships.

CHAPTER 11

ROBERT COOPER

Owner of a Computer Server Design and Support Firm

ROBERT J. COOPER, AAS

Age: 64

Resides in: Houston, TX

Occupation: Owner and vice president of a computer server design
    and support firm

Marital status: Divorced, with three children

FROM TEMPLE:

Robert became proficient in many different lines of work, such as
an upholsterer, electronics technician, military policeman, and chef.
He also experienced some tough times, becoming an alcoholic and
spending some time in jail for stealing. Unlike the other contributors
in this book, he had much less teaching and guidance on right and
wrong when he was a child. He found himself involved with the
wrong kind of "friends" that didn't help him learn proper life skills.
Robert has been married and divorced twice. His children are doing
well, and together they are looking into some of his own Asperger's
characteristics that may manifest in them. His son is a field supervisor
for a major entertainment company, and his daughters are pursuing
advanced degrees in psychiatry research and kinesiology. Today,
Robert is a successful independent computer consultant.

ROBERT'S INTRODUCTION

I have been involved in electronics of one form or another since
my godmother, Aunt Mary, gave me a Remco radio kit on my

8th birthday. I took electronic parts out of people's trash cans and collected them in "my attic"—my hideaway in my house—as a child. From there, I ordered U.S. Navy electronics textbooks from the back pages of comic books. I loved learning about electricity. In those textbooks, the electrons were portrayed with smiley faces as they moved around in the wires. This imagery worked extremely well for me, as one thing I have difficulty with is recognition of faces. Looking back now, those electrons are possibly some of the first faces I related to.

I graduated from Penn State with an associate's degree in electrical and electronic technology. Electronics made sense to me. What I appreciated most about engineering was its plain, yes-no, black-white, up-down, hot-cold logic. This was the reason I was drawn to it in the first place—an Aspie's common sense, I'd later find out. Little did I know then that logic was to be my best friend for the rest of my life.

My thought processing always occurred in nonstop pictures or moving-color film reels (another one of those "I-thought-everyone-thought-like-this" deals). I can call up a "still shot," or a short splice of film, from any moment in my life. At times, I can even smell an aroma I associate with a mental image. Little things, like catching a line from a song, can bring up such recollections.

I Was a Follower

I grew up during the Woodstock era, and what stood out to me was how people simply wanted to be friends. I didn't know I was a follower then, but follow I did, in search of that ever-elusive common sense and spirituality I seemed to lack. As I got older, while other kids delved into the popular "ups, downs, and arounds" of the recreational drugs of the times, I was intrigued only by the herbal hallucinogens. They enhanced the images in my mind. I branched off from the others and had no problem studying various plants and herbs—namely, peyote, psilocybin, and mescaline. I was so intrigued that I read all I could about American Indians and their worshipping rituals. The "party drugs" and I never did get along. But, I was sold on spirituality and anything that seemed to compliment it.

Overcoming Alcoholism

For 26 years, I worked to overcome a slow progression from first-, through second-, to eventually third-stage alcohol poisoning. I went to live with the Franciscan Friars of the Atonement in Saranac Lake, in the Adirondack Mountains, for a year. It was the greatest 12-step program I could have been a part of, except I just wasn't getting it! I went through years of Alcoholics Anonymous (AA) meetings, where the best people in the world hang out. I loved the camaraderie there, too, except I didn't connect with anyone. It must have been the alcohol, right? Slowly but surely, I kept "coming back" to AA; the relapses were less frequent, and good judgment overruled the bad. I finally made peace with my alcoholism at the age of 50.

What I've found I've always needed at a job site is some space where I can be alone, for hours at a time, just simply doing what's expected of me. When first being introduced to a new team of engineers, the inevitable invitations to lunch and after-work socials don't seem to stop. I have finally taken it upon myself to explain to others that I'm in no way trying to be rude, but they need to please try to understand that I'm most comfortable being left alone to do what's expected of me.

My Kids Are Doing Amazingly Well

I have three beautiful children from two marriages. Graham, 33, is my son from my first marriage. He is a successful field supervisor for a large entertainment company. He has two sisters from my second marriage, Brittany, 24, and Brianna, 22. Brittany is attending the University of Florida to obtain her master's in public health and epidemiology, and Brianna will graduate soon with her master's in kinesiology. My kids are doing amazingly well right now, and they are my biggest fans and advocates.

The Logical Simplicity of Computers Made Sense to Me

In the early 1980s, computers were beginning to move front-and-center into engineering communities. Besides personal computers, which were appearing on everyone's desktops by that time, a man named Ken Olsen had been grooming a company called Digital Equipment Corporation since 1957. Ken was a simple man who was pivotal in the development of mainframe computers. Ask any engineer who worked with Ken's mainframes, beginning in the early 80s, and the first thing you'll get is a smile. I don't know of any system since that has so eloquently incorporated pure logic with common sense. I once told my boss, "If you can think it, I can write it," in reference to the ease, simplicity, and depth associated with programming on that computer system. I'll forever be indebted to Mr Olsen!

His computers ported well to new engineering tools, such as computer-aided design, manufacturing, and electronics. I was responsible for helping to homogenize this new equipment into a working engineering environment. Because of Ken's logical simplicity, I took off with his operating system and never looked back.

Today, I Work as an Independent Consultant

Today, I still work with those same systems as an independent consultant. My days at work are rarely in conflict with being an Aspie. My Asperger's syndrome tends to play a role when I first meet new people at work or when I relocate, as most contractors have to do when a particular contract ends. I have a slew of readymade excuses for not being able to go to lunch with the gang or meet up with the guys after work. The excuses came long before I was aware of my Asperger's, but at least now I know why I needed them.

In my line of work, I can sit at a monitor and keyboard and do a full day's work without ever leaving my chair—an Aspie's dream! I have one staff meeting a week, with 10 other staff members. Even today, I find myself nervously wishing for a system problem just to avoid that meeting. But I made a decision after learning of my Asperger's about a year and a half ago that my boss (and no one else) needed to know about my condition. I'm capable of saying some off-the-wall remarks or fumbling through explanations of the absurd at any time. But, my boss is the only one I feel may need to know why. He's more than appreciative, as, in my initial interview, he stated that he was in need of some "outside-the-box thinking." Well, being an Aspie, I *live* outside the box.

EARLY YEARS

I was pretty much a recluse within my family. I can remember having some interaction with my older brother, but he was with his own friends most of the time. We had an empty lot just behind our house that was a city playground at one time. After the playground was torn down, we were left with a huge lot with only some swingset poles left behind. I spent a lot of time going "to the playground," where I loved to join in a small baseball game or practice my casting (ie, "fishing") by placing a Hula-hoop about 100 feet away on the ground and trying to cast into it. I was pretty good with the casting and was so-so on the baseball. Those were fun times.

I Had Little Interaction with Other Kids

I had almost no interactions with other preschool kids, as far as I can remember. Mostly I was on my own, just trying to be content in my own skin. I didn't get along with other kids. Of course, that was "all their fault." I can vividly remember throwing a fit and writing "shut up" with chalk on every wall, door, and sidewalk for others to see, before sneaking into my basement for solace.

I can remember almost no interactions between myself and my two brothers and sister. The great attic we had became my "house." It had a floor nailed to the rafters, which was unusual in that most homes only had rafters in the attic. I could stand upright in most of the attic. I moved old furniture and any old electronics I could find out of the neighbors' garbage cans and into my attic. I would be quite content to talk about that attic for days on end.

My Parents Were Concerned I Was Different

I believe my parents felt I was "different," but they never spoke to *me* about it. I occasionally heard my older brother whispering to my mom in the kitchen, which was my clue that I had somehow screwed up again. He was the first tattletale of my childhood, and surprisingly he still holds that distinction even today.

I first became aware of my parents' concerns when, totally out of the blue, and without my asking, my Uncle Tom left a full-bred

Boxer dog to "my guardianship" for an entire summer (read: my parents arranged it). She was a beautiful dog, with a full white chest and four perfect white socks to compliment her golden brown coat. I cared for her "in my world." I even ran away with her once, in the throes of my very first "anger at another family member" mood. I can remember that feeling vividly, because I stopped processing mental images and felt a tightness in my gut for one of the few times in my life. At such moments, I had "the woods" to retreat to just a half-mile up the alleyway. Between my attic and the woods, life was pretty good. I also had a complete understanding of the fact that this was specifically *my* dog, and not my brothers'. I knew I had this dog for a reason, and deep down I knew what the reason was. I was different—I was made aware of that on a daily basis with other kids—and evidently my parents knew it, too. I believe my parents got me the dog so I could maybe get close to it as a friend. But I simply didn't have a good sense of *why me, and not the others too.*

I Raised Myself, and Dad Was an Aspie

I'd always referred to my upbringing as having "raised myself." Aside from the usual day-to-day interactions, I don't remember a single thing that either parent taught me directly. They were not bad parents, I just never asked them about much. They argued constantly, mostly because my mom initiated it. Only now can I see that my dad was simply an Aspie. He was a beautiful man, and I just didn't know it. I was taught to dislike him by my mother, who even told me at the age of 6 or 7 that he had thrown a knife at her. She pointed and said it stuck in the kitchen wall by the stove, next to her head. I looked and looked for that knife marking in the wall where she pointed. I tried really hard to find it, to prove to myself that she wasn't lying to me, but to no avail. Inwardly, I hated her for trying to pit me against my father, but I never spoke a word of that to anyone. I became my mother's keeper, as I was the only one in the family that seemed to know how to use a hammer and screwdriver.

SCHOOL YEARS

Learning from Books Was a Pleasure

My parents sent us to a great parochial school, just three blocks up the hill, and later to a wonderful parochial high school. Right from the start in elementary school, I didn't feel like I knew anyone. But everyone feels like that, right?

It was a pleasure to learn from books, every single day. At times it was a nightmare to get along with the other kids, though. I turned out to be a fairly good student, especially with science, math, and English. Aside from those two subjects, though, by the end of high school, my grades in my other classes ranged from A's and B's to D's and F's. I had a harder time with the other subjects, I suppose because I just didn't care about them as much as I cared about science and math. This resulted in getting called into the office of the principal, Sister Felicia. She warned me that I would flunk the year if my grades didn't improve. I had noticed the fluctuation of my grades myself, but being held back couldn't happen to *me,* could it? Still, I saw that my inattention to my other subjects could have serious consequences. So I crammed for every test after that and managed to get out of there with high "C" or low "B" averages.

I Had Anxiety Attacks When I Read Aloud to the Class

Looking back, that happened at the same time I had my first anxiety attack in front of my fellow students. Of course, at that time, I thought my "attack" was simply caused by my "fear." I had religion class first thing every morning. In it, we took turns reading from the catechism, the Holy Roman Church's answer to all those dirty pictures in the Bible. (I liked the pictures better.) One day, as per usual, I stood to read a few paragraphs to the class. I took a deep breath to read, but when I went from the bottom of the left page to the top of the right page, my eyes "hopped" around each word and I was unable to "translate" what the words meant. I could not speak, and my breath started to hurt from inhaling so excessively. It was hard for me to exhale at all.

You must appreciate that this incident occurred at an age and in an environment where "the greatest generation" won wars and didn't cry. I was so sure this episode had happened strictly because I was scared of reading aloud—and no boy at that time admitted fear. I asked the teacher, Sister Mercia, if she would please not call on me to read ever again. She asked why, but I wasn't able to offer any explanations, other than the short and emphatic, "You don't call on me, and I don't make a fool out of myself in front of the entire class." She kept that promise for exactly 1 week and then asked me to read aloud one more time. This inability to read aloud was the most embarrassing and haunting thing that happened to me in this stage of my life. I had to put a stop to it. If I didn't have to read, I didn't get scared. If I could be spared from reading, then none of my classmates would know just how frightened of it I was. This transpired halfway through my senior year. I figured that in college, a student would never be asked to read in front of the class—so I only had to make it to June without having to read again. After a third such incident, Sister Mercia realized I was in earnest, and she left me alone. Today I find it very odd that no one had any idea it could be biophysical in nature.

I Have Memories on Film in my Head

It was only a little over a year ago, when I was busy doing some self-analysis, that I realized I have exquisite memories "on film" in my brain. I can recall, in vivid detail, almost everything in my life, as a rolling film in my head. Recently, I recalled my first panicked reading incident and was able to "see" the first two words at the top of the page on the right. Because my eyes were jumping around the words, I was not able to "identify" the words clearly enough to say them. "Nystagmus" is what this is called now. Back then, it was only a feeling of, "I'm scared to death!" I still live with the fear of reading to a group. I attempted it a few more times in my life to find out if it was just a phobia from my youth—but it wasn't.

Around that same time, a small bald spot, about the size of a dime, formed on the back left side of my head. I remember feeling it to see if the hair roots were still there, but hair never grew on that spot. It lasted for about 3 years and then went away. For those 3 years, I found it pretty difficult to go to a barber and ask that he not cut the hair just above that area. I slowly grew my hair long enough to drape it over the bald spot to cover my embarrassment. I was absolutely positive it was a "bad mark" that only shows up on bad boys. I believe it's called "alopecia" now.

I can explicitly remember wishing a "big kid" would take a liking to me and show me where I was going wrong with making friends. I remember even picking one kid out to be my friend. I knew him from my paper route. He was 2 or 3 years older, and he seemed to fill the bill in terms of what I wanted for my first friend. While I was never able to make friends with him, I can remember the "wish" being very strong. I felt I would have a "safe" feeling if only we could be friends.

I Loved Word Associations, Numbers, and Angles

I had a secret crush on my 6th grade teacher, Sister Helena. She was very young. She was a newly ordered nun, and I remember thinking how pretty she was. She complimented me on my homework of arcs and angles and said, "You must really like geometry." When I asked her why she made that remark, she simply said my homework stood out from the rest of the class. I loved anything to do with arcs, angles, and numbers. Drawing those shapes and angles was fun for me, so I probably turned in a few masterpieces, comparatively speaking. Additionally, only recently am I beginning to realize just how important words are in my world. I remember looking forward to English classes, especially because I liked analyzing and diagramming sentences. I aced every test on that material, and I just couldn't get enough of it. With my Asperger's syndrome, as well as that of my Aspie friends, I'm finding that we're emphatically literal in what we say to others and in what others say to us.

EMPLOYMENT

I Learned to Make Money at a Young Age

At 10, I was a paperboy. I was actually a paperboy's *helper,* eagerly awaiting his graduation so I could take over his route. Making money *made me independent.* I was hooked!

From there, I worked as an upholsterer at my uncle's upholstery factory. It was a small, four-floor building where he made and sold mattresses and furniture for mobile homes. I remember being not just a *good* upholsterer, but a *very good* one. I liked *the feel* of the fabric—I don't know how else to describe that, but I loved it. My parents expected me to earn money to buy my own clothes since grade 9, and I didn't mind that a bit. The upholstery job, the job I had at the Sunday Newspaper—*The Sunday Independent*—and the job I had up my street at the car wash were my three mainstays during my 2 years of local college.

I Earned Money to Buy a Motor Scooter

By that time, I had a special way of communicating with my parents. I never felt I was able to put words together properly, but we communicated with hints and gestures. I wound up working out an arrangement where I got "three hots and a cot" (three hot meals and a bed) in exchange for funding my own tuition and books at Penn State, where I got my associate's degree in electrical and electronic technology. I thought the deal I'd made with my parents was great. I worked 34 hours per weekend for $1.25/hr, plus car wash tips, and I had enough for school, books, dating, and a used Benelli 125-cc Italian motor scooter. I bought it from a rental shop just down the street from my uncle's factory for $125. I remember thinking "a buck a cc" was a fair deal. I wish I still had that scooter. It got 55 miles to the gallon!

I Was in Heaven Working in Technology

A large technology company hired me fresh out of Penn State to work on their Air Force Manned Orbiting Laboratory Project. They were building a "spy in the sky" that could read what brand of cigarettes you smoked from the pack label in your shirt pocket, from 150 miles up in the sky. I was 20 at the time. Working on that project, I thought I was in heaven.

Not long after, Digital Equipment Corporation built a new operating system that felt like it was built just for me. It was pure logic! With the new system, I had never felt more at home "talking" to my computers, both mainframe as well as desktop design terminals. I even developed programs to check the designer's designs for specific corruptions. For the first time in my life, I had found my "wave," and I rode it with a determination I had never felt before.

RELATIONSHIPS

As a child, I was not close with anyone, not even my siblings. I do remember wishing, for a few years actually, that I could find a friend who was older, as kids my age seemed to know very little. While it never came together, I was a little surprised by the fervor with which I yearned for a friend. My older brother could have been a friend if he wanted to, I suppose, but the older we got, the more he sided with whomever was making fun of me. While I never blamed him, it hurt. A lot.

Ever since 8th grade, I had a "girlfriend" pretty regularly. If one broke up with me, which they all did eventually, then it didn't take me long to find a new one. Looking back, I don't know why I had to have a girlfriend all the time. I suppose it was because I had no "self." In those days, I never did anything beyond kissing because we were "good Catholic" boys and girls.

My Prom Date Is Still My Friend, 35 Years Later

My senior prom date was a girl named Ruthie. Boy, could we kiss! After a year of me, however, Ruthie needed a little more "personality" than I could offer. The only problem was, I didn't pick up on the fact that she didn't want to go out with me anymore. As far as I was concerned, I was just perfect for her! That poor woman was so kind, she could never come right out and say "Get lost," which are words this Aspie can fully understand. Instead, there were I-don't-want-to-hurt-him gestures that only led me to assume I was the one true love for her. I bent over backward to stay with Ruthie, including traveling to France by myself to see her (she spent her junior year of college overseas). As it turns out, Ruthie and I are friends to this day, after a 35-year hiatus.

Jailed for Stealing, Involved with the Wrong Kind of "Friends"

A few years after dating Ruthie, I had to spend 14 months in two county jails, for the misdemeanor of "possession of burglary tools." I had been caught with a "friend," trying to break into a drugstore to steal and ultimately sell controlled substances. We broke into 38 stores during a 2½-year period. We always selected out-of-the-way plaza drugstores and went in after-hours. Oh, and we robbed one bank. I stole often, and never out of necessity. I actually had this tendency for much of my life. When I was 10, I swapped price tags on baseball gloves to save money. I thought to myself how easy it was to do this. To me, stealing was fun. My first wife was also a thief. She was a friend of the guy I got caught stealing with. I myself had no interest in stealing professionally, until I met him. I was the electronic brains behind his ideas of how to do it. We were a good match personality-wise. He even conned my future wife into stealing thousands of dollars of stereo and electronic gadgets from a giant chain store, using stolen credit cards he had come across through his girlfriend.

My future wife and I were two peas in a pod, at least as far as I was concerned. Our sex life was perfect (a first for me), just so long as I wasn't called on to make love in daylight. For some reason, I was afraid to make love with a light on—it horrified me. I "suffered" through it maybe twice in our 7 years of marriage. My future wife and I "lived in sin," as my mom would say. We didn't marry for years.

I Am a College Graduate...Why Am I Stealing?

During my time in jail, I often thought, "What the hell was I thinking, stealing like that? I'm a college graduate!" When I got out, however, I felt as lost as ever. I got a job as a short-order cook at a country restaurant, thanks to one of the deputies that knew me from jail. I worked that job like there was no tomorrow. I think cooking can be a loner's haven. That job taught me that a person's mind needs to be exercised just as much his body. We worked 6- and 7-day weeks, as the restaurant was seasonal. It closed from November through early March. I collected unemployment checks during the winter.

Shortly before getting the restaurant job, I had to face the label of "felon" for the first time. I was offered a short-order cook's job for less than everyone else was paid. I didn't refute the pay, as my future wife and I needed all we could get. But I remember feeling how anyone getting out of jail in this country must feel—like a total loser who had a record he could no longer hide. I also remember repeating to myself, time after time, "What's a college graduate doing in a mess like this?" with regard to the burglaries and the inevitable outcome.

One year later, I was first cook at that restaurant, and 6 months after that, I was asked to be chef. I studied the work of chef Auguste Escoffier, and I treated that job as both a work of art and a science. I worked 84 hours each week, taking one day off to order $30,000 of meat and $14,000 of fish weekly. I never missed a beat. In fact, I got a beautiful two-page article written about me in the local *Rochester Sunday Newspaper*.

I Loved My Baby Son

One day I came home from work and said to my future wife something to the effect of, "I don't want to play house anymore. I want a child of my own. If you're game, let's marry! If not, then maybe we should break up." I said this with no emotion—it was just pure logic. She took time to consider it, and in the end we married. She consequently gave me the closest thing to love I have ever experienced—a baby boy. He consumed 99% of my mind and heart during the following years. He could do no wrong, and I rarely left his side. My wife found an old rocking chair frame, and I drew from my upholstery days and immediately went to work renovating it into a warm, comfortable rocking chair for me to rock my son in. My wife had to rise every 2 hours at first to feed our son after he was born. I don't remember ever complaining about rocking him for her so she could get some rest. We seemed to be a perfect team.

Friction with My Wife and My Descent into Alcoholism

My old company called me around this time, asking if I wanted to return to work on a new project with my old boss. My wife and I moved from a trailer in the country to the city. The house we bought needed a tremendous amount of work. It was wired and piped as two apartments, one up and one down. I was fine with doing the renovations and did all of my own electrical work, plumbing, and carpentry. But, my wife wasn't as keen on the idea of renovating the house while we lived in it. We began to argue, at first over objections I had to certain things she did with my son. She was a great mom for the most part, but she called my son names and avoided closeness to him, which really bothered me. My son's face showed hurt when she called him names. And if I said anything to her about it—well. She was of Sicilian descent, and to this day I wouldn't attempt to win an argument with her.

The problem on my side was that my son's face was the only face in the world I felt I knew. He was certainly more important to me than any other human being. I was a great dad then, I thought. But that slowly changed as I progressed into alcoholism. Back then, it was the only relief I had from the constant merry-go-round of pictures that ran through my head. Beer made the voices stop. The pictures in my head also stopped when I drank, and I felt like I could finally be like other people. When I saw other people in my life drink when I was younger—including my father—they seemed happy, and no one fought (except my mother). However, I found myself on a slow descent into hell. I never missed a day's work because of alcohol, therefore I reasoned that I "wasn't an alcoholic." I worked a second shift that got out at midnight, and I started to avoid going home, as I found an all-night gambling place that suited me just down Bay Street. The beer, the guys, and the smoke were just what I needed, compared with the slow-simmering battle I was nurturing at home over my wife's treatment of my son.

Being Single and Raising My Son

After we divorced, I remained single for 4 years. I focused on raising my son and working. I was fortunate in that my wife didn't really seem to want to be around my son nearly as much as I did. After the divorce, I got to spend every single weekend and every Wednesday evening with him. To me, that was close to heaven. We had a small park just up the street, where football became our pride and joy. It was fun to watch a 3-year-old boy run around in shoulder pads and helmet. He was untouchable in his little uniform. I absolutely loved raising that boy. And I still enjoy him, to this day.

Married a Second Time

I married a second time, a few years later. I had bought a second house that didn't need nearly as much work as the first one, and I had settled in with my son whenever he wasn't with his mother. I wanted more children. Raising my son was the only thing I felt I was doing right, and therefore more children must be better. I registered with the county and went through a series of classes to be a registered foster parent. I was adamant about helping any and all children. To me, they were the easiest people to be around. I met my second wife just weeks after I finished that class. Regrettably, I wound up never fostering any children.

My Alcoholism Worsened during My Second Marriage

My second wife and I had two beautiful daughters, Brittany and Brianna. My alcoholism was worsening every year, and by the time my daughters reached the ages of 3 and 5, I couldn't go a single evening without a drink. After a few years, my wife and I could both see that I needed help, so I joined a group that met in a hospital a few miles away every Thursday evening. I quit drinking on the first day I joined that group, and I did not drink for 7 months. I loved going. But I quit attending the group sessions after my wife said she wanted to spend more time together. She maintained that my group sessions took up an entire evening of time we could be spending together. So I quit the group, and couldn't help noticing how eager I was to drink again after that. Within a week, I began hiding alcohol throughout the house and garage.

ON AUTISM

With age, I've come to realize that I may truly be bisexual. Personally, I feel it goes with having Asperger's. I've always noticed that, when I'm in a relationship, I don't feel jealousy or true anger. I only now know why. For me, I've noticed that sex and love are two distinct things—not one. Sex is sex, and love is everything nonsexual. I can now remember questioning my sexuality back in the early 1950s and thinking I did have a curiosity about homosexuality back then. The catholic church taught me that having those kinds of thoughts was normal, only acting on them was sinful. So I lived most of my life heterosexually. But lately I can see that, for me, sex is still just sex. Since having these thoughts, I've spoken with a couple of other Aspies about it and found some agreement.

Other People Seemed More Mature, and I Didn't Know Why

For me, one simple transition spurred my realizations about being "different." When I graduated Penn State and was hired by the major technology company, I moved from my little corner of Wilkes-Barre, PA, to Rochester, NY. I immediately noticed how much more mature my fellow electrical techs seemed, compared to me. At that point I thought their maturity must be related to the alcohol they drank, and they seemed to enjoy drinking very much. I had never considered drinking, as I didn't wish to be "like my dad," as my mom continually told me. I later tried drinking during army boot camp, where I was drafted from a military police reserve branch after missing too many weekend Army Reserve meetings.

Even though I refused to drink at that early phase in my life, I was aware of some serious differences between myself and others my same age. I felt immature, for lack of a better word, and I didn't understand why.

The speeches of Martin Luther King, Jr, inspired me in the 1960s. I felt I could relate to the issues minorities dealt with then. I listened to National Public Radio all the time, and King astounded me with the words he chose and his profound clarity. All my life I responded to race issues by saying, "I'm color blind." Little did I know that was close to the truth—I'm "face blind," to be more precise. I have always had difficulty recognizing and remembering other people's faces.

MENTORS

My first boss after college inspired me for years. As it turns out, he was in the Korean War with one of my professors from Penn State, so he took me under his wing. In him, I finally had that big brother I always wanted.

My father is becoming my hero only now. I know him now. As a matter of fact, I may be the only one who does truly know the man. He was a good, good guy. He showed every indication of having Asperger's, and had I only understood him, he could have quite possibly been my best "big brother" of all.

OUTLOOK: LEARNING ABOUT ASPERGER'S WAS A BRAND NEW DAY

One day in 2009, I visited a doctor who confirmed my lifelong suspicions that I am truly different than others. I had been driven to see her because I had "had it" with trying to "negotiate" with my brain all the time. In many ways, I thought I was going crazy. When I arrived at her office, I uttered the most difficult sentence I have ever spoken: "I've felt all my life I've had 'some retardation.'" For years I had wondered what was going on with me and hoped to find some answers, but I always failed to find a single one. Somehow, using the word "retardation" with Dr West was so much better than saying the word "retarded."

When she told me I have Asperger's syndrome, it was the end of one life for me and the beginning of a brand new day. I had found what I had been looking for—through pain, hurt, jail, embarrassment, shame, and even turning "hippie," because hippies seemed to know "the secrets of being close with others."

Years of AA meetings had taught me to pay attention to the concept of "acceptance." And I have to say that at this point in my life, "acceptance" is a wonderful realm in which to live.

CHAPTER 12

LEONORA
GREGORY-COLLURA

Autism Outreach Consultant and Dancer/Choreographer

LEONORA GREGORY-COLLURA

Age: 53

Resides in: Vancouver, British Columbia, Canada

Occupation: Autism outreach consultant and dancer/choreographer

Marital status: Married 13 years, with one child

FROM TEMPLE:

Leonora has been a dancer and choreographer since a very young age. Dancing helped her to express emotions she otherwise could not. At times, Leonora has been dealt a tough hand. She lost a daughter, and her son has experienced severe medical problems. However, she leans on a lifetime of enriching experiences to help her get through the rough patches and to assist her in touching the lives of others. She has been very fortunate to enjoy a healthy marriage with a loving partner, whom she says is like a mirror image of herself. Leonora currently operates a consulting business to help children with autism.

LEONORA'S INTRODUCTION

In 1995, I was asked to speak and create training programs for volunteers, parents, and professionals who work with and support autistic individuals. After the inception of the idea for my company, I incorporated in 1996. My company is called ANCA Consulting, Inc. I have also created a private nonprofit foundation to help educate the general public about autism in Canada. So, I effectively run two autism outreach businesses. Additionally, I have developed a bursary program for further education and career employment support.

The consulting work we do relates to educating parents and professionals about autism "from the inside out." We teach others about the way the autistic mind works and how an autistic person communicates naturally. Our programs include parent training and developmental support systems for education. We focus on how autistic persons interface with subject matter or topics of interest. Their interests can be useful for bridging the gap into the learning environment. We consult with school personnel about the most effective way to teach an autistic person, taking into account the individual's environment, family, lifestyle, and medical concerns. We also help families navigate various systems, such as education, medical and clinical arenas, and government. We aim to find the best support resources available, given each individual family's unique situation.

A vital part of our program is the monthly group activities we do with children, teens, and adults. Each autistic member of the group learns by experience, through the mirror reflection of one another. This can be an important means of developing mentorship. Our group program has three community components: holiday/winter open house, summer campout, and annual presentations. Natural interactive skills are gleaned by participating in these types of group activities, through which parents and siblings gain heightened insight into the autistic mind. Activities like these also help enhance self-confidence in each and every individual at the event, including parents.

Our annual presentation has culminated in the annual Naturally Autistic People Awards and Convention, whereby the greater global population has the ability to experience the natural interactive process. This year, we have received many e-mails from individuals thanking us for helping their child/teen/family member feel accepted in a group for the very first time, without feeling isolated or stared at. One such attendee, a 15-year-old teen with autism, said she appreciated that we are not "curists." She felt so comfortable at the convention, she spoke up spontaneously and asked to read her poem "Acceptance" at the gala dinner.

Through my consulting company, I have achieved a longtime dream: to unite the autism community with one voice—the voice of many, joined together as one. You can read more about our mission statement at *www.naturallyautistic.com.*

I Love Working with Autistic Children

I love working with autistic children, teens, and adults. I dislike working with ignorant behaviorists and those who try to change or "fix" an autistic individual. It can be tough to meet with educators and behaviorists who are unwilling to listen. There are many of us on the spectrum who have found success and who have a lifetime of information to share to make the learning environment a better place for the younger autistic population. In my experience, there is a great deal of ignorance in the professions that cross paths with autistic people and their families, and there can be unwillingness to "hear" the autistic child, teen, and adult. My life's work through the creative arts has been to help shift that ignorance, and I do believe we are making headway.

Another aspect of what we do involves helping parents really look at themselves and stop blaming autistic children for their own unrelated personal problems. It can be tough going when parents choose not to be honest with themselves and instead point fingers at a child's autism as their source of discomfort.

In British Columbia, certain organizations have lobbied government to implement disdainful approaches regarding the rights of autistic individuals. In my opinion, it is inhumane and corrupt to attempt to further isolate families with autism and prevent them from seeking out other autistic people to connect with. Many new families my company encounters have never heard of names like Temple Grandin or Donna Williams, and that worries me. But, they do seem to know about celebrities in the media who sell what they think they know. This can create a confusing environment for parents who are dealing with a new diagnosis of autism.

I Help Others Create Small Businesses

I love the business aspect of my company, because it has enabled me to teach others how to develop themselves and create their own small businesses. I helped one young boy open up a small recycling business in his neighborhood. He loved riding his bike and knew all his neighbors. He enjoyed making flyers and dealing with money. With our help, he was able to make use of these assets and create his own business as an adult.

I love to share ideas and support people in seeking out new experiences. The families affiliated with my company seem to cherish the way we support them. We really try to empower them by way of reaching out to the greater community and society as a whole.

There is so much I find challenging and rewarding when it comes to overcoming obstacles in this field, I could probably write a book about it. At the end of the day, the firsthand experiences we offer families through our awards convention and other annual activities make all our efforts worthwhile.

EARLY YEARS

My first memory is from when I was about a year old, when I was on a ship going from Australia to Singapore. I was taken into a room with other kids, and at that point all I could relate to was shapes. I had no names for the shapes yet, and I had been living in the jungle with my family, so I could not make certain connections or contextualize this room of noisy kids, Jell-O, clowns, and streamers. It was a birthday party, and it sent me into sensory overload. I demonstrated a sensory response, and my mother realized it and took me away immediately. From early on, it became obvious that I was not like other kids.

My brother is 5 years my senior, and I learned a lot from him. He taught me how to tie my shoelaces when I was 8. My father was a professor, and we were living in West Africa at the time. My brother drew a figure eight in the sand and showed me that the laces were like the figure eight. It was so easy for me to associate and connect to that physical analogy. He was very protective of me and somehow knew I had no fear. When we walked up our driveway after the school bus dropped us off, he looked out for alligators and other wildlife (in Africa there were all sorts of wild animals around). If necessary, he put himself between me and danger. Once, I was running and my brother saw a python slither across the front steps. He ran in front of me to protect me from the python. He always carried me across the fields when we went to other people's houses because he didn't want anything to happen to me.

My Brother Taught Me Many Skills

I always seemed to be unable to generalize my focus, and my brother somehow knew that. I learned from everything he did. He taught me to sail, ride a bike and a scooter, and play with toys. He even taught me how to cook for special occasions, such as making pancakes for our mom and dad on a special day like Easter.

My brother always had a job as a child, and I emulated that. First he had paper routes and took care of pets. Then he created a small printing company that made letterhead, return-address envelopes, and stationery. We were living in England at the time, and he got customers by placing little ads in the newspaper. He showed me the way the letters created the print on the paper. When he completed each print batch on linen paper, we boxed it and delivered the goods to his customers on our bikes.

We Had Lots of Animals

My brother always saved animals, and he taught me about birds with broken wings and helping stray cats and dogs. We both grew up with pets—he had a donkey and pig in Samoa. Then, in Singapore, we had dogs and puppies and cats and a tortoise. In Africa, we had an old parrot that we taught to speak. In England, I learned to fish and hunt for hare and rabbits with an elderly neighbor. I learned about cows from interacting with them in the fields.

My brother had another business I helped him with in the summer months in England—he collected mooring money from boaters. That was a lot of fun, because we went from boat to boat, met people, and looked at their different vessels. Lots of them had come from other countries.

My brother taught me about flags and Morse code, cowboys and Indians, and medieval times. We played with his toy horses, cattle, and armored knights. My parents bought my brother a house kit, so he could learn how to build a house with bricks and mortar. The bricks were cute, about ½ inch in length. It also came with small bags of cement. I watched my brother use this kit, and I learned how to build a house with doors, frames, windows, and a roof.

As kids, we both loved secondhand stores. We saved our pocket money and bought old-fashioned wooden telephones. He had one in his room, which was two flights up from my room, and we "called each other up" with the old phones. He showed me how to do the same with cans and string. He also taught me how to surf in Africa. My brother and I remain close to this day.

Our family listened to radio drama as a treat. Our father got us records of famous dramas. While I am not good at remembering titles of things, I have a good spatial and visceral sensory memory. I can memorize books photographically and can recall specific information that way. That's how I passed my exams in school. I also have a good long-term physical, experiential memory.

My Parents Knew I Was Different

My mother says she and my father always knew I was different. After I received a diagnosis of Asperger's syndrome and posttraumatic stress disorder at British Columbia Children's Hospital when I was 37, I asked my mother why she and my father didn't have me assessed when I was younger. She said if I had received a diagnosis by a psychiatrist when I was younger, I may have been institutionalized. She said that because of her educational background and experiences and those of my father, they understood that there are many people who learn and do things differently. She added that both her family and my father's family were somewhat eccentric, anyway.

I remember my parents spending much time finding the best schools for me. They always communicated with the principals and teachers. This continued right through to my graduation at the Royal Ballet and even with my employers as I got older. My parents always seemed to know how to support me. My father and mother knew how I learned best, and they consistently provided the tools I needed to succeed.

I Was a Hyperactive, Sound-Sensitive Child

I was hyperactive as a child. I had early onset of language and was highly sensitive to sounds, movement, and smells. When we lived in Singapore, I was enrolled in music, dance, and movement classes. My father took me swimming at the university club all the time, and he built a special sandbox for me to play in. I started nursery school at 2 years old. I remember it being fun, but I knew I was not like the other children.

When I started dance classes, I "zoned out" when it wasn't my turn. My mother called it "daydreaming." I talked too much and never really knew what I was actually saying. I absorbed the intellectual conversations my parents and their colleagues had around me before I could fully understand their meaning.

I never had much desire to play with other children. It's not that I didn't *like* to—rather, I did not *want* to. I preferred to observe them rather than play with them. From time to time, I did play ball and other games with the kids my dad arranged to hang out with me.

Mostly, I followed my brother and his friends around. I lined things up. My brother actually loved to play with his trucks and cars on the edge of the pavement around our house, and I followed him and stayed right behind him, as if I were forming a line with him. I did the same thing when I followed his friends.

In Singapore, my father made my bedroom very basic. All the toys were put in another room, so all I had were my bed and dressing table and one soft doll that was given to me at birth. He said I needed a "calm" room, and he was right.

Our house in Singapore had mosaic tiles and a circular swooping staircase. I used to sit and "get deep into" the patterns within each 1-inch square to see all the details of color within it.

I often went into the bathroom, sat on the toilet, and fell asleep sucking two of my fingers. Sometimes I locked myself in without understanding what I was doing, and the houseman had to come get me out.

I Asked Questions Over and Over

My mother used to gesture with her hand as if I were a gramophone record player, on and on, never stopping. I often wondered why she did this, but as I grew older and received my diagnosis, it all made sense. I talked nonstop and looped my speech, asking questions and wanting to know the "why" and "what" of things all the time. Round and round I went, like a gramophone record. I tend to process things out loud, not internally like many others. I was also clumsy—my mother would not allow me to wash dishes unless my brother helped me, because things slipped out of my hands and broke. It's funny that my mother thought of me as clumsy, because I thrived in dance classes. I later joined two of the most prestigious dance schools of my generation—Elmhurst Ballet School and the Royal Ballet School.

I had good spatial relationships with other bodies on a team, such as my netball team (of which I was captain), but I was terrible at grass hockey and got hit in the face many times. I did not have the same style of reflex required to play that game.

My parents always partnered me up with school friends. They had friends come to my house for birthdays and teach me activities like "French skipping" or "two ball against the wall." These friends also went with me to the local youth group, church choir, and bell-ringing practice.

My Mother Taught Me Etiquette

My mother taught me etiquette, and my father taught me practical life skills, like opening a savings account, budgeting, shopping, making lists, and developing organizational skills.

I always watched our various housekeepers, no matter what country we were in. I watched and learned and observed. They didn't seem to mind. They also didn't seem to mind my endless questions. Our hens were killed for food, so I learned about where fresh chicken came from by watching our servant kill the chickens. I also learned about the nervous system and why it still moved after the chicken's head was broken off at the neck.

In Africa, my parents had a special bed made for me on stilts. It was like a crib, with sides and locks. I think my parents were afraid I would go wandering around without the extra precautions—which I did anyway. I remember sleepwalking for a short period. What my parents did not realize was that I could get out of that bed—I just unlatched the locks. I know they were concerned about my lack of fear. Also, at night there were tarantulas and scorpions about. Once, I found myself a pet scorpion in the sand under our stilted house. My parents did not know this, and I did not know it was dangerous. I poked it with a stick and was fascinated at how it responded to me touching it.

My mother knew I did not like clothes—itchy clothes, anyway— so she started to make my clothes herself when we lived in England. When we lived in Asia or Africa, I didn't like to wear clothes at all. My parents found ways to support this preference and made compromises. I also did not like to eat, because I didn't like the sensation of using the forks and spoons. My mother fed me with her hands.

Even though I had early onset of language, I was often nonverbal in my communications. One time I hit a little boy, who was the son of my parents' friends. I hit him because he gave me green plastic beads for a gift instead of the real McCoy—emeralds. I could not explain reactions like that, but later in my childhood, I was able to start piecing things together for myself. I started to note and observe how I did things versus how other children did things, and I found the discrepancies really fascinating. This was when I started to see myself as "not the same" as my peers, before I received my diagnosis.

I Developed through Dance

I wanted to take Judo classes like my brother, but in those days it was not ladylike for a girl to do Judo. So I took ballet, movement, and dance classes instead. I was very interested in dance and the mechanics of movement in the human body. I found the study of these concepts useful as I matured and developed.

My parents and their friends thought I must be a dancer because I walked on my tiptoes all the time. I did not like wearing shoes—I preferred to walk around with bare feet. I often stayed up late, because I could not sleep. Instead of sleeping, I played with Chinese checkers, allowing the colored pieces to fall and then spinning around the living room as I tried to balance the round checkerboard on one hand.

I Preferred Being Read to

My father was an academic and educator, so he knew my learning style and what to provide me with to help me grow through each developmental stage. Even though I could read, I preferred to hear the words—so I was read to a lot. I listened to lots of fairy tales, stories, and nursery rhymes. I loved these because they took me off into another world and another dimension. I was influenced by stories about the black swan and the ugly duckling. As I grew, I went to the English village school for a short period before going to Elmhurst for dance. There were bundles of kids who teased other children. I fought them on the playground, as I was a bit of a tomboy then. I loved climbing trees and cliffs and biking. I preferred hanging out with boys rather than girls.

I Hated Water on My Head

I hated having water on my head when my mother washed and bathed me. So, she got creative and showed me pictures of little girls in magazines that used little bubbles in their hair to keep their hair styled. I liked the analogy of how the bubbly soap put the hair in place without using hairpins, so I allowed my mother to wash my hair after that. But, she had to be very gentle and not rub too hard or make my scalp so sensitive.

306

My mother was from an aristocratic family in Thailand, with Laos heritage. My father had Scottish and Irish parents. They were scholars, teachers, writers, and landowners. Our history goes back a long way, and there is even a book about my father's family—the Gregory family. My father's family was catholic, and my mother's was Buddhist. Both of my parents were educated at university. My father worked for the United Nations and the World Health Organization and was sent to different countries on United Nations business. For example, he was working for the United Nations in Yugoslavia during the Tito Revolution. My mother was in politics and was later a diplomat. Both spoke several languages, so we all learned to speak the language of the country in which we were living. We had a strong sense of etiquette, values, and beliefs on the basis of our religion, culture, and family history. My father was also a Quaker. Even though we grew up with servants, we learned how to support and appreciate the Quaker culture. We had to learn to make our beds, put laundry away, clean up our rooms, set the table, and the like. Our houses were never messy—everything had its place and was labeled accordingly. Both of my parents were extremely well organized and orderly. We were taught not in words but rather in actions what was expected of us in a household, a family, and a community—even in society in general. I didn't understand it in words or language; it was just a way of life demonstrated to me through experience, expectation, and physical interaction.

I went to the High Church of England School, where I excelled in religious knowledge as an "A" student. My parents had friends, colleagues, and acquaintances of all religions, races, and cultures— mainly in the arts, film and television, publishing, writing, journalism, politics, and academia. They knew diplomats, consulates, and other intellectual types. I went to school with the aristocracy and children of self-made business families.

We All Ate Meals Together

Responsibilities were modeled for us and were part of our family structure. We always ate meals together, even when I did not want to eat because I was a picky eater. Usually, Mom made me what I liked, but I was never forced to eat. It was expected that we would all eat together and try new foods—or at least taste them. We always walked as a family after dinner. Our household structure was not rigid; rather, it was an integral part of growing up that a child could count on. It provided safety and a sense of belonging. We shared conversations during mealtimes and discussed politics, our interests, and what we had done during the day.

At one point, I told my father I wanted a guitar. He suggested that I get one from the secondhand store and said that if I saved up my pocket money and showed interest and potential, then I might get lessons. The same went for the piano. While we already had a piano, my father said I would only get lessons if I showed deep interest and consistency first. Nothing was given to us unless we demonstrated a purposeful interest in it, consistent with achievement. Otherwise, it was considered a passing phase, well worth experiencing but not worthy of financial investment. With my dance classes, my parents saw my deep interest and understanding. It was worth the investment.

Even though we had servants, my parents did household chores. Dad liked to sweep the front walk every week, even though we had a gardener. He liked to burn the old papers and magazines and organize the recycling, which he taught to my brother and me. We learned about plants and gardening—we grew roses, flowers, trees, vegetables, and fruit—and we learned about why trees are important. My mother took what we grew and bottled and jarred it. She made jam and all kinds of great baked goods, as well as homemade ice cream, cream, and butter. We learned that running a life, a family, and a household is how you learn organization and communication skills, values, and responsibility.

At age 11, I had to learn how to make checklists to pack my trunk for boarding school. I had to figure out what train to catch, how to book my trunk on the train, and the like. My parents never did these things for me.

Learning to Consider the Life of Another Person

In Arica, we had a lovely male servant named Dosa, whom I loved. When we had to leave suddenly because of the revolution of Incruma, I wanted my father to bring Dosa with us to England. He said he wouldn't bring Dosa because there were no black people in England at the time, and he didn't want Dosa to feel isolated and different. Through this experience, I learned that my parents considered the life of another and the impact of changing that person's life by bringing him to an all-white country at that time. Dosa had a son who was about 32 years old, and he came around our property from time to time. He was different. He paced all the time and could not work or get a job. My father arranged for him to go to a special school to learn basic skills, so he could work when his father became too old. My father financially supported Dosa until his death and paid for his son to go to the special-skills school so he could be employed. I saw that my parents cared about people and understood the bigger picture. They shared what they had, even though we lost everything during the revolution. I have lived my life much like this over the years. From my parents, I learned that it is the duty of those of us who are more fortunate to give of ourselves, in terms of service to others and to the community.

SCHOOL YEARS

Starting at 2 years old, I attended a private nursery school, then village schools and British Schools in Africa and England until I was accepted at the private Elmhurst Ballet School in England. Later, I was admitted to the Royal Ballet School in London. I received the equivalent of a bachelor of education degree at London University in 1979. The Royal Ballet had an affiliate program, and I could have done a 1-year practicum in the East London Schools. Instead, I came to work in Canada.

I started kindergarten in the early 1960s. I wet myself badly one day, and my mother was called. I was put in the corner to stare at the wall, and I was smacked with a ruler. When my mother arrived, she was humiliated in front of the class for being Thai, and I was called a "chink."

I used to stand up to bullies on the playground. When my brother and I went to live in England full time, we were enrolled at the local village primary school. I remember him being teased. The other kids covered him with flour when he walked into the classroom, and they called him "Donald Duck." My brother was my hero—I learned so much from him and looked up to him. To witness this event at school was horrible. My father immediately enrolled him in a private school in the north, instead. Then, when I saw the village bullies go after others in my age group, I took them on and fought them.

I also connected with a little boy who came into our Friday art class for raffia (fiber weaving) and needlework. He arrived on a special bus, and later I learned he came from an institution. I knew he liked me because he always came charging up to me. I believe he was nonverbal, as he never spoke to me. However, I remember that he came running up to me with a raffia needle, and when I put my hand up to stop him, it went into my hand. A time before that, he poked the inside of my knee with a pencil. I have never forgotten him in all these years.

In school, the most difficult thing for me was language. It was daunting to me how language was used in communications, especially in lectures and in mathematics. My easiest subjects were history, geography, English literature, theology, anatomy, art, and music. I was excellent at geometry, trigonometry, algebra, and logarithms. We studied basic biology and sciences, which I loved. But, attending an arts school, I didn't delve into anything beyond the basics. French was easy, for the most part. I understood French grammar better than English, and that is how I was able to finally begin to understand English grammar. I was also good at Latin.

Choreography Became My Passion

Drama, theater, the stage, and set design were very interesting to me. Improvisation was scary. I loved voice and elocution, and I had a powerful voice but difficulty with inflections. Choreography became a passion at age 11. I used music and movement to begin to decipher cognitive function. The first ballet I produced and choreographed was called "Neurosis." It was about which part of the brain is which, what part is something else, what part is made up of thoughts, what part is "feelings," and so on. I made each dancer a character of the brain's function. I must have understood the filing system of the thought process then, but I didn't know how to communicate it in language to have a conversation about it with others. So I turned it into a dance. I got honors for that piece of work, which was judged by critics from Fleet Street. After that piece, I wanted to perfect the use of choreography but was unsure how to go about it. I just kept developing pieces as I went along.

From age 8 until I was about 13 years old, I created many small events with kids in my neighborhood during school holidays. I used my mother's silk cocktail dresses to make costumes and put on plays in the cellar of our house. Then I took the shows to the neighbors and the old folks' homes, and they paid sixpence each to watch our performances.

EMPLOYMENT

I began babysitting when I was 8 years old. I also did some shopping for elderly persons who needed assistance. I helped out in two stores in the village borough. I worked for my dad, taking mail to the post office, collecting his "fan mail," and typing manuscripts for him. He also taught me how to make maps when he made them for geography books.

As I got older, I worked in a variety of stores and learned about retail and sales. I looked after pets and helped take care of people who were elderly and sick. I taught ballet (freelance) and did choreography for pageants, gymnastics, and ice skaters. I waitressed and modeled.

I Was Respected for the Quality of My Work

I made many acquaintances through my career in dance and the performing arts. Before long, I was doing choreography for hair product companies and hair stylists. I started choreographing commercial works. The people I worked with accepted me and my idiosyncrasies and nuances. I was very good at what I did, and I think they respected that about my work. A handful of students and professionals from those early days remain in my close circle of friends today.

My Diagnosis Explained Being Both Intellectual and Childlike

When my friends and colleagues found out about my diagnosis, they were delighted, because they finally had a "context" for me. They always saw me as creative, and they viewed my creative abilities and my unusual background as the cause for my eccentricities. Now they also had an explanation as to why I seemed highly intellectual one moment and like a child the next. It was good to know why.

Aside from my work, I volunteered at church, which took a variety of forms. When I was younger, I helped out with weddings, bell-ringing, and singing in the choir for special occasions. I have never really stopped doing volunteer work. I suppose that is why my husband and I have a philanthropic attitude toward our work, our vision, our goals, and our objectives.

I Turned My Life Around after My Baby Died

My best career experiences have been running my own businesses. There is always a creative element attached, and I can follow my dreams, pursue my passions, and help others while constantly being challenged to think creatively. My dance and choreographic experiences have been the backbone of my life. Everything I learned developed skills that were transferable to other areas of my life, no matter what my situation. Some years ago, I had a baby girl, and she died. The grief I experienced from this event caused me to lose my mental health, the dance school I'd started, and my home, and I was 24 hours away from being out on the streets. However, I was able to dig deep inside myself and draw from my educational background, my skill sets, and my life experiences. I used those skill sets to turn things around. (My mother politely said, "I won't help you—your father and I gave you the best education and the best schools in the world, now go figure it out!) I had to get clear on what I was doing in life, and I did. Three years after losing my child, I had turned my life around.

The ability to choreograph large bodies of work demands many skill sets. Those same skills sets can open up all kinds of doors. I have introduced the element of choreography into everything I have done and continue to do so, only now it's on a more international scale. I use it to help a community I feel so comfortable with and with whom I feel so connected. I belong with the autistic community.

In my career, I have enjoyed all manner of work. Nothing has ever been above or below me. Every job has been an asset toward running two very successful businesses.

RELATIONSHIPS

As a young child, I was surrounded by lots of different children, but I did not necessarily interact with them the way other children do. I did like them, but I did not understand them. I was often termed "bossy," but what I was actually doing with my interactions was learning how other kids functioned. I observed them. From my observations, I figured out how I could communicate. One such time was when we lived in Africa part time and in England part time.

My birthday was always in England. So one afternoon, when we were in Africa, I decided to ask my classmates to my home for a birthday party. It was not about the birthday or the gifts or anything of that nature. I wanted to know if they would all show up. They did, much to the dismay of our head servant and also to the curiosity of my parents, upon their return from the university. Dosa, our head servant, rallied and started to prepare food. My parents immediately went to the shops to buy beverages and refreshments. Once the children arrived, I took off to hang out with the servant children instead. The party went on without me. I played games in the dirt and gravel with the servant children, and we climbed trees. These children liked what I did. They taught me things about nature and our surroundings, like walking to the sugar plantations nearby. We picked and tasted root vegetables from obliging fields.

On some of the ships we traveled in, I preferred to seek out the adults, like the kitchen chef and the engineers. I liked to observe what they did on the ship. I never played with the children on those voyages.

I Interacted with Children by Getting Them to Do Things

At school, I did not really have "friends," other than those I interacted with for specific purposes. I coordinated with some children who were in my cellar productions. What it boiled down to was that I liked getting other children to do things. In the Africa days, I got them to climb up a high ladder in the kitchen and eat the dried milk. I did interact with other children when we visited friends of my parents or when we were invited to special occasions or gatherings. My parents invited children to my birthday parties, and sometimes my parents coordinated holidays between school terms in which children would come stay with us, or I went to stay with them at their homes.

When I attended the Elmhurst Ballet School, I often spent time on my own, sitting on a bench on the school grounds. Unbeknownst to me, my father spoke with the headmistress and asked her to have another student keep me company, which she did. I had no idea this was a coordinated event. There were many other such occasions.

As a teenager, I developed some friendships at Elmhurst, as coordinated by my parents with school personnel. It was the same at home, as with the children of my parents' friends.

I Did Not Understand Why Others Thought I Was Aloof

After I graduated from the Royal Ballet School, I came back to Canada and reconnected with ballet friends and local neighbor friends. They started to call me names and said I was "aloof" and a snob. I did not understand why. I did not like how it made me feel in my body—so I didn't connect with them again. I put all my energy into my art, theater, dance, teaching, and choreography. I had lots of energy, so I could work continuously, with little or no sleep, to meet the production deadlines. The people I worked with—dancers, models, musicians, stylists, and designers—became my "friends." But, I do not think I really understood the meaning of having friends or friendships.

Prior to this, my father had connected me with many of his local and international students, who took me under their wing when we traveled abroad or when I simply hung out at my dad's college. Later, I found out that he had also arranged this, as he was always worried I might get myself in trouble somehow, being in London on my own. One such person has remained my friend and comes to Canada to visit about every 3 years.

I Never Understood Dating

I never understood dating. I had lots of male friends and associates, and I always connected with my brother's friends. Otherwise, I was not interested in boys except for observation purposes or to connect with one of their particular talents, such as sailing, music, performance, nature, hiking, or biking. My dad always said I was attractive and that so-and-so liked me, and when I worked in London, I saw guys look at me. But I really did not know what that meant. My dad tried to orchestrate that as well, but to be honest, I was clueless. I did like men, because it seemed to me they were less complicated than women. Gay people liked me and seemed different than straight people. At first I was uncomfortable with their touchy-feely ways, but it was a different kind of touch than with others, so I began to connect with them. I learned a lot from my gay acquaintances. I have also always loved to be around older people.

I was engaged to a musician in the 1970s, and, later, another potential marriage came about through my work in the arts. But I never followed through. I had my son as a single mother, because I did not want to marry my son's biological father. My father always said I should follow my career and that marriage would not be a good thing. He thought that being pregnant would interfere with my career, as well.

I Had a Son with Brain Damage

When my son Anthony was born, it opened up another chapter of my life. He was born with brain damage at birth, owing to medical negligence. My education and training in anatomy and physiology enabled me to work with him, however, and he has developed remarkably, against all odds. Anthony went to an integrated preschool at 2½ years of age, and I was invited to teach dance arts to both special-needs and typically developing children there and at other preschools.

I consequently lost my second child, Catherine, to another medical negligence issue. I broke down. I lost everything. I nearly lost my life and my son's life as well, because of suicidal tendencies. I found a good psychiatrist at British Columbia's Children's Hospital and received a diagnosis of Asperger's syndrome and posttraumatic stress disorder.

I started weekly psychotherapy in an attempt to understand myself better. I worked with other adults with my condition to try to find the connecting links between us. Even though we all had different backgrounds, we had this one thing in common, and I wanted to learn more about "what that was." I knew this would help me understand myself and be able to support others.

I Found My Husband

I also wanted a male friend for my son. He came in the form of a community worker named Charlie. Charlie and I connected over common interests. Our intellects matched. Anthony says he knew that the three of us all had something in common. Then, out of the blue, Charlie said he could not work with us anymore. I just about died because I had found a real friend for the first time. What he had difficulty saying and communicating was that we were experiencing the same thing and that what he felt for me was more than friendship.

A relationship was developing. I had prayed to meet someone like me, and now I had. My husband Charlie is like a mirror image of me.

MENTORS

I had many teachers along the way whom I consider mentors because they really seemed to understand me. One that stands out is my nursery-school teacher from when I was 2 years old and living in Singapore. She knew what I knew, but I couldn't speak it. I had no language or words as a context to put my experiences into. After school, I often had to wait for our chauffeur to come and pick me up. My teacher had a large glass jar of shiny, colored objects. I saw other kids take some when they were offered, but I had never taken any and did not make the connection that they were candy. I just liked the way they looked, so I stared at them, taking in all the details. I got drawn in to the configurations of all those little objects in that large jar. One day, my teacher saw me doing this (today, it might be referred to as an autistic child "fixating"), and she opened the jar and offered to put my hand in it. I did, and I could feel the colors and textures of all those shiny objects. I did not want to eat them, as I still didn't know I could. I had never had candy before.

Anything new like this within the context of my developmental stages was fascinating to me. My nursery-school teacher really seemed to understand me.

Mrs Weeks, the school secretary at my village primary school in England, gave me jobs to get me away from the crowd. My principal and head teacher in Africa helped me with language comprehension by using the Dick and Jane books. The director and prima ballerina director at the Royal Ballet saw and encouraged my gifts in choreography, as did the music director. One teacher, Joan Lawson, witnessed my understanding of communication through dance and suggested that I had a unique understanding of the human body. She said I could see within the body and through it and that she had never had a student with this ability.

I Expressed Emotions through Dance

My Spanish teacher was someone who could draw emotions out of me—for the first time in my life. Until then, I just could not manage it. But, the power of her movement was like the power of my speaking voice, and somehow she was able to bridge the two for me. She got me to finally "speak" through dance in an emotive way, which I had not been able to do before. She knew I had the technique for the rhythm and a feel for the voice, and somehow she got me to connect the two. I am extremely grateful to her for that. My passion for dance turned into a love for choreography as a result.

My parents often told me that there is always someone worse off than yourself. And, if you have a brain that can think, communicate, differentiate, and evaluate, and you have two arms, hands, and legs, you can always live and survive—especially if you have a good education. Additionally, you can always help others with fewer advantages. I really could not have asked for two more supportive and thoughtful parents. For me, as an autistic child growing up, it made all the difference.

CHAPTER 13

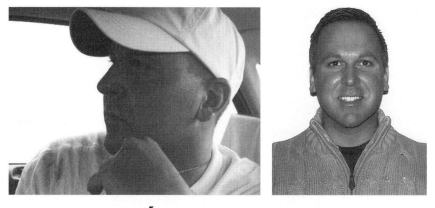

SEÁN JACKSON

Successful Real-Estate Executive

SEÁN JACKSON, BIS

Age: 33
Resides in: Owensboro, KY
Occupation: Executive for a real-estate investment firm
Marital status: Single

FROM TEMPLE:

Seán learned how to sell at an early age. He sold more chocolate rabbits than any other kid in his school. Learning this skill helped Seán become more outgoing and used to dealing with people. He admits he still struggles somewhat with personal relationships and feelings of isolation and that he had a hard time getting the answers he needed regarding his troubles. Over the years, he repeatedly reached out for help but had difficulty arriving at a diagnosis that fit. He doesn't keep in touch with much of his family; instead, Seán's friends have always provided him with the "family" he needed. He has a positive outlook and keeps developing his own philosophy of life by reading books and traveling to other countries to learn about other cultures. The most significant decision of Seán's life was to go to college when he had absolutely no money. Fortunately, he was able to wipe out his debt by serving in the military. Today, Seán works for a successful private investment firm that buys real estate.

SEÁN'S INTRODUCTION

I am currently an executive for a company I created in 2006, because working for someone else does not make sense for me. My company is a private investment firm that specializes in the acquisition of real estate. Which is to say, I facilitate the purchase of middle-income single-family units to be remodeled and rented out to generate cash flow and equity appreciation.

There are several aspects to my job: investor relations; asset allocation; locating, inspecting, and purchasing suitable properties; rehabilitation and remodeling; and property management. Each aspect has its appeal, but the common underlying thread is a schema for making money that allows me to enjoy my creativity without answering to a supervisor. The acquisition of real estate is conducted by identifying purchase capital (cash), attaining several months' worth of reserve funds (such as cash, silver, or gold), generating cash flow from existing properties, and—when possible—leveraging the power of financial institutions.

Locating, inspecting, and purchasing property is not difficult if you partner with a reputable real-estate company that can streamline the process, particularly when property management is included. I look for distressed properties that fall within an established price range. Once a specific home is identified, I put a contract on it and inspect it. After a while, you learn what to look for, but it is always good to hire an unbiased home inspector. It is imperative to stick to the business plan and never get in over your head. After the inspection, an acceptable appraisal, and closing, it's time for the real work to begin...renovation!

For me, remodeling a house is like playing with an adult set of Legos. It's a puzzle. I have a certain standard that each house must meet before being placed into service, yet each one is unique. This, in combination with keeping a close eye on profit margins, creates inherent problems within a specific situation. I conduct a thorough assessment, which I document and color code on a spreadsheet. As I am highly visual, this allows me to move blocks about as timelines flow and projects are finished. Houses are like people, and it takes time to get to know them well. Going from room to room to discover a home's personality is just as important as managing costs. If you take care of a house, then it will take care of you—possibly for the rest of your life.

EARLY YEARS

I have no siblings, or at least none that know of me. I do have two half-sisters from my father's first marriage. However, he lost contact with them after returning to Owensboro. It is a little strange knowing you have two sisters who are completely unaware of your existence, but this is actually typical for my family. My father's side views me as the "black sheep" of the family. I think they believe I'm white trash like my mother's side. My mother's relatives think I am arrogant and controlling. So, I basically don't talk to anyone outside of my immediate family. As a result, I have always considered my friends to be my family. This has been the case from the beginning.

I was raised in a subdivision called Carriage Park, which had a lot of kids. These were the kids I spent most of my time with before middle school. They were my "brothers and sisters," and their families were like aunts, uncles, and grandparents to me. My subdivision, however, was thought of as being on the "wrong side of the field." Across a large field directly in front of my house was another subdivision, ironically called Thoroughbred Acres, where the "middle class" families lived. There was a difference between the neighborhoods for sure, but I couldn't describe what I knew as a kid until much later. Families in Carriage Park were blue collar, whereas families in Thoroughbred Acres were largely white collar. I didn't really come to know the kids from Thoroughbred Acres until I went to middle school. I suppose I had always known them, but where one lived just wasn't important in elementary school. You had friends at home, who were also at school, and then you had friends who were only at school. In middle school, the social relationships between everyone seemed to change. Groups were formed. Whom you spent your free time with was now of paramount importance, because it said something about you. I can't say I was oblivious to popularity. I do have eyes and ears, and it's a little hard not to notice. What mattered to me, what I saw clearly, was that the kids who came from stable homes, dressed well, and did great in school were largely from Thoroughbred Acres.

I Was Attracted to Students from Stable Homes

I began gravitating toward these students. There was a distinct difference between my home friends and my school friends—a distinction that became more prevalent as we got older. As it turns out (which I'm sure will come as no surprise), the kids from both neighborhoods perpetuated their parents' social status, except for me. I crossed over.

My Parents

I had blonde hair, like Sabrina-the-Teenage-Witch blonde. My father had black hair and a full, dark beard. So when friends of his teased him about how I looked nothing like him, he said, "He's got his mamma's looks and his daddy's brains!" He didn't know just how true that statement was. I'm about 100% certain that my father was also an Aspie. My mother used to tell me, "There's the right way, the wrong way, and Dave's way. We always had to do it Dave's way." My dad, Dave, was quite rigid in his thinking. This was one of the many things I picked up on at an early age, and I realized that it cost him dearly. The best example was that he had been married three times and divorced just as many.

My mother tried her best, but the descriptor that repeatedly comes to mind with regard to her parenting style is "permissive." Which is to say she tried, but she really never knew what was going on in my life because she was too busy. This led to custody being switched over to my father when I was 13.

My father's parenting style, on the other hand, was authoritative. He was a good man and a good parent—not that my mother was a bad parent. He just did a better job of raising a son. I believe it was because I was so much like him. I doubt he thought I was any more different than he was. Apparently, my father was teased unmercifully in the navy because he was 5 foot 7 inches and weighed only 125 pounds. He was noticeably "different."

I Was Teased in Elementary School

I often came home from elementary school crying. My father asked me what was wrong, but I couldn't explain it to him. All the teasing was a blur. I do remember coming home one afternoon, and I said, "I hate all three of my names!" Both of us have the first name, "Cary," so he understood that one. He said, "What's wrong with 'Jackson'?" I said, "They call me Michael." As you can imagine, in the early 1980s, Michael Jackson was very popular. He asked me what was wrong with 'Seán,' and I said, "They call me 'Seen the Green Bean'!" My father handled situations like this well.

My teachers all said, "Seán wears his feelings on his sleeve." I couldn't understand why the other kids treated me differently. I mean...I wasn't a complete social misfit. I did have a couple of friends here and there at school, but they were more acquaintances than friends. I had a hard time starting and maintaining friendships. Today, I still have difficulty maintaining friendships that go beyond superficiality.

Jealous Students Spread Cruel Rumors about Me

When I was in the 8th grade, a kid who was jealous of my meteoric rise in popularity started a rumor about me. In my yearbook is written: "Sorry about the rumors, Brent paid me." The rumor was that I was gay, which is absurd, but in small-town America in the 1980s and 90s, if you were different, then you were considered gay, period. That rumor followed me all the way through high school and into college. At my high-school graduation, in the midst of thousands of people, the two guys sitting behind me made antagonizing gay comments. It took everything I had not to stand up, fold the metal chair I was sitting in, and bash it onto their heads. So, that is what I think of when I remember my high-school graduation, instead of the accomplishment of 12+ years of education.

We Were Practical People

I was baptized in proper catholic fashion as an infant. I am told we went to church when my parents were still together, but I don't have any recollection of it. My parents divorced when I was 4, and my mother and I began attending a Baptist church. I was made fun of for not knowing the stories of the Bible. I refused to go back when I was about 7 years old. Religion did not play a significant role in my family. We were very practical people. When you are poor, there is a certain moral flexibility built inherently into one's character. Which is not to say I was a heathen. I was taught responsibility at an early age. My father constantly pushed me to do things properly, presumably the way he was taught. He came from a solid, middle-class, entrepreneurial family and joined the navy. My mother largely raised herself within her large, segmented Roman Catholic family.

I Learned to Interact Socially by Watching TV

To be perfectly honest, I learned how to interact socially and ethically from watching television more so than from my family members. I watched "The Cosby Show," "Growing Pains," "The Facts of Life," "Who's the Boss?", "Star Trek: The Next Generation," and cartoons like "The Smurfs," "Transformers," "Inspector Gadget," "GI Joe," and reruns of "Donna Reed," "The Patty Duke Show," and "Mr Ed." These were my Ten Commandments, my Noble Eightfold Path. I learned vicariously. Although life rarely plays out like a sitcom, watching various morality plays over and over again seemed to effectively drive home the point…sometimes a little too well. I remember my dad being concerned because I wanted the "Decepticons" to win on "Transformers." He asked why, and I said, "Because it's boring when you know what's going to happen each time. I'd just like for them to win once, so I could see something different." This is the earliest I recall being a contrarian. It was rare, however, for my parents to correct me for a moral violation, mostly because I kept to myself, but also because I thought about consequences a great deal.

Playing the Nintendo was the first time I remember thinking, *Whoa, I need to get a grip before I hurt myself or damage something,* because I had meltdowns over not playing well. One game in particular got me seriously worked up, and I hurled things across the room. In general, I was careful not to destroy my toys, and, as a result, I had them for a very long time—unlike those of my neighborhood friends.

My Innate Moral Compass

I have always had an innate moral compass. I prefer to tell the truth. I never liked getting in trouble, disappointing others, or pain—physical or emotional. As a result, I was a good student and, according to my parents, not a difficult child. I was the moral conscience among my friends, which was great when we were little, but it became off-putting in high school.

I wasn't particularly straight laced. How could you be, growing up in Carriage Park? But, I had a certain intuition for doing what I wanted and avoiding trouble, which is to say I was masterful at exploiting specifics and effectively bending the rules. Plus, I already had experience with sex, smoking, and alcohol long before my high-school friends did because I tended to hang out with the older guys in our neighborhood. In all honesty, when friends in high school wanted to do the normal partying, I wasn't all that interested. I wanted the social interaction but not the risk of doing things I just wasn't into, like drinking. Unfortunately, more often than not, that immediately makes you different. Different is suspect, and suspect will get you excluded from the group. So it was always a difficult line to walk.

As an adult, spiritually, I find Buddhism to be the most comfortable fit for me where morality is concerned; however, one can never escape one's upbringing, and the religion of Catholicism is still a comforting practice too.

SCHOOL YEARS

I Experienced Difficulties but Excelled at Certain Things

I have always placed a premium on learning. Education, both formal and informal, sits at the top of my value set, just above loyalty.

I think I realized I was different from others for the first time when I made a detailed tree topper that looked exactly like King Friday from "Mr Roger's Neighborhood" in the 3rd grade. Then, for the next Christmas, I made a highly detailed church out of Legos— the plain ones, not a specialty set. That same year, I was the top seller of chocolate Easter rabbits in elementary school. This was also the year I won a state conservation poster contest (4th grade was a big year for me). Academically, I received my first poor grade, and I really did think my dad was going to kill me. I made a "D" in math class because of the timed multiplication and division tests. That was also the first time I refused to do schoolwork. The teacher assigned weekly glossary work, and I had a hard time remembering what to copy. (I later had difficulty with the same task in the 9th grade.) I had to flip back and forth rapidly between the glossary and the front of the book because my capacity for short-term memory was quite low.

While everyone else was reading *The Boxcar Children* books, I was not reading anything at all. In fact, I avoided reading beyond what I had to for schoolwork, and even then I had a hard time with it. The first book I read from cover to cover, aside from the *Berenstein Bears* books and *Dr Seuss*, was *The Firm* in 9th grade. I was so pleased with myself, I immediately read *Jurassic Park*.

I Transposed Letters, and a Graphing Calculator Helped

I often transposed letters and numbers. I used a graphing calculator to do math, so I could see the numbers being entered and go back and check the input, as well as the output, if needed. I also did weird things with letters, groups of letters, and whole words—and I still do.

In elementary school, I was never in the gifted and talented program, I never made the honor rolls, and I never understood why. Others evidently couldn't see my cleverness, but this wasn't the only thing I couldn't comprehend. The most difficult thing about this period of schooling was the vicious cycle of being alone, and then being thought "weird" for being alone, which made me just want to be alone. I was comfortable being by myself. I enjoyed the company of others, and I had "friends," but I didn't fit in—particularly with the kids I wanted to be with. The disparity between my neighborhood friends at home and my "friends" at school progressively grew. My friends at school came from stable families who were solidly middle class, which translated into security and comfort. I always felt like I was looking in from the outside.

I Memorized Everyone's Names and Faces from the Yearbook

My middle-school experience was atypical for an Aspie. Often, it can be the hardest time, but I found it to be the best. I studied the yearbook and memorized everyone's names and faces. I then called people by name, acting like I knew them—which, believe it or not, actually worked. Occasionally, I got the *How do you know me?* look or the *Why are you talking to me?* stare of disdain, but, usually, people just said "Hi" back.

I took band in middle school because it was an alternative to gym—all but one semester of it. I didn't like gym because certain kids tried to start fights in the locker room, which was a confined space lined with perforated metal lockers set just 3 feet apart and lacking in adult supervision. The rumor about me being gay drew unwanted attention to me, as you might imagine. I had started playing soccer, however, and the other guys on the team were supportive during gym class.

Band class was the place to be in middle school, unlike high school. It was like a daily end-of-school party. All the most popular kids were in band, which included most of my friends at the time. I never was any good at playing the clarinet, but I did learn to sight-read music. I have come to find that just being exposed to an experience, such as music, allows me to relate that experience to other aspects of my life. It gives me additional areas of common ground to share with other people. My inability to form strong relationships tends to center around a lack of recognizing appropriate reciprocation, as opposed to a lack of common interests. The friends I have kept over time are compassionate and overlook (or admire) my many idiosyncrasies.

Middle school changed everything for me. Certain teachers took notice of my abilities in English and math. English was the easiest subject for me, because writing allowed me to collect my thoughts, break through "the fog," arrange the pieces, and express them in a succinct manner—sometimes even playfully through repetition, floating opposites, and clinching with the one that's not like the others. Words have always made sense to me.

Rejected by a Best Friend

Science was my favorite subject, and I made a good friend who, as it turned out, lived just on the other side of the field from me. Trent and I became close friends—true friends—*best friends* for 3 years. We were practically inseparable. We built high-intensity magnifiers ("lasers") to burn things with, ran electronics to spy on his sister, and rode bikes all over. Then, after the rumor Brent started about me being gay, Trent disappeared. I mean he *vanished*. It was the second most hurtful thing I have ever gone through in my life. I think what made it worse was that he acted as if we hadn't been friends at all. We simply became acquaintances after that. Once, when we were juniors in high school, I asked why he stopped hanging around me and why he disappeared. Trent looked away and said he didn't know what I was talking about. He looked visibly uncomfortable, like he'd been caught with his hand in the biscuit tin.

I Was Totally Stressed Out in High School

By my junior year, I was completely stressed out! I went to our school guidance counselor and asked her if she could test me for attention-deficit disorder. I knew something wasn't right: My brain was spinning, I was overly sensitive to noise (specifically conversations in class), and I had great difficulty articulating my thoughts. She sent me on my way and told me I couldn't possibly have anything wrong with me because I was in the honors program.

Senior year was worse, because I felt socially isolated, as I did in elementary school. I was also worried about my dad's health and how I would pay for college. I just wanted a tall, tall cliff with beautiful scenery and a hard surface below. I actually remember verbalizing this, but no one ever took me seriously. I graduated from high school with honors, which is odd because I was always the dumbest kid in the smartest classes.

I went away to college at the University of Louisville, and I did everything backward. I took just enough general-education courses to get into both the psychology and sociology departments. I concentrated on those subjects almost exclusively with a double major.

Other People's Perception of Reality Was Different

Around this time, I began to realize that other people's perception of reality was different than mine. I noticed things in lectures that others didn't. I made connections between theories and concepts, often across disciplines. This was helpful when I did research in the sociology department.

In the end, owing to many unforeseen circumstances and a distinct lack of resources, it took me years to complete my bachelor's degree. My dad died in 1999, and for a while now I have been taking care of my grandmother, who is dealing with Alzheimer disease. After I left the University of Louisville, I also attended Central Texas College, Mary-Hardin Baylor (while I was in the army), and, finally, Western Kentucky University.

While taking a business course at Central Texas College, I was forced to rewrite a paper because the instructor said it was too detailed and "over his head." He said that because the paper didn't sound the way I speak in person, I couldn't possibly have written it—even though I had. I asked him how he could know my writing potential, as it was the first thing I had ever written for him. Then I went on to state the obvious, that people often don't write the same as they speak. One is formal, and the other is rather informal. Additionally, the extra time required to write one's thoughts down allows a person to fix many if not all errors. I was furious, but he did give me an "A" after I rewrote the paper to make it "sound the way I speak."

I took the Myers-Briggs Type Indicator at a leadership conference, which showed me to be "INTP" (Introversion, Intuition, Thinking, Perceiving). The conference participants moved about the room, grouped according to the results, and it was clear that I had consistently different results from everyone else, except for maybe one person—but it was *never the same* one person. I started to get depressed about being different.

I Cannot Remember Sequences

While taking an astronomy exam at Western Kentucky University, I became frustrated because I continually have issues with conceptualizing things in their proper order (for example, knowing all three of Newton's Laws of Motion but not remembering their proper sequence). I left that exam in such a strop; I called the psychology department and asked to be tested for dyslexia. After the test, I was told the results were marginal and I would, therefore, not be considered dyslexic. I was indignant. I knew the diagnosis fit. I also knew that it didn't account for everything going on with me; however, the umbrella term "dyslexia" covered a great deal. I started to search for better answers.

Employment and Learning Entrepreneurship

The first "work" I did was in sales. I sold chocolate rabbits for school. In fact, I sold the most chocolate rabbits of anyone in the entire school. Then again, I sold all sorts of things in those days: mechanical birds, Styrofoam airplanes, vibrating pillows, water-filled insoles for shoes, and panty roses—yes, panties rolled up on a stem to resemble roses for Valentine's Day. My family sold seemingly anything and everything during the "off season" at kiosks located at various malls. The "off season" was the time of year when my mother's swimming-pool business was closed. She taught me about entrepreneurship, which is likely why I had the confidence to start my own business.

Selling Things as a Child Helped Me Meet People

Selling everything under the sun was easy as a cute little kid. Doing so forced me to become more outgoing, or at least to get comfortable being around other people and talking to them. It didn't help me understand people beyond a certain superficiality. But, it did open the door for the "bull by the horns" way I went about meeting people in middle school, which, again, didn't help me maintain relationships. I have a theory that sales got me used to being around people, and just being around people allowed me to pick up certain understandings. It's akin to the way I learned of opportunities that others didn't, just by virtue of being in honors classes.

I Was Successful at Work but Felt Like the Help

One summer, I volunteered to clean the grounds at a private swim and tennis club to demonstrate my work ethic. The next year, I became a lifeguard at 15. During summers at the club, I worked 7 days a week, from 7 AM until 4 or 8 PM, cleaning the pool early in the morning, teaching swim lessons, and then lifeguarding all day with sporadic breaks. I can't say I didn't enjoy it, because I did, but I always felt like "the help."

I worked at the club for four summers and at the YMCA during the winters. The last summer, I had to literally beg for my job at the club. I was pleading with the swim coach and de facto assistant manager. I remember telling her that I didn't know what I had done wrong. I later discovered it was partially due to the rumor about me and largely due to internal politics. I hadn't done anything wrong except naively believe that hard work alone would get you ahead. The summer after that, I left the club to work at the Boys & Girls Club as their swim team coach. I doubled the size of the team by bringing with me all the home-schooled kids I knew from the YMCA and various friends from high school, many of whom were also on my local U.S. swimming team. It caused quite a stir in our aquatics community.

My favorite job by far is working for myself. When you own your own company, you make your own rules. No longer are you hemmed in by others—you are only limited by your resources. Additional jobs I enjoyed were performing research, marshalling aircraft, and managing an office.

Fun Jobs I Had

For a time, I served as a research assistant to a couple of professors at the University of Louisville—I loved reading academic journals, and the work was interesting. I felt appreciated, and working as a research assistant helped me both academically and socially. I spent a great deal of time collaborating with graduate teaching assistants, in addition to my professors.

To support myself during college, I worked as an aircraft marshaller for a shipping company, which was just plain fun. Randy Pausch said to "never underestimate the importance of having fun," and standing out on a sea of concrete, with the smell of jet fuel washing by and a 747 bearing down on you, hanging on every wave of your hand, was by far one of the coolest jobs I've ever had. It was definitely fun. Additionally, I learned firsthand about union versus corporate interests. I learned I didn't want to be a part of either.

Objective-Oriented Work Is Best

I also spent some time with the U.S. Army. Upon my final redeployment, in the last few months of my enlistment as a biological weapons specialist, I was retasked as an office manager for the 13th Chemical Company. It was rewarding work, knowing that I was doing something so important for the rest of the unit. The thing I liked most, though, was being left alone to complete my assigned tasks. It was objective-oriented work, where I wasn't micromanaged. The commander expected results. I was given a certain amount of respect and a little bit of slack, because I was the one who could do people "favors" (which, in the army, where everyone who outranks you is your "boss," is really nice).

Awful Banking and Office Jobs

My worst job was working as an office manager for a private clinical practice. The training was cursory and probably would have been fine for a neurotypical person, but I got hung up on minor details that precluded me from executing some of my responsibilities. I asked for clarification, but I wasn't given the information in a helpful manner. Therefore, my employer and I were both frustrated. My employer's husband, who was gracious enough to get me the job in the first place, was very good about it after the fact. He talked to me one afternoon and wanted to make it clear that he valued the work I did for him in spite of what happened with his wife. It's no wonder he was one of my favorite professors. Lord knows I wasn't an easy student.

Another least-favorite job was being an account executive for a subprime mortgage lender. The number of cold calls we had to make was excruciating. The micromanagement was unbearable. Getting blamed for my supervisor's errors was unacceptable. But, hey, I did get to see the Rolling Stones and Alice Cooper on the company's dime, so it wasn't all bad.

For a time, I was a general manager for a clothing store. This turned out to be a situation where I had unrealistic expectations placed upon me. I did learn how to manage people, though. I have always been a natural leader. I'm sure it has something to do with everything always having to be done my way and my inability to understand others' ways of doing things. But, this was something altogether different. It was a trial by fire, but after 2 years, I had worked out a system that allowed me to run my store comfortably, while other general managers were tearing their hair out.

I worked as a loan processor for a major bank, where again I had unrealistic expectations foisted upon me. When you are told in an interview that you will only be given 20 loans to manage—25 maximum—but then are given 48, there's a breakdown somewhere in the supervisory chain. When you are at your performance review and you question the only low marks you're given, and you're told, "I didn't train you on those, but I have to mark you down anyway," then, again, there's a problem.

I also worked as a fire fighter, but I never really fit in as one of the guys. They could tell I was different, and, again, different isn't good. I was teased because I was slower than the others. I think my motor skills, perfectionism, and lack of "good 'ole boy" social skills were problematic. I was proficient but not accepted. An example of how autism affected my job directly can be illustrated through my difficulties with hearing. I have more trouble than most discerning auditory detail, and I couldn't understand the garbled transmissions on the old pager devices. The day I received a pager with a repeater button was a good day. Being able to hit the repeater to hear what was being said helped immensely.

Auditory Processing Problems

My auditory detail problem is most evident in music. This was an issue I noticed as a kid around the 4th or 5th grade. I didn't understand at first—I just thought it was strange that I couldn't make out the words to songs that everyone else understood so clearly. When it comes to music, I listen to a song first for the music. Then, later, after many months and literally hundreds of plays, the words begin to come into focus. I still have to look at liner notes sometimes, though, because the music makes the words fuzzy. It's like trying to listen to one person in a crowded room of talking people. I encountered this problem in classrooms all throughout my school experience.

Relationships and Getting a Diagnosis

I talked with a doctor at the Veterans' Affairs (VA) medical center, who said that since I have a good understanding of Asperger's syndrome, I should be able to make changes accordingly. I find this to be faulty reasoning. Knowing you *want* to get from point A to point B doesn't necessarily help you *get* there.

Sometimes I feel like it's not worth being around other people if it's going to require so much effort. I went back to the VA for a doctor's appointment not long ago and made a comment to the nurse that the doctor seemed to be the only person in the world who cared about my well-being. While I do, in fact, have many people who care about me in their own ways, sometimes I do feel as though no one cares, and, moreover, that no one would notice if I were gone. I can't say I'm depressed about it—it's just an honest assessment of how I feel about my relationships with other people.

It's Hard to Decipher Conversation

I find myself screening calls because I often do not have the energy to decipher a conversation or say the right thing. Additionally, I still have a phone that only makes calls—I do not do texting or anything else on a phone. It's too much for me. I prefer doing things face to face. This extends to business but is especially true for personal relationships. People lie. To be more specific, people aren't always completely truthful, which is easier to see on their faces than it is to hear in their voices. All of my long-time friends are aware that sometimes I misinterpret things when talking over the phone, and they are forgiving when miscommunications arise. Because of this, I feel more comfortable talking to them on the phone than I would an acquaintance that might not give me the benefit of the doubt. Fortunately, most business I conduct takes place in person.

It's Difficult to Gauge Where a Relationship Stands

I do have difficulty with realizing that not everyone is my friend. So for me, it can be difficult to gauge where a relationship stands. Be it an acquaintance or a family, business, or romantic relationship, my aptitude for distinguishing whether or not someone is being sincere, civil, or smarmy is the direct result of a vicarious education. Since I was raised on television and movies, I sincerely believe that watching these shows is the reason I was able to function at the social level I did. I lived in front of the television. When I stayed with my mother, if I wasn't at a friend's house, I could be found in my room, watching TV. I also spent a good deal of my childhood at my dad's apartment, stationed in front of the television with a giant box of Legos.

I Organized Memories by Music

Until my 20s, I seemed to organize memories according to music, which in turn made me think of relationships I had had at one time or another. It's difficult to explain. When I hit my 20s, music seemed to lose its cohesiveness. MTV stopped playing music, radio station formats changed so significantly that I stopped listening to them altogether, and CDs gave way to playlists and downloads. My relationships with women also seemed to be less consistent. Larger and larger gaps appeared between them, what I call "dry spells." There would be a long period of no dating, and then suddenly, as soon as I found myself dating a woman, several other opportunities presented themselves in quick succession. Dating is exciting for me at first, but it quickly fades once I realize the other person and I have significantly different goals in life.

Recognizing incompatible life aspirations, however, is not as difficult as seeing dissidence in intimacy. I believe I've made progress in dating, though. Now, if I find I don't feel loved, I begin looking for the door instead of remaining in an unhealthy relationship.

Understanding Relationships

Dave Chapelle says it best in the film "You've Got Mail": "I always take a relationship to the next level. If that works out, I take it to the next level after that, until I finally reach that level when it becomes absolutely necessary for me to leave."

I used to not be strong enough to recognize that I needed to leave a relationship and execute the steps necessary to do it. I used passive aggression to get the person I was dating to end it, which ensured I wouldn't go out with her again. Now I don't do that, because I am far better at recognizing an unhealthy relationship and I end things when it becomes apparent the relationship won't work out. Someone taught me a long time ago that you end relationships face to face—not via multimedia of any sort. It's just the right thing to do. In fact, it's the least you can do for someone else and for yourself. It's about respecting the person you have chosen to date and providing closure for both of you, which requires character. There's just something dishonest about not ending a relationship face to face.

When it comes to beginning romantic relationships, I tend to go all in. There is no halfway. If you go in halfway, you get hurt. I've been told I can be intense, not because I come on strong, but because I want to be with someone who challenges me—someone I respect. I'm clear about what I need, which is something I've come to notice a lot of people older than me still don't know.

Realizing a relationship is over usually isn't problematic. There's a moment, a feeling, a look, when you know. At that point, I find it's best to just walk away. I have a firm policy that once I've left a relationship, I don't come back, because it never works out. And of course, there's a difference between an argument, a misunderstanding, a fight, and the obvious end of a relationship.

I Saw Too Many Bad Marriages, So I Avoided Getting Married

I've always said I wanted to be married, but the closer I come to it, the more I want to run screaming in the opposite direction. From a rational standpoint, I've seen far too many marriages that didn't work out, and not many at all that did. Of the marriages I have seen that appear to be good, very few seem to be worth the sacrifices both people have to make. A spouse should enrich your life and allow both of you to grow, but more often than not, I see the exact opposite. I'm not willing to make those types of sacrifices. It's tantamount to compromising my personal integrity.

I was talking with financial speaker and writer Diane Kennedy recently, and we agree that people say opposites attract, but in reality, like attracts like. The question is whether or not your strengths and weaknesses overlap and compliment. She said, "Two halves don't make a whole; two wholes make a whole."

Social Interaction Is a Rubik's Cube

I view social interaction as a Rubik's cube. My friends have always teased me about this. They have historically come to me for solid advice because I'm brutally honest and exceedingly analytical, but when it comes to my own relationships, there should be large yellow cones all around me. My emotions completely screw things up. It has taken years for me to work things out emotionally, and I'm still unsure. It makes me seriously concerned about my future marriage prospects because I do see the advantages of being married if it's to the right woman. I suppose my take on relationships is to have fun and take chances, but still be mindful.

I've learned that once you reach the age where having sex is expected, not having sex can make a relationship just as complicated as having it. So, again, have fun, take chances, but be careful. Which brings about an interesting point—how experience of all types is gained through doing. There is only so much you can learn vicariously. Thinking only gets you so far. There comes a point where you have to *do*, because there are myriad situations where you *think* you know how you might react, but you never *know* until you are in the situation yourself.

When it comes to opportunities, seize them! (Or *Carpe carp*—seize the fish!) I make it a point to try to recognize and take advantage of every opportunity that presents itself. To me, the importance of this approach in life is immeasurable.

ON AUTISM

Diagnosis Connected the Dots

Since learning I have Asperger's syndrome, much of my life has been brought into focus. Many events that seemed like disparate dots on a page now connect to form a coherent picture. I have always felt different from seemingly everyone else. While I was accepted among my friends in the neighborhood, it was clear to them that I was different. I know it sounds arrogant to say I was smarter, but that was the case. The same perceived difference was true for my friends at school, but not because of giftedness. Rather, it resulted from social awkwardness. This has been a running theme for every group in which I have been a part, including my fraternity, the fire department, the army, and every job I've ever had. I am generally more comfortable around women, because they are less openly

Chapter 13: Seán Jackson

hostile to someone who is perceived as being different. They tend to be more accepting.

I remember occasions when I have been wronged for quite some time, or even points of injustice in which I am only tangentially involved. Often, I think about the experience as if it has just occurred. This can result in a sense of near paranoia, unless rationalized. Think of it as being hit with a stick each time you encounter a certain person. After only a few times, you feel anxious in the mere presence of the aggressor. It is a conditioned response; however, the response is stronger in animals that have a longer memory.

Similarly, I often communicate in ideas or symbols. Many times, I cite cultural references, events, and people to convey a broader connotation or a deeper meaning. My friends say I speak my own language. I suppose this is why, at times, I will leave out seemingly important details during conversations. I assume the information was inferred.

I Hate Small Changes in Routine

Small changes in routine can disrupt my entire day. Also, transitions are extremely difficult for me at times. Even today, I can have significant trouble with this. With regard to inflexibility, I have preconceived ideas of how things are going to work in any given situation, and when they don't meet my expectations, I can become quiet and snappish. In all honesty, I am very easygoing when I am comfortable with my environment. It's when I get anxious or tired that I become more rigid in my thinking. An early example of this is when I was little, and my dad sold Christmas trees. I was about 6 years old. It was cold and uncomfortable in the little shack I had to hang out in while he worked, but there was a small television (of course). Each afternoon, my dad picked me up from school and took me to work with him. I was excited to watch my favorite cartoons, "Inspector Gadget" and "Voltron." Often, however, we arrived after "Inspector Gadget" had begun, which I did not like. Then, to add insult to injury, "Voltron" had a different format than I was expecting. I became snappish for the rest of the evening, and my dad never understood why. I couldn't have explained it then, but looking back, it all makes perfect sense now.

In my search to ascertain why I am different, I took a Buddhist Religious Traditions class and went to Indiana University to see the Dalai Lama speak when I was 30. Spiritually, I felt comfortable in a way I had never experienced before. A year later, I went on a pilgrimage to the Vatican, where I came face to face with the pope. He walked right up to me during the Christmas mass, stood in front of me, and gave a blessing. It was surreal.

I Learned Coping Mechanisms to Appear Normal

I went to Canterbury, England—one of my favorite places—the next Christmas. I met a lovely psychologist named Anne, who told me I seemed to have innately picked up the coping mechanisms she normally teaches to her dyslexic clients. She said if I were employing these strategies during testing, then it would be no surprise at all for me to appear "normal." This might explain why no one had ever been able to assign an accurate diagnosis for my condition when I was in college. While in England, I met a nice couple from the Netherlands, one of whom was dyslexic. I met even more dyslexic individuals in London. Evidently, dyslexia is identified earlier and more often in the United Kingdom than in the states.

Listening to Randy Pausch's famous "Last Lecture" prompted me to live more in the present. I decided to take an integrative yoga therapeutics course for anxiety, insomnia, and posttraumatic stress disorder, taught by a man named Bo Forbes. This program took place at Kripalu Yoga Center, located in the Berkshires of Western Massachusetts. The program happened to coincide with a master's guitar class that Steve Vai was teaching. Bo provided insights to my thinking and how it relates to the body. Similarly, Steve Vai echoed several of Bo's teachings. Both of them articulated many of the same philosophies as the Dalai Lama, but in more practical detail. We spent hours discussing how beliefs and values are incorporated into our daily routines. The entire week challenged me to view the world differently. Plus, the yoga was fun, the food was fresh, the people were pleasant, and autumn in the Berkshires is amazing. Hanging out with a rock legend was pretty cool, too.

I Saw Videos of People Like Me and Read Books about Autism

The first time I recall hearing about Asperger's syndrome in anything other than a tangential way was when I watched the ESPN program "E:60," with Aspie surfer Clay Marzo. I related to some of what he said, but what struck me the most was how "normal" he was. It never occurred to me that I was like him, however, until several months later when I watched the interview again. Something clicked when Clay talked about his cup overflowing. He articulated feelings that I had been trying to describe to others for years. Then I watched several people on YouTube, including musician Maja Toudal, who stated my thoughts and feelings over and over again, often using the same phrasing. It was truly bizarre. I felt I had finally found my tribe!

Next, I bought Tony Attwood's book *Asperger's Syndrome*, which read like a personal biography. What I had felt before was now confirmed. All the pieces fit. Since I have a degree in behavioral science, I have quite a few friends who are counselors. I consulted with a friend about the possibility, and we agreed on the diagnosis on the basis of the preponderance of evidence.

Psychologists Wondered Why I Wanted a Diagnosis

I worked the VA system, speaking to several different clinicians. None of them denied that I have Asperger's syndrome, but they could not wrap their heads around why I would want the label if I seem to be doing so well. But just how well am I doing? I have mostly superficial relationships. I'm not married. I don't have kids. I can't work for someone else longer than 2 or 3 years without having to take a break, which just destroys any chance at a career wherein one climbs the corporate ladder. I have next to no family. It took 13 years for me to obtain a bachelor's degree. And the list goes on. If I hadn't wasted so much time trying to compensate for deficiencies, there is no telling where I could be by now. I'll never know just how much my social inequities have limited my ability to capitalize on opportunities that have come my way.

MENTORS

My Father Was a Mentor

As with many gifted people, it is difficult to find people who "get it" and who "get me," especially within a tight geographic location. Fortunately, television and books broaden one's options when it comes to mentors. While you may not be able to give back to them, they often have a significant impact.

First and foremost, my greatest mentor was my father. He not only showed me how to live by demonstration, but he took the time to explain "why" in nearly every situation. We watched television together, and he asked me questions and pointed out why TV characters should or shouldn't do the things they do.

Any time I was to do something, I was also told *why* it was to be done. This was clearly frustrating for him at times, because when he told me to do something, for instance, "Go get my cigarettes off the headboard," I often came back with questions, such as, "I didn't see them. Are you sure they're in the bedroom?" Meanwhile, the cigarettes were right on the nightstand in plain view. I remember having this sort of conversation with him often, and he turned puce at times because he didn't understand why I couldn't see them sitting out in the open. What he didn't realize was that he had told me to look elsewhere, so cigarettes on the nightstand simply did not compute.

I Learned from TV Personalities

There have been many TV personalities whom I've thought of as mentors. I used to spend hours watching Bob Ross paint his "happy little trees." It was extremely relaxing and taught me to self-calm. He also taught me patience, specifically the value of putting time into something. Steve Vai reinforced this idea. Bill Cosby showed me what a normally functioning family looked like. The impact of his show on my life cannot be understated. George Carlin stated thoughts I had been carrying around for years but had never heard anyone say openly. His honesty was refreshing. For someone like me who processes in patterns, it was amazing to hear him consistently express what I had been thinking. There was an instant connection.

> **Note from Temple Grandin:**
> *Today, many characters on TV exhibit really bad behavior and values. I, too, learned from TV characters that were good role models, such as the characters on "Star Trek." The shows I loved had good values. I am worried about what kids are learning today from the media.*

I had several teachers who did a great deal for me. Mrs Woolard recognized my talent for English in the 6th grade and placed me in her honors English class. This led to honors algebra with Mr Firkins, who spent a great deal of time helping me understand variables.

Mr Morton, our middle-school band teacher, taught me about music, but also about family. He and his wife had adopted several children, and that was unusual to me at the time. They were a concrete example of how family has more to do with behavior than genetics. I later found out that my own father was adopted. Mr Morton's son, Teddy, played soccer with me in high school and generously gave me soccer shoes when all I had were flats to play in.

Coach Camp taught me not only about soccer but also how to work *with* others as a cohesive unit. I showed up at practice one day and sat by the edge of the field in the 8th grade. Coach Camp walked over and asked if I wanted to play. That was it. He never gave up on me. Which is to say, I was behind the curve but improved rapidly. Everyone else had been playing for years. My previous experience playing soccer consisted of shooting out all the slats in the stockade fence around Perry Pound's backyard while passing the ball back and forth. Perry was like my older brother. He is the one who encouraged me to go to that practice. I learned a lot more than soccer from him, and I'll probably never fully understand how much he helped me.

A Teacher Instilled a Love of Words

Other teachers mentored me in high school. Mrs Nall, who taught advanced placement (AP) U.S. history, showed me that you could travel to Asia without knowing English, which made a huge impression on me when I was a kid. This later prompted me to visit The Great Wall when the opportunity to go to China presented itself. Mrs Riney taught AP English, and she gave me the best writing feedback I've ever had. She is in no small measure why I'm writing this now. There was one other teacher who was a mentor to me on many levels, Mrs Hart. She instilled within me a love for words that I had never known before her freshman English class. Beyond the many English lessons, she was a friend. She recognized certain qualities that led me to be the stage manager of our drama department for 3 years. We spent a lot of time working on plays together, which gave us time to talk. My dad's health was in decline as I progressed through high school, and I often stayed late to work on sets.

Guidance on my Philosophy of Life

I wouldn't know where to begin describing all the ways in which learning about Benjamin Franklin helped me. His grasp of religion, his practicality, and his tenacity were all an inspiration—especially to a small-town kid who felt quite isolated at times.

Author Robert Kiyosaki explained the difference between business and personal taxation and how to create a real-estate business that yields enough passive income so I would not have to be "employed" in the traditional sense. He showed me how to own the corporate ladder instead of climbing it.

The late author and speaker Randy Pausch showed me how to live life to its fullest and to do it now, because there may not be a tomorrow. He also offered very practical advice about morals, values, and achieving one's dreams. I can't think of him without also thinking of Temple. They both have inspiring philosophies on life.

Guitarist and songwriter Steve Vai was gracious enough to talk at length to me and others about his life, his writing process, and the music industry. He gave me a concrete understanding of how to be successful that I will never forget.

Sheryl Cooper, wife of rock-star Alice Cooper for over 35 years, gives me hope that there are women who will stand by their husbands no matter what and that marriage does mean something. Successful marriages are not something I have seen a great deal of in my life.

Recently, model and musician Maja Toudal has become a mentor of sorts. Aside from having a wonderful voice and the most endearing pronunciation of certain English words, Maja helped make the connection between Asperger's and myself by explaining things I had been trying to tell other people for decades. Her YouTube blogs on Asperger's syndrome have been invaluable, as have others in the Aspie community, such as Temple, Diane Kennedy, Rebecca Banks, Claire LaZebnik, and Kerry Cohen.

My Friend Katie Taught Me Morals and Ethics

I can't speak of mentors without mentioning my dear friend, Katherine Long Duvall. Katie is like the little sister I never had.

Over the past several years, we have spent hours discussing all kids of moral and ethical situations. I have often said that she has an uncommon sense of proper morality. While we don't always agree, our talks are enlightening without exception. Her compassion and understanding far exceed her years.

Last but not least, my realtor and property manager Rose Castlen, of Rose Realty, is the very definition of a fine Christian woman. She has known me since I was 5, when my father had rental property. Rose leads by example every day, in both her work and her private life. I am truly blessed to be counted as one of her friends.

OUTLOOK

Living Life for Today While Planning for Tomorrow

In my adult life, the events that changed my outlook on who I am and what I've become began with leaving Owensboro, Kentucky. The decision to go to college when I had absolutely no money was likely the most significant decision of my life. Choosing to travel would be next on the list. There is no better way to nullify egocentrism than to talk with other people in other cultures about how they live and what they think about where you live. It's an exchange of ideas that no book, movie, or lecture could ever compete with. The decision to use the army as a means to wipe out college debt and get my financial house in order was paramount. Concurrently, the effect of reading Robert Kiyosaki's *Rich Dad, Poor Dad* showed me an entirely as-yet-unknown perspective. All of these things, one building on the other, allowed me to be in a position to help my grandmother cope with Alzheimer disease, create a successful business, and follow my passions. I now choose to live life for today, while planning for tomorrow.

CHAPTER 14

STEWART FORGE

Partner and Creative Director of an Advertising Agency

STEWART FORGE

Age: 47

Resides in: Sunshine Coast, Queensland, Australia

Occupation: Partner and creative director of an advertising agency

Marital status: Married, with one child

FROM TEMPLE:

Stewart was a good student and a go-getter, and he has enjoyed a successful career in radio and advertising. However, he had difficulties when he moved into higher-level management jobs. Getting a diagnosis of Asperger's has helped bring understanding to his marriage. The diagnosis has enabled Stewart and his wife, Trish, to better understand his condition and make necessary adjustments. He concludes, "Our relationship has not fully recovered, but we're still trying. Compared with many people on the spectrum, I guess you could say I'm a success. From my perspective, it's a work in progress. I may never understand the neurotypical world completely, but I'm absolutely determined to keep trying."

STEWART'S INTRODUCTION

I'm not sure that I would characterize myself as an Aspie who "made it." More accurately, I am one who has "survived" in a world I wasn't cut out for. Determination might have something to do with that.

I have very few personal memories. I haven't worked out if that's an Asperger's characteristic or not. Perhaps it's got something to do with the fact that I don't "see pictures" in my head like many people do. (Some Aspies, like Temple Grandin, excel at this.) My skills lie with words—both verbal and written. So I'll tell you what I do remember, and what others have said took place, like the story of my mother and I battling over a broomstick.

I rode around the room on what, to everyone else, appeared to be a broomstick. To me, it was a magnificent white horse, carrying me to safety from the clutches of the savage Apache hordes from the cowboy movies my father loved. I was 2 or 3 years old. When I finished with my game, I dropped the broom and went off to do something else. "Stewart," my mother admonished, "Pick up that broom and put it back where you got it." Hands on my hips, I asserted, "No—not gonna."

Fifteen minutes later, after an escalating war of words, threats, and smacks, the broom still lay on the floor. My grandfather walked in and watched the battle ensue before intervening. "Mary, come here a moment." My harried mother came to him, fire in her eyes. "You might as well forget it," he counseled. "You could smack that child all day long, and he'll never pick up that broom. He is too damned determined. You'll never win. He'll die before he picks it up."

EARLY YEARS

I Grew Up in a Farming Family

The few memories I do have are of an idyllic childhood, growing up as the eldest son of a farming family in northwestern New South Wales in Australia. I was born in 1964, long before anyone in a small Australian country town was aware of something called

"Asperger's syndrome." According to my family, there were some early indications that I was a little different from other children. As a baby, I did not crawl. Instead, at 9 months of age, I stood up and walked. I first talked at 12 months and was speaking in sentences by the time I was 18 months old.

As I matured, my parents found that I had good physical coordination, but my balance was quite poor. My vocabulary expanded very quickly, and I was soon capable of having detailed conversations with adults. I was intensely curious as to how things worked, and my mother was often frustrated to find me disassembling the vacuum cleaner or radio or table lamp in an effort to discover how they worked. Once I understood what made them function and why, I was utterly disinterested in putting them back together again. The mystery had been solved.

My sister Fiona was born when I was 2. At the age of 5, I went to primary school (or elementary school, as Americans call it), and my father still delights in recounting my arrival at the school. Apparently, I informed him that the kindergarten class was full of little kids and that he had made an error—surely it would be a better idea to enroll me at the high school only a few blocks away.

I Was Naive and Gullible

My early years at school produced no notable problems. I made one or two friends. There was a tendency to want to control the other children playing with me. I had a higher level of naivety and gullibility than most kids my age, and there were a few instances where I refused to do what the teacher told me and left the classroom to walk home. But, according to my school reports, I performed very well academically. In fact, I was nicknamed "the little professor" by my teachers.

My father was a share-farmer and was often away working for weeks at a time on a remote property. At the age of 9, my parents decided to move to this remote location full time so we could spend more time together as a family. The principal of my school met with my mother and expressed her concern about this. The school had just performed IQ tests on all the students, and my results were "the highest she had ever seen in many years of testing." She was worried that the environment of a one-room schoolhouse (where children from 5 to 12 years of age were all taught by a single teacher) would be a waste of my potential. Nonetheless, off we moved to a 10,000-acre wheat farm, and I attended the tiny local school.

Academically, the new school wasn't too bad, as I finished my 4th-grade work by lunchtime and then did all the 5th- and 6th-grade assignments in the afternoon, effectively completing 3 years of schooling in one. But it was here that I became conscious of difficulties in fitting in with the other kids. It's my first memory of being "a square peg in a round hole." I had a good relationship with my two younger sisters but was much more comfortable in the company of adults than children.

I Had Difficulty Controlling Emotions

The older I got, the more difficulty I had with controlling my emotions. There were many outbursts when things didn't work out as I wanted them to or when I was forced to do something I didn't want to do. My mother cleverly controlled these situations by diverting my attention, distracting me, and channeling my rage into more productive areas. I struggled with authority figures, especially those who demanded blind obedience just for obedience's sake. "Respect your elders," I was told at school. I replied, "Just because you've managed to avoid death for longer than I have doesn't make you better or smarter than me, it just makes you older. I respect my *betters,* not my *elders.* " This went over well, as you might imagine.

I Was Given a Good Moral Template

My family were good country people. They always gave me support and encouragement. We were taught the difference between right and wrong, the meaning of personal responsibility, the importance of manners, the value of truth, and a belief in God. Looking back now, I believe this moral template had a lot to do with my capacity to integrate reasonably well with a society that I didn't quite fit into. In that respect, I think the most important of these factors was manners. Manners provided me with a framework for social etiquette, demanded that I interact with people, and came with a series of "scripts" to follow when forming polite conversation with those I didn't know.

My family purchased a farm at Gunnedah when I entered 6th grade, and it was there that I entered high school a year later. The early years of high school were difficult ones for me. While the breadth of curriculum provided more intellectual stimulation, the more complex social structures that teenagers create perplexed me. Being a farm boy, I was used to having lots of space (and no people) around me. Each day after school, I happily retreated to our 1,100-acre sanctuary. Controlling my emotional responses in a busy, complex world was becoming more difficult in the school environment, and it was a relief each day to be out of it. I got on well with many of my teachers but found the students to be largely shallow, self-interested, and stupid.

I Learned to Fit in Socially with Humor

Over time, I learned how to appear to fit in with peers. One of the most useful tools in achieving this was humor. With my quick brain and strong verbal skills, I taught myself how to be funny and became accepted through my capacity to mimic teachers, write and deliver funny poems, recall and act out scenes from TV shows, and make witty remarks. It became easy to deflect attention from my own inadequacies by highlighting those of someone else. In retrospect, I could be quite cruel at times.

Bullying was never a great problem for me. Being a farmer's son, I worked hard on the farm after school, and I was larger and stronger than most of the other students. However, relationships between males and females were a complete mystery to me. I had several female friends, but now I understand that I could not read the social cues that could have taken those relationships further.

Dislike of Authority Figures

I did have problems with authority figures. I consistently argued with my teachers, and in one case, I punched the sports teacher. These struggles usually resulted from one of three things: *(a)* an overdeveloped sense of social justice, which led me to fight in situations I perceived as being unfair to someone; *(b)* illogical or irrational behavior by others; and *(c)* demands for obedience for obedience's sake—in other words, a power trip. One example I recall of this was being asked to write an essay of 700 words on the causes of World War I. On handing in my work, the history teacher reprimanded me because my essay was only 300 words long. "Did I identify and explain all the reasons why the war came about?" I asked. "Well—yes," he acknowledged. "Were there any mistakes in the essay?" I demanded. "No," he admitted. "Then why do I need to pad it out with another 400 words?" I replied. "Because...because you have to!" was his frustrated response.

In general, I enjoyed subjects like history, agriculture, English, and French. I also enjoyed mathematics but found it frustrating when my teachers didn't explain concepts in sufficient detail. I joined the school debating team and won many competitions. I thoroughly enjoyed being part of the drama group and won several regional acting awards. Obviously, these areas appealed to my strong written and verbal skill set.

I Was a Good Public Speaker and Was Elected School Captain

In my senior years, I was elected senior prefect and then school captain. Looking back, this was evidence of my capacity for public speaking and the skills I was developing for manipulating a crowd. More public speaking followed, in the form of representing my school at conferences and functions and doing radio interviews. I was named Lion's Club "Youth of the Year" and the Australia Day Junior Citizen of the Year in 1982. I was learning that dealing with large groups was easy for me. I learned how to tune in to an audience's emotions and their need to "follow the herd." I could easily manipulate a crowd. Making a large group laugh, cry, or get angry was simple stuff. However, dealing with individuals was another thing entirely.

I graduated from high school with above average, but not stellar, exam results. Then came the important question—what to do for the rest of my life? I had no idea. I had acquired no work experience during my schooling, unless you counted editing the school magazine or writing an occasional article for the local newspaper. I had learned to work hard on my family's farm, driving tractors, fencing, spraying, and planting. While a career as a farmer was something my father would have liked to see me do, I was an asthmatic, and the dusty environment caused frequent asthma attacks.

When asked what my ambition was, I usually answered, "To do nothing." This wasn't strictly true—it was more a case of being in a position where I didn't *have* to do anything I didn't want to. I didn't want to be controlled. I guess I still didn't want to put the broom away just because somebody else wanted me to.

EMPLOYMENT

Radio School and First Jobs

My father offered me the chance to go to university, but the last thing I wanted to do was endure 4 more years of a school environment. After a few months of indecision, I finally chose to attend radio school in Sydney. I had enjoyed doing several radio interviews in the past, and it seemed I was pretty good at communicating with an audience. So, off I went to learn the arcane arts of back-announcing songs. Living in Australia's largest city was a bit of a challenge for an introverted country boy, but since I lived alone and had full control of my time, it was a surprisingly pleasant experience.

Twelve months later, I began my first job as a radio announcer at a small country station. The work ethic and strong sense of responsibility instilled by my parents stood me in good stead. I quickly learned how to prepare my program, spin records, read news, interview people, write commercials, and do voiceovers. I liked talking to people via a microphone—it was infinitely better than dealing with them in person. While I formed friendships with a couple of the other announcers, my problems with authority figures continued. I had a very rocky relationship with my manager, which may have had something to do with going over his head to the board of directors and getting his wife sacked as office manager for her bullying behavior.

I began to drink heavily in social environments. I now understand that this "lubrication" allowed me to interact with people more easily, appear to be "one of the boys," and feel less stressed in social situations.

A Client Was Thrilled with My Radio Advertisements

Then, one of those moments of serendipity occurred that altered my life. A local retailer asked me to write a radio advertising campaign for him. He had overstocked his plant nursery. He had tried other advertising methods, but with little success. I went back to the station and wrote and produced a humorous 60-second commercial that was put on the air. It was a huge success! His nursery stock cleared in 1 week, and everyone around town was talking about the commercial. The client was thrilled and insisted I do all of his commercials from then on, which were very successful campaigns. As a major advertiser, his influence gave me "protected status" with my boss. It was then I realized that convincing people to buy things they didn't know they wanted might be a viable career option.

After a couple of years working as a full-time junior copywriter for another radio station, I had honed my craft. I was writing more than 120 commercials each week. I won a couple of awards for the commercials I wrote and was eventually offered a job at one of the major international advertising agencies in their Brisbane, Queensland, office.

I Learned Advertising Strategy

It was here I learned advertising strategy. How to position a product. What its inherent benefits are. The theory behind the emotions that lead people to do irrational things. The psychology of purchasing fascinated me, and I quickly developed a talent for it. At the initiation of each task, we received a "briefing form" from the agency, on which the core question was, "What is the one single thought or idea we are trying to communicate?" This appealed greatly to my single-minded focus. My capacity to work hard was a distinct advantage in an environment where workweeks of 60+ hours were the norm.

I loved coming up with advertising concepts. More than that, I enjoyed presenting them to the marketing managers or to clients' boards of directors. The agency put me through presentation skills training to further polish my natural talents in front of an audience, and I loved the planning and structure that went into a good presentation, followed by the high-wire thrill of actually delivering it. I thoroughly enjoyed thinking on my feet to promote and defend the concept against challenges, with hundreds of thousands of dollars hanging in the balance.

My employers appreciated my skills and dedication, too. I was paid very well. The personal eccentricities I displayed (such as not wearing shoes, drinking at lunchtime, and only shaving every few days) perturbed no one in the "creative-is-king" world of advertising. I *almost* fit in.

My Mind Works Differently

It was during this period I began to fully understand that my mind worked very differently than that of other people. I could think faster. I could see the ramifications of different courses of action much more quickly. I was not influenced by the emotional influences that affected others. I had a much more systematic and methodical approach to things. I had a high level of perfectionism. Whilst these skills were a distinct advantage in my job, I began to feel more and more separate from the rest of the world. My few romantic relationships didn't survive long.

I began a course of "biblio-therapy." I had always been a voracious reader (I still read an average of five books per week), but I decided to embark on a more specific search to better understand myself and my place in the world. I began at the beginning, with Socrates of Athens—the father of logic, philosophy, and critical thinking (along with his student and biographer, Plato). Here was a man I could identify with. He understood how little he knew, as opposed to those who considered themselves wise. He created the Socratic method, examining an issue from every angle through simple questions. And, he refused to bow to the political correctness of the masses. His inability to compromise his ethics or dumb down his position ultimately cost him his life—a price he was willing to pay.

Seneca, Giordano Bruno, Copernicus, Michelangelo, Michel de Montaigne, Machiavelli, Arthur Schopenhauer—I found these men and their ideas inspiring. I suppose this was largely because they reflected back my own self-image—an intelligent outsider who threatens the status quo and is condemned for his nonconformist ways.

Difficulties Arose When I Was Promoted into Upper Management

After a few very enjoyable years working as a copywriter in Brisbane, I quit working for the agency. They had asked me to fill an account service position to stop a major account from leaving the agency. I grudgingly said I would do it for 12 months, until they found a quality replacement. At the end of the 12 months, they realized they were making much more money from that client than they were previously, and they didn't want me to return to copywriting. I didn't want to stay in account service, where I had to interact with clients, suppliers, and staff all the time. They offered me a position in Melbourne, apprenticing to the national director of strategy (which, in retrospect, I should have taken), but I left and went back to radio on the Sunshine Coast to launch a new FM station. After 3 years back in radio, the station was taken over by another company. My closest friend, who was the station manager at that time, left. A few months later, I left too, and we set up our own marketing and advertising company. Fifteen years later, we're still doing it.

I Am Currently an Advertising Creative Director

I am currently a partner in and the creative director of said advertising agency on the Sunshine Coast. We are a boutique operation, with four full-time staff members, several contractors, and multiple suppliers in specialist fields.

Here's a basic overview of what my job entails:

- Taking briefs from clients on what they wish to achieve
- Choosing the media that will be used to communicate their message to the target audience

- Creating an advertising strategy—why should customers purchase this product and what is the best way to communicate that

- Coming up with an advertising concept to communicate the message

- Writing the message, whether it is for a radio commercial, a newspaper or magazine ad, a television commercial, a Web page, a direct-mail letter, a brochure, or a billboard

- Briefing my designers or other creative help to create the layout and "look" of the communication

- Reviewing their work and suggesting improvements

- Estimating the cost of production for the communication

- Presenting the concept to the client for their approval

- Making any modifications the client requests

- Directing the production of the TV, radio, or press ad

- Dispatching the final advertisement to the media

Having Asperger's syndrome is very helpful for some aspects of my job. Attention to detail is useful when proofing jobs for errors. A high IQ is a strong positive when coming to terms with briefs on complex products or services. A single-minded focus is beneficial when tackling major jobs with tight timelines. A logic-based thinking style is advantageous when coming up with strategies. Being very objective is necessary in accurately assessing the value of an idea.

Dealing with Less Rational People Is Stressful

Other aspects of Asperger's are distinct disadvantages in a creative career. Having to spend large amounts of time in meetings with clients, staff, and suppliers can be uncomfortable. Dealing with others who are less objective and less rational can be stressful. Having to assuage the creative egos of my team can be challenging. And retaining the necessary clarity of purpose when faced with multiple jobs with competing time constraints can be difficult for someone with weakened central coherence.

RELATIONSHIPS

Meeting My Other Half

It was when I returned to the Sunshine Coast that I met Trish, the woman who would become my wife. She asked me out to a dance. We were inseparable after that. A very different style of person to me, Trish was spontaneous, feisty, fun loving, and a risk-taker. She quickly became my other half. Additionally, in the early years at least, she allowed me the freedom to decide whether I'd "pick up the broomstick" or not. Our son, Ethan, came along a few years into our relationship.

When I began working for myself, I struggled at first, both from a financial perspective and in terms of coming to grips with running a small business. Until this point in my life, my talent and ability to work harder than anyone else had always meant that people were willing to overlook my differences. In the days when I worked for a large agency, however, I was cocooned—by the creative environment, the huge resources at my disposal, and the major clients I worked with who understood that anyone who could contribute to the bottom line was worth listening to.

In contrast, working in a small agency means working with smaller clients, where you deal with an individual rather than an entity. This means dealing with personalities. To provide an example of the frustration this leads to, a client might give me a brief for a press campaign and explain that he wants his ad to "really stand out." So I proceed to create an advertisement that fulfills his brief and stands out. The client will watch me present it, horrified, and then say, "But I don't want to stand out THAT much!"

Dealing with Clients' Petty Emotional Needs

The more I dealt with individuals who ran their own businesses, the more frustrating inconsistencies I stumbled over. Like the 50-year-old man I worked with who ran a youth-oriented store but would only accept an ad to please his own age group, heedless of the 15–25-year-old target audience. Clients who want to voice their own radio commercials, despite the fact that they sound like Jerry Lewis after inhaling helium, damage their brand any time they approach a microphone. People will sign a written brief, get an ad that isn't what they were "expecting," and then deny ever asking for what they wanted in the first place. For a long time, the levels of subjectivity, hypocrisy, and egotism I encountered stunned me.

Like the determined 3-year-old I had once been, I refused to put the broom away. I kept on trying to create advertising that actually sold the client's product instead of meeting their petty emotional needs. I kept banging my head against a proverbial brick wall by giving them what they needed, not what they wanted. This caused a lot of arguments with my business partner. And, to my friend and partner's chagrin, it was making us broke.

I Became Frustrated and Depressed

It was also making me very depressed. A black cloud settled over me. I was difficult to be around, both at work and at home. Realizing that I couldn't continue this way, I (as usual) tried to "think" myself out of the problem. I researched depression and psychology. I underwent Myers-Briggs personality tests. I was also treated by a psychologist. That treatment was unsuccessful. Hypnosis was attempted, but I couldn't be hypnotized. Some cognitive therapy was tried, but that didn't work, either. Of course, this was in 1996, before there was a great deal of professional understanding of Asperger's syndrome in Australia. Eventually I was prescribed antidepressants, which were effective.

One day, my friend and business partner, Mark, saw an article in our local newspaper about a boy with a condition called "Asperger's syndrome." As he read through the symptoms, he thought, "This sounds a lot like Stewart. The inability to see other people's perspectives, the capacity for detail, the fascination with process— hmmm." He showed me the story, but I didn't think the boy in the article seemed like me, because he was further along the spectrum than I am.

Mark spoke to his wife, an experienced schoolteacher who had received some training on handling Asperger's and children with attention-deficit/hyperactivity disorder. She concurred that Asperger's was a possibility.

Desperate to Learn Why I Thought Differently

Desperate for an answer as to why I felt so different and why I *thought so differently* from other people, I began to read everything I could find about possible conditions that fit what seemed to be going on with me. I read about everything from narcissistic personality disorder to sociopathy to autism spectrum disorders.

After contemplating all this new information, I came to the conclusion that I probably have an autism spectrum disorder. The narrow focus, the importance of process, the comfort of repeating things the same way, echolalia (my ability to mimic), the obsession with logic, my confusion at the emotions of others—all these symptoms rang true, along with a few others, such as over- and underresponsiveness and a degree of face-blindness.

Over the years, I had always struggled with my emotions. It wasn't that I didn't *have* emotions—rather, sometimes I had them too strongly. As I matured, I managed to overlay them with logic and keep most of them under control, except for flashes of anger or depression.

On the Surface, I Seemed Normal

I found it difficult to meet new people. On the surface, I seemed "normal," but this was simply another role I played, like the Shakespearean comedies of my youth. I had developed a series of tricks and techniques to survive social situations. At parties I constantly circulated, ate, had a quick word with someone, looked for an ashtray on the other side of the room, then went to adjust the music volume. Repeat. I was like a shark—if I didn't keep moving, I would drown. Staying on the move kept me from having to sustain long and awkward social conversations or having to chit-chat with people I didn't know well about things I don't care about.

My Marriage Started Falling Apart

Soon, the cracks began to appear. My relationship with my wife began to take a dive. Naturally, with the birth of our son, she focused her attention on him, and she started to pressure me to earn more money. We had different values, which only became apparent once there was a child to raise. From her perspective, I provided little emotional support.

A warm, loving marriage deteriorated into an ever-increasing onslaught of verbal abuse about my lack of ambition and practicality, my stupidity, and my inability to provide. My wife threatened to leave me. Looking back, I suspect these were attempts to goad me into action. But that was never going to work with the broomstick kid.

It got to the point where I could no longer handle being told how useless I was. My self-esteem couldn't take the battering. I went away for a few days. Let me be clear—I love my wife dearly. I love my son even more. He is the center of my universe. And for these reasons, I went to see a counselor in an effort to save my marriage. My wife also attended a few sessions independently of me. I mentioned to the counselor that I thought I may have an autism spectrum disorder, but he knew little about it. Counseling was an interesting process, but ultimately an unsatisfying one for Trish and me.

My wife would not accept that I had Asperger's syndrome unless she was handed a written diagnosis from someone qualified. I was finally able to track down a psychologist who had worked with professor Tony Attwood's Hearts & Minds Clinic in Brisbane. (Autism training and support are less available in Australia than in either the United Kingdom or the United States.) This psychologist diagnosed my condition as Asperger's. Her opinion was that I was very intelligent and very well socialized for someone with the condition.

My Diagnosis Was a Great Relief

The diagnosis was a great relief to me. At last, I knew why I had felt so different all of my life. I knew I wasn't just an individual "weirdo"—about 1% of the population are "wierdos" with me!

I found a clinical psychologist near my home on the Sunshine Coast who had done a lot of work with children with autism spectrum disorders—Dr Sally Lock. She was a godsend. Understanding, warm, and caring, Sally worked with me on a weekly or bimonthly basis to help me understand the practicalities of how I think versus the way neurotypical people think. Best of all, she listened without judgment—and given how verbose I am, that's a task in itself.

Dr Lock arranged to have my IQ tested at a university where she lectured. She suspected that I was very smart and that my skills were verbal. She was right. I tested in the 98th percentile, with extremely good verbal skills but a limited processing speed compared with others of the same intellect. Along with the Asperger's syndrome, this helped to explain my frustration with others. Sometimes it wasn't the Asperger's that caused the difficulties—it was simply that I expected them to be as smart as I was. (I had always thought that a lot of other people I knew were "dumb" and that I was "average.")

Getting a diagnosis has made my work life somewhat easier. I still get frustrated with people, but at least I understand that I will never be able to see things the way others do. My partner Mark and I have worked out ways of getting the best out of what I am. I attend client meetings for short periods of time and then excuse myself before my internal stress levels get too high. He tries not to overload me with too many considerations at once and gives me time to think about things. And I acknowledge that there are some areas where my decision-making is not relevant, because I cannot see things from an emotional perspective. It's still a struggle, but it's easier than it was.

My Marriage Has Improved and Is a Work in Progress

My marriage has improved somewhat, but it's still a work in progress. If neurotypical people are a mystery, neurotypical women are an utter enigma. Trish has also made some changes to adapt to the way my brain works. She no longer springs as many surprises on me and gives me more time to consider the ramifications of choices. She knows that social situations are very stressful for me, so she tends to have lunch with friends without me. Our relationship has not fully recovered, but we're still trying.

So, as a person with Asperger's, have I "succeeded"? Compared with many people on the spectrum, I guess you could say I am a success. But, as the American industrialist Henry Ford said, "If there is any one secret of success, it lies in the ability to get the other person's point of view and see things from that person's angle, as well as from your own." From my perspective, understanding the viewpoint of another individual is something I am still working on and have not yet mastered.

I'm a work in progress. I may never understand the neurotypical world completely, but I'm absolutely determined to keep trying.

GET CREATIVE ABOUT FINDING JOBS

DEVELOP A PORTFOLIO AND USE CONNECTIONS

I always found opportunities for work by locating the "back door." I never landed a single job by filling out a job application or doing a formal interview. I got my freelance business started by showing potential clients a portfolio of my work. Another thing I learned very early is that certain people could open the door to opportunity. Often I found these people in places where I least expected them. In the HBO movie made about my life, called "Temple Grandin," a scene shows me meeting a lady who was the wife of the plant manager. In the movie, this enabled me to get into the meat plant, where I undertook my first big project. The reality of it happened in a similar way. I was at an Arizona cattle reception, wearing a Western shirt I had hand embroidered. A woman came up to me and said she liked my embroidery. We got to talking, and I expressed interest in getting into the Swift meat plant. (It was named "Abbot" in the movie.) This woman turned out to be the wife of the plant's insurance agent, and he knew the plant manager. That was the connection that got me in. At the reception that night, I was wearing my portfolio and didn't even realize it.

The normal approach of doing formal interviews often does not work for autistic individuals. Both parents and professionals need to look for alternative means to identify the specific people who can open a door. Often, people fail to see the door. I heard about an artist who had a big gallery owner stop at her house because he was lost. The artist had many pieces of her artwork in her house, and she failed to show him her artwork. She gave him directions, and then he left. A door had opened up for her briefly, and she failed to walk through it. Autistic individuals need to start recognizing the doors when they appear and take it upon themselves to walk through them.

Find a Mentor

Around the time I attended the reception where I met my connection into the Swift meat plant, I was making a few bucks painting signs for local businesses. One big client was the Swift plant, where I combined cattle handling and sign painting. I always carried a black notebook that contained photos of signs I had painted. Another large client was the carnival attraction at the Arizona State Fair. I took my notebook to the fair and met an old sign painter named Pat. When I showed him my photos, he had me start painting signs. He showed me how to use the correct type of brushes and taught me tricks of the trade that can only be learned from an experienced instructor. For example, the best brushes only work if they are soaked in lard oil and carefully shaped. I invented paper cones to store them in so their carefully shaped tips would not get bent. My experience with Pat illustrates the importance of getting mentoring and instruction. The role of other mentors in my life is discussed extensively in my books *Thinking in Pictures* and *Developing Talents*. Some of the signs I painted were for Jimbo the Giant Steer, the Country Western Museum, and a ridiculous exhibit that was billed as a real prehistoric iceman frozen in a chest full of ice.

Know Your Audience

My aunt worked at Fort Huachuca in Arizona, and she used her connections to secure me an opportunity to present my sign portfolio to a military officer who needed signs. With this potential client, I learned the importance of putting the right examples in my portfolio. The material has to be appropriate for the customer. I made the mistake of showing him a sign I had made for my aunt's 3rd-grade classroom. He liked the sign I painted for the implement dealer, but unfortunately, the officer had already been turned off by the collage I had made of animals living in a barn. I learned from my mistakes, and after that, I made sure I put items in my portfolio that were appropriate for the client. Another mistake I avoided was putting in too many examples. Usually I showed one large drawing and five to 10 photos. It has to be presented neatly, and only the really good stuff is displayed. A good portfolio should get a big "WOW" out of a client within 30 seconds.

One Small Project at a Time

I also did odd carpentry jobs, such as building a spare room in a friend's house. Everything I did started with one small project at a time. Writing for *Arizona Farmer Ranchman* magazine helped me gain respect within the cattle industry. It started out with one article, and then I wrote articles for free for 6 months. Finally, they started to pay me. The press pass I got was very valuable. It enabled me to gain free access to major national cattle conventions that had very high registration fees. It was a ticket that helped me to contact cattle equipment design clients. Writing articles for both *Arizona Farmer Ranchman* and national magazines gained me name recognition and attention to my cattle behavioral work. The articles were valuable free advertising.

Niche Career

My work designing cattle-handling facilities was the perfect career for somebody on the spectrum. I became an expert in a highly specialized field where I had little competition. I hunted for potential clients by reading all the meat magazines and looking for news of new plants being built or plants that were undergoing expansions. I attended cattle meetings, where I did a good amount of "card hunting" and "badge reading." I landed a major job on the floor of the convention center at McCormick Place in Chicago during an American Meat Institute meeting. I saw a badge that had the name of a plant that was expanding, and I showed my portfolio to the representative. I had to be discreet, because reporters are not supposed to sell on the trade show floor. The portfolio I used was a black folder that also contained my legal pad for taking notes at meetings. Nobody could see the pictures I brought until I opened my portfolio. (Today, making a portfolio would be so much easier. Instead of having a bulky notebook, I could have my pictures and drawings on my smart phone or tablet computer.) I always sold my work instead of myself, because when people utilized my designs, they worked. After I landed jobs, I got them done immediately. In fact, I got the drawings done so quickly that I could sit on them for a few days before I submitted them to the customer. I did not want the client to know how quickly I was able to do them.

Today, there are many tools for social networking, but many people fail to see that the door to opportunity awaits right there on the computer. To show off, portfolios, Web pages, social networking sites, and many other things can be used. Business networking sites can be a very valuable asset when it comes to networking and finding employment.

STEVE JOBS—A "DIFFERENT" KIND OF GUY

Steve Jobs, the late head of Apple Computer, got started by going in the "back door." An article in a special Steve Jobs memorial issue of *Bloomberg BusinessWeek** made it clear that young Steve was a different kind of kid. The word autism or Asperger's was never mentioned in any article connected to Steve, but I began to wonder as I read the entire special issue of *Bloomberg Businessweek*, along with articles in *Time*, *Newsweek*, and the *Economist*, if Steve may very well have been on the autism spectrum.

Steve was a bright and unchallenged elementary-school student who disrupted the classroom, once even letting snakes loose in class. His classmates thought of him as a weird loner. He dropped out of college after 6 months but still attended classes. He became a barefoot, grubby hippy who ate a weird fruitarian's diet and slept on the floor of a friend's room. To obtain money for food, he collected aluminum cans. During this same time, he sat in on a calligraphy class. His interest in calligraphy led to the development of all the beautiful printing fonts that we use on computers today. Steve was not an engineer—he was an artist, and he was obsessed with creating a beautiful computer that was easy to use.

A grungy, rude Steve Jobs managed to talk his way into the video game company Atari. The other employees hated the "arrogant weirdo," so they allowed him to come in during the night to avoid conflict. Steve needed a partner to do the engineering side of making

---

* Aley J. Steve Jobs: The beginning, 1955 to 1985—the high school loner who figured out what the world wanted from technology. *Bloomberg Businessweek*. October 6, 2011.

his computer. He found one in Steve Wozniak, a hard-core nerd who did the programming side of computing.

Steve Jobs is legendary for the charismatic way he introduced new Apple products. He had to work on public speaking. For him, it was not easy. When he went live on an early national TV broadcast, he was so nervous he almost vomited. I can relate to that. When I was in graduate school, I had to teach a class, and I became so nervous that I had to walk out.

I shudder at what might happen to Steve Jobs in today's school system. I imagine him so spaced out on inappropriately prescribed medications that he would be like a "zombie." Yet, Steve Jobs, the "weird" kid who terrorized his elementary school with snakes, became the head of the most valuable company in the United States. I think it's fascinating that everything he did was achieved through unconventional ways.

TOO MANY YOUNG PEOPLE FIXATE ON AUTISM

People on the autism spectrum usually get fixated on their favorite subjects. My fixation on cattle chutes motivated me to find clients so I could design their systems. Fixations, when they are channeled in useful ways, can be huge motivators for success. I am concerned that many young autistic people are getting fixated on autism itself, instead of fixating on some useful outside interest, such as art, computer programming, or history.

Most of the people who contributed chapters to this book gained great insight when they received their diagnosis of autism, especially when they learned of their condition later in life. It explained many of their problems in terms of getting along with other people and their relationships with spouses. However, if autism is a person's major focus in life, I think it becomes a hindrance. It troubles me when a 9-year-old walks up to me and all he or she wants to talk to me about is his or her autism. I much more enjoy hearing about his or her history projects or robotics project. Autism is a significant part of who I am, but I consider myself a designer, college professor, and scientist first. I am often asked, if I could snap my fingers and be cured of autism, would I do it? My answer is "no." I like myself and my logical way of thinking. So, while autism is an integral part of who I am, I feel it's important that I'm not totally defined by it.

MANY INDIVIDUALS WILL NEED A BUSINESS MANAGER

I have looked at the portfolios of many individuals who have very marketable talents, but they have no idea how to make a business out of their skills. They desperately need someone to help run the business side of doing freelance work. Today, it seems like setting up a business is more complicated than it used to be. When I set up my freelance business, I had help from my building contractor friend, Jim Uhl. Today, the paperwork requirements are three times what they were in the 1970s. I have to fill out W9 forms and vendor forms for many clients. Failure to attend to these forms would result in not getting paid. One talented freelance artist I know failed to be reimbursed for $30,000 worth of travel expenses because he wouldn't fill out the required paperwork.

The services that are available to help individuals with autism get jobs often have a "one size fits all" approach. For some individuals, training to be janitors or grocery-shelf stockers is a good fit, but for other individuals, it is completely inappropriate. There is a need for services to help people on the spectrum with marketable talents get businesses started and assist them with running their business. Even though there are huge technology companies run by undiagnosed Aspies, most of these people have a neurotypical "suit" manager to hold the business together. This usually becomes essential when businesses grow large. People who are skilled in the fields of art, writing, and the like need similar business support. There are several ways this can be done.

One way is for a person's siblings or children to run the business. A parent is also a possibility, but the problem with a parent running the business is that the person on the spectrum loses his or her business manager when the parent dies, unless the parent prepares for a transition to a new manager.

Additionally, agencies and other businesses can be enlisted to run the business side of freelance work, such as filing expense reports and doing the more complex taxes that are associated with freelance corporations.

Another option is that, rather than having an autistic individual run his or her own business, he or she can find work in a conventional company with a boss who understands autism and can manage a person on the spectrum. Oftentimes, in these instances, parents and professionals can contact managers via the "back door" to get people placed. However, it is possible a job can be lost if one's manager changes jobs.

One creative mom I know of got her autistic daughter on the right track after she was suspended from school. She contacted a friend who managed a local McDonald's and set up an informal "job coach" program for her daughter there. Whenever her daughter skipped school, her mom called the McDonald's and requested an increase in the number of hours that her daughter had to work.

On the technology side of things, there are businesses that specifically hire people on the spectrum to do software testing, phone applications, and other types of computer work. Two established ones I know of are Aspiretech and Specialisterne. These firms were set up by parents of children on the autism spectrum.

PEOPLE ON THE SPECTRUM CAN KEEP PROGRESSING

One of the contributors called his life and marriage "a work in progress." He is continually learning and developing a better understanding. Charli, the tour guide, gradually learned to become better and better at her job. Too often, individuals are looking for a single, "landmark" turning point. Instead of a turning point, however, more often there is a gradual gain in greater insight. In my own life, I have continued to change as I have gained more and more experience along the way. People on the spectrum need to be "stretched" and encouraged to try new things. As demonstrated by the outstanding individuals in this book, it is never too late to start.

A NOTE FROM TEMPLE ABOUT THE DSM

Proposed Removal of Asperger's Syndrome from the Diagnostic and Statistical Manual of Mental Disorders

The American Psychiatric Association is proposing to eliminate the diagnoses of *(a)* Asperger's syndrome and *(b)* pervasive developmental display—not otherwise specified from the *Diagnostic and Statistical Manual of Mental Disorders*, or DSM. They would instead classify these two diagnoses as autism spectrum disorder. This proposed change would occur when the new diagnostic guidelines are published in the upcoming 5th edition of the DSM, or DSM-V.

The association is also proposing to create a new diagnosis, independent of autism, called *social communication disorder*. The description of the symptoms for social communication disorder would be similar to that of Asperger's syndrome. Some of the features of social communication disorder would include difficulty in the social uses of verbal and nonverbal communication, as well as social communication problems that have a detrimental effect on employment and social relationships.

To receive a diagnosis of autism, an individual must also display additional symptoms, such as sensory problems, fixated interests, or repetitive behaviors. It is my opinion that social communication disorder is a part of the social-impairment continuum of the autism spectrum. My fear is that many individuals who have Asperger's syndrome will be reclassified as having this new diagnosis when school districts grow short on funding, to cut costs on services.

The way I see it, the proposed changes in diagnostic criteria would probably cause the most problems for older children who possess a full range of verbal capabilities, have a normal level of intelligence, and are diagnosed in late childhood or adolescence. For example, I have observed many individuals on the spectrum who receive a diagnosis that switches back and forth between attention-deficit/hyperactivity disorder and Asperger's syndrome. Another problem is that some individuals could receive an incomplete or imprecise diagnosis, such as conduct disorder or oppositional defiant disorder, which would ultimately prevent them from being able to improve or progress.

We must bear in mind that diagnosis on the basis of the DSM, either the current version (DSM-IV) or the proposed revised edition, the DSM-V, is not an exact science. It is not like arriving at a diagnosis for bacterial infections, where precise lab tests can be used. Diagnostic labels for psychiatric conditions are determined by means of both scientific study and the opinions of committee members, who get together and attempt to reach a diagnostic "consensus." Over the years, as new information and insights have been obtained, many psychiatric diagnoses have changed accordingly.

Scientific studies have clearly shown us that the social problems that occur in autistic individuals represent a true continuum. When individuals receive a label that falls on the milder end of the spectrum, it must be remembered that the following terms—*Asperger's syndrome, Aspie, social awkwardness, mild autism,* and *social communication disorder*—can all point to the same thing.

Indeed, it is likely that some of the autistic individuals who tell their stories in this book would be diagnosed as having social communication disorder, if the proposed DSM-V criteria were used.

FURTHER READING

Constantine JN, Todd RD. Autistic traits in the general population: a twin study. *Arch Gen Psychiatry.* 2003;60:524-530.

Constantine JN. Intergenerational transmission of subthreshold autistic traits in the general population. *Biol Psychiatry.* 2005;57:655-660.

Dubin N. *Anxiety.* London, UK: Jessica Kingsley; 2009.

Grandin T. *The Way I See It.* Arlington, TX: Future Horizons; 2011. [Contains information on medications for anxiety and panic attacks.]

Grandin T, Barron S. *Unwritten Social Rules.* Arlington, TX: Future Horizons; 2005.

Grandin T, Duffy K. *Developing Talents.* Shawnee Mission, KS: Autism Asperger Publishing; 2004.

Kennedy DM, Bank RS. *Bright not Broken.* San Francisco, CA: Jossey Bass (Wiley); 2011.

Ledgin N. *Asperger's and Self Esteem.* Arlington, TX: Future Horizons; 2002.

Reversen AM, Constantino JM, Volk NE, Todd RD. Autistic traits in a population-based ADHD twin sample. *J Child Psychol Psychiatry.* 2007;48:464-472.

Robinson JE. *Be Different.* New York, NY: Crown Archtype; 2011.

Simone R. *Asperger's on the Job.* Arlington, TX: Future Horizons; 2010.

Kim YS, Leventhal BL, Koh YJ. Prevalence of autism spectrum disorders in total population sample. *Am J Psychiatry.* 2011;168:904-912.

INDEX

A *p* indicates a photograph.

ABOUT THE AUTHOR

© Rosalie Winard

As a child, Temple Grandin could not speak. She lived a silent existence, broken only by rhythmic rocking and occasional fits of screaming and thrashing. Temple's mother, caregivers, and teachers eventually helped her grow to become one of the autism community's most beloved success stories. Temple is a popular international lecturer on autism and the author of *Emergence: Labeled Autistic, Thinking in Pictures, Animals in Translation, Unwritten Rules of Social Relationships, Animals Make Us Human,* and *The Way I See It.*

One of the world's leading experts in livestock facility design, more than half of the cattle in North America are handled in facilities Temple designed. She credits her visual thinking and her systematic mind, which are both characteristics of autism, as giving her the ability to be "the woman who thinks like a cow."

The subject of the award-winning 2010 HBO movie "Temple Grandin," which is based on her life story, Temple continues to be an inspiration and role model to millions. She was recently named a "hero" and selected as one of *TIME Magazine*'s top 100 most influential people.